ORACLE® *Oracle Press*™

Oracle8 Architecture

Steve Bobrowski

Osborne **McGraw-Hill**

Berkeley New York St. Louis
San Francisco Auckland Bogotá Hamburg London Madrid
Mexico City Milan Montreal New Delhi Panama City
Paris São Paulo Singapore Sydney Tokyo Toronto

Osborne/**McGraw-Hill**
2600 Tenth Street
Berkeley, California 94710
U.S.A.

For information on translations or book distributors outside the U.S.A., or to arrange bulk purchase discounts for sales promotions, premiums, or fund-raisers, please contact Osborne/**McGraw-Hill** at the above address.

Oracle8 Architecture

1234567890 AGM AGM 901987654321098

ISBN 0-07-882274-2

Publisher	**Proofreader**
Brandon A. Nordin	Pat Mannion
Editor-in-Chief	**Indexer**
Scott Rogers	Rebecca Plunkett
Acquisitions Editor	**Computer Designer**
Scott Rogers	Mickey Galicia
Project Editor	**Illustrator**
Mark Karmendy	Lance Ravella
Editorial Assistant	**Series Design**
Ann Sellers	Jani Beckwith
Copy Editor	**Cover Design**
Tim Barr	Elysium Design

About the Author...

Steve Bobrowski is the CEO of Animated Learning, Inc., a company that specializes in training Oracle professionals through its web-based information hub OraWorld (www.oraworld.com), and multimedia courseware (www.animatedlearning.com). Steve is an award-winning author who also writes and edits magazine articles for several industry publications, including *Oracle Magazine, DBMS, OReview, SELECT Magazine*, and *Database Programming & Design*. Previously, Steve worked for Oracle Corp., where he assisted in the development of Oracle Server and Oracle's own documentation for Oracle7 and Oracle8.

ALI FAROKHI

Contents

PART I
Introduction to Oracle

PART IV
Oracle8 Software Architecture

PART V
Specialized Oracle Environments

Foreword

echnological progress has often driven society through great changes, from ancient times through Gutenberg's invention of the printing press and the Renaissance, from the Industrial Revolution to the Atomic Age and the Space Age. Each era was marked by new opportunities in the world of commerce, new challenges in the military, political, and diplomatic landscape, and dramatic changes in the daily lives of ordinary people. Today it is impossible to contemplate the existence of modern society without computers for banking, manufacturing, or any number of other business areas. The seeming omnipresence of computers and instant television coverage of global events has led to a feeling of information overload and years of talk about the Information Age.

In the Information Age, possession, access, and analysis of information will be even more important than possession of more tangible assets. In business and economics, the Information Age will bring electronic commerce, global trade, and totally efficient markets. Ubiquitous, low-cost, and easy-to-use personal computing and universal access to information should improve education and facilitate free speech and democracy. The Information Age could be seen as a New Renaissance, marked by rapid and dramatic changes in every aspect of society, affecting the lives and interactions among individuals, businesses, economies, and nations.

XV

However, the Information Age is not really in full swing. In the United States, only 30-40 percent of homes have personal computers, and in other countries the presence of computers in homes is dramatically lower. Despite frequent improvements in the performance, cost, and ease of use of personal computers, they are still too expensive and too complex for most people to own and operate. The situation in most schools may be even more discouraging, since very few schools can afford to provide each student with access to a computer for educational purposes. Even in large automated enterprises, some might claim the Information Age has not really arrived. In many organizations, incompatible and hard-to-use systems make it impossible for employees to gain immediate access to the information they need to carry out their jobs.

Now, however, emerging computing and communications technologies are poised to accelerate the advent of the Information Age. One of these is the Internet, and another is a paradigm shift from client/server architectures to network computing.

It's been said and widely believed, "The Internet Changes Everything." Millions of people daily use the Internet and the World Wide Web to access the latest news, to search for information on and purchase goods and services, and to exchange electronic mail. Many organizations today have created an "intranet," using communications products based on Internet standards, to connect all their systems and users, providing access to information and applications. It has become clear that the Internet, combined with other communications technologies like television and telephone, will be a central technology of the Information Age.

A new information systems architecture, network computing, will also help enable the Information Age. In the dominant computing architecture in the1960s and 1970s, large and expensive mainframe computers supported centralized batch processing and structured online access to applications through limited function terminals. These systems were secure and reliable and offered good economies of scale for supporting large databases of information and large numbers of users for applications like transaction processing, but were complex and hard to use.

With the client/server model that became popular in the mid-1980s, the application logic runs on a personal computer (PC), and uses a network to access databases stored on a mid-range server machine. Because of the PC's user-friendly interface and open systems hardware and software components, many managers hoped to reduce the cost of their computing infrastructure with client/server computing. However, the total cost of ownership for client/server systems has proven to be higher than expected. High costs result from limited security and reliability, the need for frequent upgrades of PC software and hardware, and the need to manage a complex distributed environment.

In the mid-1990s, a new computing architecture emerged called "network computing," which in place of personal computers uses low-cost and simple client access devices called "network computers" (NCs) that require no administration. These "thin client" devices, or "network appliances," offer the ease of use and multimedia capability of personal computers, but without their complexity and cost. Applications software is downloaded across the network to the NC as needed, so no data or applications are stored locally, thus eliminating the need to manage the configuration of the client access device. The idea of network computing is to retain all of the advantages of both centralized mainframe-based computing and the client/server model, with none of the disadvantages.

With low-cost, easy-to-use network access devices free of an administrative burden, more homes and schools will be able to afford to connect to networks for applications and for information access. In enterprise environments, network computing will permit rapid deployment of new and revised applications that users can conveniently access from anywhere in the enterprise via the intranet. Together with the Internet, network computing makes accessing information more like using the television or telephone network. Simple, low-cost network access devices network provides access to any and all information, anywhere in the world via the professionally managed network, in a secure, scalable, reliable, and economical manner. The complexity of the system resides only in the network, not on the client device. The Internet and network computing together promise to finally provide the near-universal information access throughout commerce, communities, and education, that will fully bring about the Information Age.

In late 1996, Oracle Corporation introduced its network-oriented approach for designing and deploying applications: the Network Computing Architecture (NCA). This vision includes a three-tier architecture, comprised of thin clients, middle-tier application servers, and data servers. NCA is based on industry standards such as the HTTP protocol, and emerging object technologies such as Java and CORBA. Object languages like Java will permit more rapid development of applications that can run anywhere in the network computing environment, whether on the NC, a PC, application server, or indeed, within the database manager itself. The CORBA (Common Object Request Broker Architecture) specification developed by the Object Management Group promises to facilitate the interoperation of application components and the incorporation of existing legacy applications into new distributed environments.

Oracle's entire product family is becoming Web-enabled and designed for network computing. At the very heart of the Network Computing Architecture is the Oracle8 database management system.

The Information Age and network computing place new demands on a database management system to support more users and more data, and do so faster and at lower cost than ever before. The intranet and Internet make accessing information so easy and efficient that database systems will need to support very large populations of users. Employees will become "self-service users", accessing the corporate human resources database via the intranet, for example to check on their vacation balances. Businesses will increasingly use the Internet to communicate with one another to support just-in-time inventory management. Millions of Internet users might access a database for travel reservations from anywhere in the world. Databases must be available around the clock to support such users.

In the Information Age, databases will grow very large in order to store all the information needed by users, whether that be accounting data or multimedia images and text that describe goods and services available from an online vendor. All types of information, including video and audio, will be stored in databases, along with traditional numbers, characters, and dates. Companies will create ever-larger data warehouses of operational data for analysis to support business decision-making.

To address the data management challenges of network computing, in June 1997 Oracle Corporation released Oracle8. Building on the strong technical foundation of Oracle7, the most widely-deployed database management system in the industry, Oracle Corporation invested over 500 person-years over nearly four years to design, develop, and test Oracle8. While Oracle8 includes performance and functional enhancements in all areas of the product, the new release was focused on two principle areas: scalability features for high-end transaction processing (OLTP) and data warehouse applications, and extending the relational model with object technology for enhanced application development capability.

For the first time, with Oracle8 open systems technology can meet the requirements of the most demanding mission-critical OLTP and data warehouse applications, which heretofore could be deployed only on proprietary mainframe platforms. Oracle8 can support tens of thousands of simultaneously connected users. Oracle8 supports databases as large as 100 terabytes, and can process data warehouse queries many times faster than its predecessors. The impressive scalability of Oracle8 is critical for mainstream enterprise computing, and the suitability of open systems technology for high-end mission-critical applications is an important development.

Some observers may place even more significance on the introduction of object technology in Oracle8. With these features, instead of storing only the rows and columns of the relational model, an Oracle8 database can represent business objects—complex entities such as purchase orders, customers, or insurance policies—more naturally and completely, and make those objects more easily accessible to programs using object oriented techniques. Oracle Corporation's evolutionary, pragmatic, and integrated approach preserves customers' investments in existing relational applications and allows them to gradually incorporate object technology into existing environments. Oracle8, as a robust object-relational database management system, will appeal to Oracle's large existing customer base, as well as to new customers, and will accelerate the adoption of object data management technology.

The breadth of functionality in Oracle8 presents a challenge for application developers and database administrators: learning about all its features and understanding how to use them. This book is a great place to start, regardless of whether you are familiar with database management systems in general or Oracle7 in particular, and regardless of whether you expect to develop applications or administer databases based on Oracle8.

Steve Bobrowski has provided an excellent overview of the capabilities of the Oracle database management system, including the new features introduced in Oracle8. As a very experienced consultant, author, and educator on the use of Oracle technology, Steve has presented Oracle's technology in a conversational and easy-to-read style. He places each feature in an appropriate context of its use, and avoids presenting details that are unnecessary to a basic understanding of the technology. This book reflects Steve's deep understanding of Oracle8, developed over several years through early hands-on access and his close relationship with the developers and product managers associated with the product. I am proud to have worked closely with Steve over the past decade, and I am honored to be able to call him my friend.

Oracle Corporation has been the leader in relational database technology and an early and consistent leader in the era of client/server computing. The company is again leading the industry through a time of significant technological change and promise in popularizing object-relational database management and network computing. The Network Computing Architecture and Oracle8 are fundamental technologies designed to implement Oracle's stated strategic intent, to "Enable the Information Age through Network Computing."

The end of the 20th century marks not only the development of important new digital technologies, but also a real renaissance and a time of great economic and social change. The Information Age is upon us! It may well have as much impact on all parts of our society as the Renaissance, the Industrial Revolution, the Atomic Age, and the Space Age all rolled into one. As Gutenberg and Galileo may have known in their times, and as we surely know in ours, it's an exciting time to be alive!

Ken Jacobs
VP Product Strategy
Oracle Server Technologies
June 1997

Acknowledgments

ypically, the author of a book gets all or most of the credit for writing the masterpiece itself—think about it, how many of you can name Stephen King's editor? However, what most people do not understand is that producing a book is the collective effort of several people working toward a common goal. The words that follow are an attempt to thank formally the many people who have helped me write, edit, and print this, my second commercial book. Hopefully, our work has produced a publication that helps you accomplish your own personal goals in working with Oracle8.

First of all, I'd like to thank my partner Kathleen O'Connor. Without Kathleen to help me, I'm afraid that my writing and organization of thoughts would not be nearly as clean as they exist on the pages in this book. There were many long days and late nights necessary to produce this book, and Kathleen challenged me to be the best that I could be in putting my words together so that everyone who reads this book has a clear understanding of Oracle8 and its concepts. I owe her an immeasurable debt of gratitude.

Next, I'd like to thank my many colleagues at Oracle whom I am happy to also call my friends. The technical expertise and reviews of Mike Hartstein were instrumental in making this book a comprehensive and accurate guide about Oracle8. Ken Jacobs, one of the most well-known and loved professionals at Oracle and in the database community at large, wrote a superb foreword for me that includes substance and insight, not fluff—I encourage all of you to read his words if you have not already done so. I'd also like to thank Julie Gibbs for personally recommending me to Osborne/McGraw-Hill as the author for this book. Julie and I have been friends for many years since we worked together at Oracle during its formative years. Numerous others at Oracle, knowingly or not, also made significant contributions to this book, including Marsha Bazley, Tom Bishop, Kevin Canady, Sandy Dreskin, Ed Miner, Tom Portfolio, Gordon Smith, Leslie Steere, Milton Wan, and Wynne White.

The folks at Osborne/McGraw-Hill also deserve many thanks for publishing this book. I'd like to thank Scott Rogers, who demonstrated enormous patience as the pages of this book trickled in throughout the spring and summer of 1997. Ann Sellers was instrumental in getting all of the book material to the correct place at the right time. Mark Karmendy was a pleasure to work with in editing the prose in this book.

Introduction

his book is a concise, intermediate-level presentation of the terminology and concepts related to Oracle8 Server, the latest version of Oracle Corporation's relational database management system. The following sections explain important information that you should understand before beginning to read the body of this book.

This Book Covers ...

Oracle8 Architecture teaches you the concepts of how Oracle8 works. Whether you are a database administrator, application developer, or an application user who simply wants to understand more about how Oracle8 functions, this book is for you. Oracle8 is a sophisticated database management product that is challenging to master, no matter what background you have with computers, software, or information management technology. After reading this book, you will have a tremendous perspective of everything Oracle8, including the structure of Oracle8 databases, how Oracle8 Server's software architecture manages access to shared databases, and other concepts about Oracle8.

This Book Does Not Cover ...

Database technology, application design and development, and information management, not to mention computers and software, are all immense topics to which no one book could ever be a complete guide. Consider this: *Oracle8 Architecture* focuses on presenting the terminology and concepts specifically associated with Oracle8. Accordingly, this book does not explain general topics that relate to Oracle8 such as operating system functionality, relational database theory, and so on.

Again, this book is a guide to the terminology and concepts related to Oracle8 Server. To be successful as an Oracle8 database administrator or application developer, you must have a clear understanding of the information that this book presents. However, *Oracle8 Architecture* is not a reference guide to the procedural tasks that you perform as an Oracle8 administrator or developer. After reading this book, you should turn to other books in the Oracle Press library to learn the step-by-step instructions necessary to administer or develop applications for an Oracle8 database system.

This Book Assumes ...

Oracle8 Architecture assumes that you are new to Oracle8 and want to learn all about its features and functionality in some depth. However, given the intended scope of this book, it also assumes that you have a general knowledge of database systems, especially relational database systems. Because Oracle8 is a relational database management system, some general experience with relational database systems will most certainly make this book easier to read. For example, if you already understand some of the basic concepts of a relational database system such as tables and views, you will simply have to focus on how Oracle8 implements the relational database model. If you have no background with database systems, I suggest you read the classic books *An Introduction to Database Systems, Volumes I and II* (Addison Wesley), written by one of the founders of the relational database model, C.J. Date.

Now that you know where this book will take you, let's begin learning all about Oracle8 and how you can use it to manage information.

PART

I

Introduction to Oracle

CHAPTER
1

Introducing Oracle8

ost everyone has heard the cliché, "information is power." And is this ever true. When you think about it, one of the most important assets of any institution is its information. For example, a typical business must keep track of its customers, sales orders, product inventory, and employee information for obvious reasons. Additionally, the analysis of pertinent business information can help make a company more competitive. For example, a sales analyst can use current sales data to forecast future sales and identify trends that might help to improve overall business profitability.

Information Management

In today's world of high technology, computers manage most information because they make it easy to organize, store, and protect valuable data. The proliferation of powerful personal computers and networks has made it possible for all businesses, large and small alike, to quickly and safely make information readily available to people that require access to it.

Databases

Most typically, computers store and organize large amounts of information within a database. A *database*, whether or not a computer manages it, is nothing more than an orderly collection of related information. A database safely stores information and organizes it for fast retrieval. For example, a business can use a database to store tables of customer records, corresponding sales orders, product parts, and employee lists. Various workers can then use the database to efficiently perform their jobs. For example, salespeople can quickly enter or look up sales orders, advertising executives can study and forecast product sales, and warehouse personnel can efficiently manage product inventories.

Types of Databases

Databases come in many varieties. *Inverted list, hierarchic*, and *network database models* are older types of database systems that, in general, are inflexible and difficult to work with. These types of database systems were originally designed primarily for prescribed transactions that input data rather than dynamic environments where data analysis is critical.

The very weaknesses of these earlier systems are exactly why *relational database systems* now dominate newer information management systems.

Relational databases are easy to understand, design, and build. Relational databases store and present all information in *tables*, an easily understood concept. Furthermore, relational databases hide the complexities of data access from the user, making application development relatively simple when compared to other types of database systems.

Object-oriented databases are a relatively new type of system that supports the object-oriented development paradigm. The primary goal of object-oriented thinking is to raise the level of abstraction so that it is more natural to design and build an information management system. For example, in an object-oriented database, complex data structures called objects closely model the entities in a business system while methods match the business operations that act upon the objects in the system. So, rather than store tables of, say, customers, orders, and order line items, a database stores instances of customers and sales order objects. Associated methods stored in the database describe how to add, change, and delete customer and sales order objects.

Database Management Systems

A *database management system (DBMS)* is computer software that manages access to databases. A typical multi-user DBMS performs the following tasks and more:

- A DBMS safely manages shared access to a single database among multiple concurrent users. For example, a DBMS locks data as users add and update information so that users do not destructively interfere with one another's work.

- A DBMS leverages computer resources wisely so that a large number of application users can perform work with fast response times for maximum productivity.

- A DBMS protects database information in such a way that it can reconstruct work lost due to everything from a simple power outage to catastrophic site disasters.

You can purchase any one of several commercially available DBMSs to build and manage databases. The market-leading DBMS in use today is Oracle Corporation's *Oracle Server*, also known simply as *Oracle*. The latest version of Oracle Server is *Oracle8*. Oracle8 is an *object-relational database management system (ORDBMS).* That is, Oracle8 is a database server that offers the capabilities of both relational and object-oriented database systems. The goal of this book is to teach you all about Oracle8 and how it works.

Oracle8, Building on Oracle7

Oracle8 builds on the strengths of its predecessor, *Oracle7 Server.* Oracle7, originally released in early 1993, sets a lofty standard for high-end relational database management systems. Oracle7's many features made it a potent database server for all types of common business applications, including:

- *Online transaction processing (OLTP)* applications—applications that process many small update transactions such as banking, reservation, and order-entry systems.

- *Decision support (DSS)* applications—applications that query targeted information from a database for the purposes of data analysis.

- *Data warehousing applications*--applications that access large, read-only databases that are specifically optimized for fast access to even the most esoteric bits of information.

Oracle8 Server adds many new features to extend the power of Oracle Server and make it suitable for even the most demanding and complex application environments. The next few sections briefly explain the principal areas of focus for Oracle8's new features.

NOTE
If you are already familiar with Oracle7 and want to concentrate on learning only new Oracle8 features, make sure to use the chapter references in the following sections as your map to "what's new."

Oracle8 and High-End Database Environments

A high-end application tests the upper limits of a DBMS, and can be characterized by one or more attributes. For example, database applications with the following qualities could be considered high-end systems:

- A database system that manages a *very large database (VLDB)*, perhaps hundreds of gigabytes or terabytes of information

- A database system that provides database access to many concurrent users, perhaps a thousand or ten thousand users

- A database system that must guarantee constant database availability for a *mission-critical application*, no matter what, 24 hours a day, 7 days a week, 52 weeks a year (24 x 7 x 52)

With certain exceptions, most high-end database environments are not controlled by today's most popular *relational database management systems (RDBMSs)*. High-end database environments continue to be controlled by mainframe computers and non-relational database systems. Why? Certainly not because businesses want to spend exorbitant amounts of money maintaining and upgrading proprietary mainframe computer hardware, software, and operating systems. And not because people prefer to work with older, hard-to-use database management systems such as *IMS*, a hierarchic DBMS for IBM mainframes. The unfortunate reality is that while RDBMSs are relatively easy to use and manage, most RDBMSs that are available today cannot manage enormous amounts of data or perform adequately under demanding transaction loads. Consequently, expensive mainframe-based solutions are the only choice to manage high-end information systems.

Without question, Oracle Server has always been an RDBMS on the forefront of supporting VLDBs and other types of high-end database requirements. With the release of Oracle8, Oracle can now support even larger and more demanding OLTP and data warehouse applications than

Oracle7 and other RDBMSs. Oracle8's newest features for high-end systems make it possible to migrate databases previously confined to inflexible and expensive mainframe systems. The following sections briefly introduce the new features of Oracle8 that help to support high-end OLTP, DSS, and data warehouse applications.

Partitioned Tables and Indexes

Managing large amounts of data can present many administrative and database performance challenges. Oracle8's *data partitioning* features help to minimize the problems specifically associated with very large tables and indexes. For example, consider the following problem scenarios that large tables and indexes can create or magnify because of their size and storage characteristics:

■ A query requests Oracle to complete a full table scan of a very large table. Application and system performance suffers while Oracle reads the numerous data blocks for the corresponding table.

■ A mission-critical application depends primarily on a single large table. The table becomes unavailable when just a single data block in the table is inaccessible due to a disk failure. A *database administrator (DBA)* must recover the entire tablespace that contains the table before the table and corresponding mission-critical application can be brought back online.

Data partitions allow Oracle Server to store a large table (and its indexes) in smaller, more manageable *partitions* (pieces) rather than as one large chunk of data. Partitioned tables can yield many benefits, including

■ *Performance*—A large partitioned table can deliver exceptional application performance because Oracle can access its multiple partitions in parallel. Additionally, Oracle's optimizer is "partition aware" such that it automatically eliminates searches on partitions that do not apply to a particular SQL query.

■ *Availability*—The intact partitions of a table remain accessible to applications, even when a disk failure causes the data in one or more isolated partitions to become unavailable.

■ *Manageability*—Because partitions of a table are individual storage areas, a DBA can manage individual partitions autonomously for more targeted and efficient administrative operations such as database backup and recovery.

To learn more about Oracle8's new data partitioning features, read Chapter 7.

Management of Large User Populations

Large numbers of concurrent users can tax the performance of any computer system, including Oracle database systems. To better support large user communities, Oracle provides its *multithreaded server (MTS)* process architecture that dramatically reduces the overhead associated with maintaining many concurrent database sessions. Introduced as part of Oracle7, an MTS server configuration uses a small number of server-side processes to efficiently manage the requests of hundreds or even thousands of connected clients. Now, with Oracle8 and its companion networking software *Net8* (formerly known as *SQL*Net*), several features allow Oracle client/server environments to avoid operating system constraints that can limit the number of open network connections to a server. Net8's *Connection Manager* component allows for more efficient use of network resources through *multiplexing, connection pooling*, and *concentration of application requests*.

To learn more about Net8's features such as the Connection Manager, multiplexing, connection pooling, and more, read Chapter 8.

Advanced Queueing

In typical client/server database application environments, applications attempt to execute user database requests immediately, as soon as a user presses the OK button. The client then waits for the results to return before continuing work. However, some systems might prefer or even require that an application queue user requests for deferred execution. For example, demanding client/server systems might want to queue and defer the execution of low-priority transactions to less taxing off-peak hours. This allows the system to perform more critical work optimally during normal business hours. Workflow dependent applications, where the completion of one step in a business process cannot take place before another step completes, are another type of application that can benefit from the deferred execution of user transactions.

Applications that need deferred transaction execution can employ *transaction processing monitors (TP monitors)* or *message-oriented middleware (MOM)* to support their requirements. However, the use of such third-party solutions that are external to the DBMS can introduce several problems. For example, TP monitors often do not log their queues and thus cannot recover deferred transactions when a system failure occurs. Furthermore, the distributed transactions that are necessary to maintain the integrity of TP monitor queues and database information create processing overhead that can detract from application performance.

Oracle8's new *advanced queueing* feature is a database-centric alternative for applications that would like to defer the execution of database transactions. Oracle applications can use Oracle's PL/SQL-based *application programming interface (API)* to queue transactions for deferred execution, prioritize their execution, set acceptable execution times for transactions, and more. Clients can review deferred transaction results after execution occurs. Meanwhile, queued transactions are automatically protected by Oracle8's backup and recovery mechanisms.

To learn more about advanced queueing and PL/SQL, read Chapter 4.

Parallel Processing Enhancements

Multiprocessor computer systems and parallel processing environments are often necessary to support the most demanding types of business applications. The following sections explain the Oracle8 enhancements to Oracle's parallel query and parallel server features.

Parallel Query Enhancements

Parallel query processing allows Oracle to take full advantage of all available server processors and provide excellent response times for even the most CPU and I/O intensive application queries. For example, DSS and data warehousing applications typically submit demanding queries to an Oracle database server. To return results quickly to a user, Oracle divides a SQL request into subtasks, then allows multiple processors to process subtasks in parallel. Oracle merges results from each subtask and returns them quickly to the user.

With Oracle8, Oracle supports the execution of all DML operations in parallel, including INSERT, UPDATE, and DELETE operations. All queries, including those based on index scans, can also be run in parallel. To further reduce response times for SQL requests, Oracle8 automatically takes advantage of partitioned tables and indexes should they be available.

- Oracle8 can perform *intra-partition parallelism*--parallelize operations that occur within a specific table partition.

- Oracle8 can perform *inter-partition parallelism*--parallelize operations that occur among different table partitions.

- Oracle8's optimizer is *partition-aware*. That is, Oracle8 automatically eliminates searches of partitions that could not possibly contain data for a query's result set to reduce unnecessary disk I/O and boost application performance.

Parallel Server Enhancements

Oracle's Parallel Server option allows multiple database servers, or instances, running on different nodes in a loosely-clustered multiple processor system, to concurrently access a single physical Oracle database. By creating multiple avenues of database access for application users, a parallel server can provide fault-tolerance for database access should an individual node experience a software failure.

Several new Oracle8 features improve system performance and availability in an Oracle Parallel Server configuration:

- A new *distributed lock manager* coordinates database updates among the nodes of a massively parallel machine or clustered SMP machines.

- *Reverse-key indexes* eliminate block contention among the nodes of a parallel server.

- *Transparent application failover* automatically migrates user connections from a failed node to an intact node. Consequently, a parallel server can provide continuous application availability and connectivity for mission-critical applications, even in the wake of unscheduled outages.

To learn more about Oracle8's parallel query and parallel server enhancements, read Chapter 12.

Oracle8 and Oracle's Network Computing Architecture (NCA)

Most modern information management systems are based on open, standards-based network computing models. No doubt, the ability to mix and match products in an open client/server world can lead to elegant customized solutions. However, the same advantage of choice in a client/server world also introduces significant challenges. For example, with literally hundreds of application development, networking, and database products available, how does an organization identify and deploy the best products for their particular information management system? And if various system components originate from different vendors, how do you integrate, manage, and support the system so that it actually works?

To solve the dilemmas associated with deploying network-based application environments, Oracle has introduced its *Network Computing Architecture (NCA)*. NCA incorporates the needs of both network-centric computing and object-oriented development methods. The two key Oracle products that support NCA are Oracle8 Server and Sedona.

Oracle8, the Object-Relational DBMS

With the introduction of several new Oracle8 features, Oracle Server can now be considered a powerful object-relational database management system (ORDBMS).

Oracle8 Object Types and Methods

Typical business applications allow an organization to manage data and process related operations. For example, an order-entry system safely manages customer records and sales orders, and allows salespeople to input and retrieve corresponding information. Object-oriented development environments allow developers to define objects (data structures) and methods (operations) that correspond directly to an application. Consequently, object-oriented applications closely model an enterprise's business.

To support object-oriented applications, Oracle8 includes many new object-relational features that follow the SQL3 standard such as custom object types, methods, and object views. <u>A database developer builds *object types* in an Oracle database</u>. Associated *methods* define the manipulation operations available for objects of the type, and can be implemented using Java, C/C++, or Oracle's own PL/SQL. *Object views* provide a way to smoothly migrate pure relational applications to object-relational environments.

Large Object Datatypes (LOBs)

Oracle8 provides several enhancements <u>for multimedia</u> database applications with the introduction of several new character and binary *large object (LOB)* datatypes. Oracle8 LOBs can be stored separate from a table's data segment within the database, or can be stored external to the database to avoid the generation of rollback segment and log information.

To learn more about Oracle8's object extensions and multimedia datatypes, read Chapter 2.

Sedona, Oracle's New Application Development Environment

To support NCA, Oracle8's new object-oriented development environment is *Sedona*. Sedona allows for the rapid development of applications using CORBA, OLE, COM, Java, PL/SQL, ActiveX, and C/C++ objects. This book does not specifically address application development with Sedona.

Oracle8 Database Management and Security

Administration of large Oracle database systems is a challenging job. Oracle8 introduces several new features that make database administration easier and more manageable.

Backup and Recovery

Backing up databases to protect data from possible failures is perhaps the most routine job of an Oracle database administrator. On the other hand, recovering a database from a failure such as a disk crash is a challenging and sometime scary task that is by no means routine. Oracle8 and its companion management tool, *Oracle Enterprise Manager*, include several new features to make database backup and recovery more automated, easier to use, and faster.

Server-Managed Backup and Recovery

An Oracle8 Server can now maintain detailed information about recent database backups. When a database recovery is necessary, Oracle8 automatically analyzes the state of the database, determines the actions necessary to repair the system, and then automatically recovers the damaged database. In summary, Oracle8's new server-managed backup and recovery features simplify database backup and recovery by reducing the possibility of human error.

Incremental Backups

In addition to its already rich set of database backup options, Oracle8 now supports incremental backups. An *incremental database backup* can minimize backup time and size because Oracle backs up only the data blocks that have changed since the most recent backup.

Point-In-Time Recovery of Individual Tablespaces

Point-in-time recovery is often necessary to recover a database to a previous state that existed before some type of error occurred. With Oracle8, administrators can now recover complete databases as well as individual tablespaces to a specific point in time.

To learn more about Oracle8's new database backup and recovery features, read Chapter 10.

Password Management

All computer systems should draft and enforce a security policy that explains the protection of the system from intruders. Oracle8 introduces several new features that allow you to automatically enforce a database security policy's guidelines for user password management. For example, an administrator can configure an Oracle database to automatically verify that a user's new password has sufficient complexity and is not a recycled password. For distributed database environments, Oracle8 also adds support for current user database links. *Current user database links* make it unnecessary to embed a password in a database link definition.

To learn more about Oracle8's user password management features and database links, read Chapters 6 and 11.

Oracle8 and Distributed Databases

Database applications at work in networked environment can often benefit from distributing data as well as processing tasks. A *distributed database* is a collection of databases that appears to an application as a single, local database. Releases of Oracle Server prior to Oracle8 support many distributed database features, including

- Remote and distributed queries

- Distributed transactions protected by two-phase commit

- Robust data replication features such as read-only and updatable table snapshots, as well as multi-master replication.

Oracle8 enhances current distributed database support with several new features.

Replication Enhancements

Replication is the copying and maintaining of database objects in multiple databases of a distributed database system. Replication can improve the performance and protect the availability of database applications because alternate access options exist. For example, an application can normally access a local database rather than a remote server to minimize network traffic and achieve maximum performance. However, if the local database server experiences a failure, the application can continue to function because other servers with replicated data remain accessible.

Oracle8 provides several enhancements for replication environments.

■ Oracle8 can dramatically improve throughput performance when replicating data. To start with, Oracle8 <u>reduces the amount of replicated data propagated over the network.</u> And Oracle8's new *parallel propagation* feature parallelizes the movement of a replication transaction stream to transmit replication information among sites more efficiently.

■ Oracle8 now supports the fast refresh of most *subquery snapshots.* Consequently, applications such as sales force automation can easily configure subsets of data that Oracle can maintain efficiently for mass deployment.

■ Oracle's *Replication Manager* makes it easier to configure advanced replication systems that use multi-master replication and updatable snapshots.

To learn more about Oracle8's new data replication features, read Chapter 11.

Distributed Security Domains

Traditionally, it's a challenge to manage the security of client/server systems, especially when they encompass multiple databases. To provide users with cross-database access, all servers in the network must manage redundant database user account information. When hundreds of users must have access to multiple servers, simple account administration quickly becomes a nightmare.

To simplify the management of user authentication in a distributed database system, Oracle8 introduces <u>distributed security domains</u>. An Oracle8 *distributed security domain* is a collection of selected Oracle8 database servers in a network. The distributed security domain employs a central authority, such as an *Oracle Security Service* or a third-party product such as Kerberos or DCE, to register and manage *global users* and *roles* in the domain. Servers can trust each other because of mutual authentication and because all network packets are secured using Net8's Secure Network Services option.

To learn more about distributed security domains, read Chapter 11.

Heterogeneous Data Access

Heterogeneous distributed databases correlate information from various data sources. For example, a distributed database system might support an application that must access databases managed by Oracle Server and *foreign systems* such as IBM's DB2. Oracle8's new *Heterogeneous Services* allows database applications to access a foreign data system just as though it was a local Oracle8 server.

To learn more about Oracle8's new Heterogeneous Services, read Chapter 11.

Onward ...

Oracle8 certainly is a powerful product that you can use to manage information. Now that you have the "big picture" of what Oracle8 is all about, the remaining chapters in this book present Oracle8's architecture and essential concepts so that you can more clearly understand how to better use Oracle8 for information management.

PART

II

Oracle8 Fundamentals

CHAPTER
2

Basic Relational
Database Structures

very database application is built upon a set of related database objects that store the application's data and allow the application to function. This chapter introduces Oracle8 database objects such as tables and views. This chapter discusses only the logical concepts of database objects. Discussions of data storage (storage parameters, partitioning, etc.) will come later in more advanced chapters. This chapter's topics include:

- Schemas

- Tables

- Integrity constraints

- Views

- Indexes and data clusters

- Sequences

- Synonyms

Schemas—Organizing Database Objects

It is easier to solve most problems in life when you are organized and have a well-designed plan to achieve your goal. If you are unorganized, you will most certainly realize your goals less efficiently, if ever at all. Designing an information management system that uses Oracle is no different.

Databases organize related objects within a database *schema*. For example, it's typical to organize all of the tables, views, and other database objects necessary to support an application within a single database schema. This way, it's clear that the purpose of a certain table, view, or other database object is to support the corresponding application system. Figure 2-1 illustrates the idea of an application schema.

Schemas, An Entirely Logical Concept

It's important to understand that schemas do not physically organize the storage of database objects. Rather, schemas *logically* organize related database objects. In other words, the logical organization of database

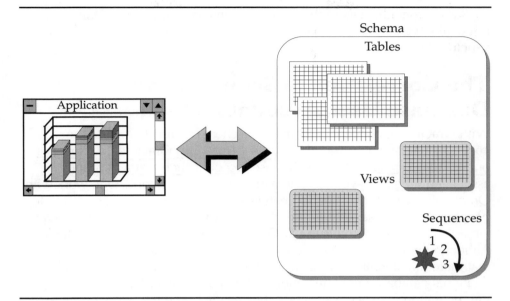

FIGURE 2-1.   *A schema is a logical organization of related database objects.*

objects within schemas is purely for the benefit of organization and has
absolutely nothing to do with the physical storage of database objects.

The logical organization that schemas offer can have practical benefits.
For example, consider an Oracle database with two schemas, S1 and S2.
Each schema can have a table called T1. Even though the two tables share
the same name, they are uniquely identifiable because they are within
different database schemas. Using standard dot notation, the complete
names for the different tables would be S1.T1 and S2.T1.

If the idea of logical versus physical organization is confusing to you,
consider how operating systems organize files on disk. The layout of file
folders and files in a graphical file management utility, such as the Microsoft
Windows Explorer, does not necessarily correspond to the physical location
of the folders and files on a particular disk drive. File folders represent the
logical organization of operating system files. The underlying operating
system decides where to physically store the blocks for each operating
system file, independent of the logical organization of encompassing
file folders.

Subsequent chapters of this book explain more about how Oracle can physically organize the storage of database objects using physical storage structures.

The Correlation of Schemas and Database User Accounts

With Oracle, the concept of a database schema is directly tied to the concept of a database user. That is, a schema in an Oracle database has a one-to-one correspondence with a user account such that a user and its associated schema have the same name. As a result, people who work with Oracle often blur the distinction between users and schemas. For example, people commonly say things like "the user SCOTT owns the EMP and DEPT tables" rather than "the schema SCOTT contains the EMP and DEPT tables." Although these two sentences are more-or-less equivalent, understand that there might be a clear distinction between users and schemas with relational database implementations other than Oracle. Therefore, while the separation between users and schemas might seem trivial for Oracle, the distinction might be very important if you plan to work with other database systems.

The Data Dictionary—A Unique Schema

Every Oracle database uses a number of system tables, views, and other database objects to keep track of *metadata*—data about the data itself in a database. This collection of system objects is called the Oracle database's *data dictionary* or *system catalog*. Oracle organizes a database's data dictionary within the *SYS* schema. You'll learn more about specific tables and views in an Oracle database's data dictionary throughout the chapters of this book.

Database Tables

Tables are the basic data structure in any relational database. A *table* is nothing more than an organized collection of *records*, or *rows*, that all have the same *attributes*, or *columns*. Figure 2-2 illustrates a typical CUSTOMERS table in a relational database.

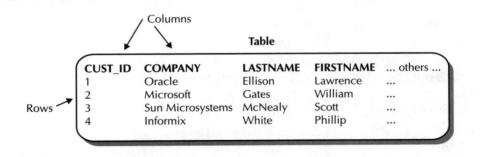

FIGURE 2-2.   *A table is a set of records with the same attributes.*

Each customer record in the example CUSTOMERS table has the same attributes, including an ID, a company name, a last name, a first name, and so on.

When you create tables, the two primary things that you must consider are the following:

- The table's columns, which describe the table's structure

- The table's integrity constraints, which describe the data that is acceptable within the table

The following sections explain more about columns and integrity constraints.

Columns and Datatypes

When you create a table for an Oracle database, you establish the structure of the table by identifying the columns that describe the table's attributes. Furthermore, every column in a table has a datatype. A column's *datatype* describes the basic type of data that is acceptable in the column. For example, the CUST_ID column in the CUSTOMERS table uses the basic Oracle datatype NUMBER because the column stores ID numbers.

Oracle supports many fundamental datatypes that you can use when creating a relational database table and its columns. Table 2-1 and the following sections describe the most commonly used Oracle datatypes.

Datatype	Description
CHAR (*size*)	Stores fixed-length character strings up to 2,000 bytes
VARCHAR2 (*size*)	Stores variable-length character strings up to 4,000 bytes
NUMBER (*precision, scale*)	Stores any type of number
DATE	Stores dates and times
CLOB	Stores single-byte character large objects up to four gigabytes
BLOB	Stores binary large objects up to four gigabytes

TABLE 2-1.   *The Most Commonly Used Oracle Datatypes*

CHAR and VARCHAR2—Oracle's Character Datatypes

Oracle's CHAR and VARCHAR2 are the most commonly used datatypes that a table uses for columns that store character strings. The Oracle datatype *CHAR* is appropriate for columns that store fixed-length character strings such as two-letter USA state codes. Alternatively, the Oracle datatype *VARCHAR2* is useful for columns that store variable-length character strings such as names and addresses. The primary difference between the two character datatypes relates to how Oracle stores strings shorter than the maximum length of a column.

- When a string in a CHAR column is less than the column's *size*, Oracle *pads* (appends) the end of the string with blank spaces to create a string that matches the column's *size*.

- When a string in a VARCHAR2 column is less than the column's maximum *size*, Oracle stores only the string and does not pad the string with blanks.

Thus, when the strings in a column vary in length, Oracle can store them more efficiently in a VARCHAR2 column than in a CHAR column.

NUMBER—Oracle's Numeric Datatype

To declare columns that are fit to store numbers, you can use Oracle's *NUMBER* datatype. Rather than have several numeric datatypes, Oracle's NUMBER datatype supports the storage of all types of numbers, including integers, floating-point numbers, real numbers, etc. You can limit the domain of acceptable numbers in a column by specifying a *precision* and *scale* for a NUMBER column.

DATE—Oracle Time-Related Datatype

When you declare a table column with the *DATE* datatype, the column can store all types of time-related information, including dates and associated times.

CLOBs, BLOBs, and More—Oracle's Multimedia Datatypes

Because databases are secure, fast, and safe storage areas for data, they are often employed as data repositories for multimedia applications. To support such content-rich applications, Oracle8 supports several different *large object (LOB) datatypes* that can store unstructured information such as text documents, static images, video, audio, and more.

- A *CLOB* column stores character objects such as documents.

- A *BLOB* column stores large binary objects such as graphics, video clips, or sound files.

- A *BFILE* column stores file pointers to LOBs managed by file systems external to the database. For example, a BFILE column might be a list of filename references for photos stored on a CD-ROM.

The following section explains several other important LOB characteristics in contrast to some older Oracle large object datatypes.

Contrasting LOBS with Older Oracle Large Object Datatypes

For backward compatibility, Oracle8 continues to support older Oracle datatypes designed for large objects, such as *LONG* and *LONG RAW*.

However, Oracle8's newer LOB datatypes have several advantages over the older Oracle large datatypes.

- A table can have multiple CLOB, BLOB, and BFILE columns. In contrast, a table can have only one LONG or LONG RAW column.

- A table stores only small *locators* (pointers) for the LOBs in a column rather than the actual large objects themselves. In contrast, a table stores data for a LONG column within the table itself.

- A LOB column can have storage characteristics independent from those of the encompassing table, making it easier to address the large disk requirements typically associated with LOBs. For example, it's possible to separate the storage of primary table data and related LOBs to different physical locations (for example, disk drives). In contrast, a table physically stores the data for a LONG column in the same storage area that contains all other table data.

- Applications can efficiently access and manipulate pieces of a LOB. Alternatively, applications must access an entire LONG field as an atomic (indivisible) piece of data.

Before migrating or designing new multimedia applications for Oracle8, consider the advantages of Oracle8's newer LOB datatypes versus older large object datatypes.

Oracle's National Language Support Character Datatypes

Oracle *National Language Support (NLS)* features allow databases to store and manipulate character data in many languages. Some languages have character sets that require several bytes for each character. The special Oracle datatypes *NCHAR, NVARCHAR2,* and *NCLOB* are datatypes that are counterparts to the CHAR, VARCHAR2, and CLOB datatypes, respectively.

ANSI Datatypes and Others

Oracle8 also supports the specification of Oracle datatypes using other standard datatypes. For example, Table 2-2 lists the *ANSI (American*

This ANSI/ISO Datatype ...	... converts to this Oracle Datatype
CHARACTER CHAR	CHAR
CHARACTER VARYING CHAR VARYING	VARCHAR2
NATIONAL CHARACTER NATIONAL CHAR NCHAR	NCHAR
NATIONAL CHARACTER VARYING NATIONAL CHAR VARYING NCHAR VARYING	NVARCHAR2
NUMERIC DECIMAL INTEGER INT SMALLINT FLOAT DOUBLE PRECISION REAL	NUMBER

TABLE 2-2.   *Oracle Supports the Specification of Oracle Datatypes Using ANSI Standard Datatypes.*

National Standards Institute)/ISO (International Organization of Standards) standard datatypes that Oracle supports.

Default Column Values

When you declare a column for a table, you can also declare a corresponding *default column value*. Oracle uses the default value of a column when an application inserts a new row into the encompassing table, but omits a value for the column. For example, you might indicate that the default value for the ORDER_DATE column of the ORDERS table be the current system time when an application creates a new order.

Unless you indicate otherwise, the initial default value for a column is a *null* (an absence of value).

Data Integrity and Integrity Constraints

Data integrity is a fundamental principle of the relational database model. When a database has integrity, it is another way of saying that the database contains only accurate and acceptable information. For obvious reasons, data integrity is a desirable attribute for a database.

To a limited degree, a column's datatype establishes a more limited domain of acceptable values for the column—the type of data that the column can store. For example, a DATE column can contain valid dates and times, but not numbers or character strings. While simple column datatypes are useful for enforcing a basic level of data integrity, there are typically more complex integrity rules that are necessary to enforce in a relational database. In fact, the relational database model itself outlines several inherent data integrity rules that an RDBMS must uphold. The next few sections describe these common integrity rules and related issues.

Domain Integrity, Nulls, and Complex Domains

Domain integrity defines the domain of acceptable values for a column. For example, a customer record is not valid unless the customer's state abbreviation code is one of the fifty or so USA state codes.

Besides using column datatypes, Oracle supports two types of integrity constraints that allow you to further limit the domain of a column:

- A column can have a *NOT NULL constraint* to eliminate the possibility of nulls (absent values) in the column.

- You can use a *CHECK constraint* to declare a complex domain integrity rule as part of a table. A CHECK constraint commonly contains an explicit list of the acceptable values for a column. For example, "M" and "F" in a column that contains gender information; "AL", "AK", …, "WY" in a column that contains USA state codes, and so on.

Entity Integrity, Primary Keys, and Alternate Keys

Entity integrity ensures that every row in a table is unique. As a result, entity integrity eliminates the possibility of duplicate records in the table and makes every row in the table uniquely identifiable.

The primary key of a table ensures its entity integrity. A *primary key* is a column that uniquely identifies the rows in a table. Typically, tables in a relational database use ID-type columns as primary keys. For example, a customer table might include an ID column to uniquely identify the customer records within. This way, even if two customers, say John Smith and his son John Smith (Jr.), have the same name, address, phone number, and so on, they have distinct ID numbers that make them different.

A table's primary key is sometimes a *composite key*; that is, it is composed of more than one column. For example, the primary key in a typical line item table of an order-entry system might have a composite primary key that is described by the ORDER_ID and ITEM_ID columns. In this example of a composite primary key, many line item records can have the same line item ID (1, 2, 3, ...), but no two line item records can have the same order ID and line item ID combination (order ID 1, line item IDs 1,2,3, ... ; order ID 2, line item IDs 1,2,3, ... ; and so on).

Optionally, a table might require secondary levels of entity integrity. *Alternate keys* are columns or sets of columns that do not contain duplicate values within them. For example, the EMAIL column in an employee table might be an alternate key to guarantee that all employees have unique email addresses.

Referential Integrity, Foreign Keys, and Referential Actions

Referential integrity, sometimes called *relation integrity*, establishes the relationships among different columns and tables in a database. Referential integrity ensures that each column value in a *foreign key* of a *child* (or *detail*) *table* matches a value in the primary or an alternate key of a related *parent* (or *master*) *table*. For example, a row in the EMP table is not valid unless the employee's department number refers to a valid department number in the DEPT table. When the parent and child table are the same, this is called s*elf-referential integrity*. Figure 2-3 illustrates the terminology and concepts related to referential integrity.

REFERENTIAL ACTIONS   Referential integrity ensures that each value in a foreign key always has a matching parent key value. To guarantee referential integrity, an RDBMS must also be able to address database operations that manipulate parent keys. For example, when a user deletes a sales order, what happens to the dependent line items for that order?

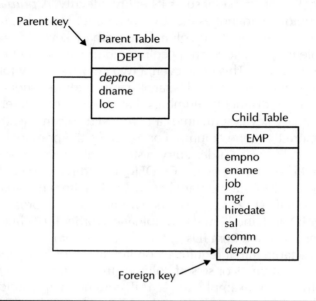

FIGURE 2-3. *Referential integrity describes the relationships among columns and tables in a relational database.*

Referential actions describe what to do in cases where an application updates or deletes a parent key that has dependent child records.

The relational database model describes several referential actions:

■ *Update/Delete Restrict* The RDBMS does not allow an application to update a parent key or delete a parent row that has one or more dependent child records. For example, you cannot delete a sales order from the ORDERS table if it has corresponding line items in the ITEMS table.

■ *Delete Cascade* When an application deletes a row from the parent table, the RDBMS cascades the delete by deleting all dependent records in a child table. For example, when you delete an order from the ORDERS table, the RDBMS automatically removes all corresponding line items from the ITEMS table.

■ *Update Cascade* When an application updates a parent key, the RDBMS cascades the update to the dependent foreign keys. For example, when you change an order's ID in the ORDERS table, the RDBMS would automatically update the order ID of all corresponding line item records in the ITEMS table. This referential action is rarely useful because applications typically do not allow users to update key values.

■ *Update/Delete Set Null* When an application updates or deletes a parent key, all dependent keys are set to null.

■ *Update/Delete Set Default* When an application updates or deletes a parent key, all dependent keys are set to a meaningful default value.

By default, Oracle8 enforces the Update/Delete Restrict referential actions for all referential integrity constraints. Optionally, Oracle can perform the Delete Cascade referential action for a referential integrity constraint.

When Does Oracle Enforce Integrity Constraint Rules?
Oracle can enforce an integrity constraint at two different times:

■ Oracle can enforce an integrity constraint immediately after an application submits a SQL statement to insert, update, or delete rows in a table. When a statement causes a data integrity violation, Oracle automatically rolls back the effects of the statement.

■ Oracle can defer the enforcement of an integrity constraint for the SQL statements in a transaction until an application commits the transaction. When any statement in the transaction causes a data integrity violation, Oracle automatically rolls back the entire transaction (that is, the effects of all statements in the transaction).

NOTE
The next chapter teaches you all about SQL and transactions.

When you declare an individual integrity constraint, you can specify the enforcement timing that you prefer for the constraint—immediate or deferred. Base your choice on specific application requirements. Typical database applications should choose the default, to immediately check data integrity after the execution of each SQL statement. However, certain applications, such as large batch jobs, must update many tables such that integrity rules are temporarily violated until the end of the transaction.

Views—A Different Way of Looking at Table Data

Once you define the tables in a database, you can start to focus on other things that enhance the usability of the database. You can start by defining views of the tables in your database. A *view* is a database object that presents table data. Why and how would you use views to present table data? The following examples demonstrate the use of views in a database:

■ You can use a simple view to expose all rows and columns in a table. For example, you might create a view called CUST that presents all customer records in the CUSTOMERS table.

■ You can use a view to protect the security of specific table data by exposing only a subset of the rows and/or columns in a table. For example, you might create a view called CUST_USA that presents only the LAST_NAME, FIRST_NAME, and PHONE columns in the CUSTOMERS table for customers that reside in the USA.

■ You can use a view to simplify application coding. For example, a complex view might join the data of related parent and child tables to make it appear as though a different table exists in the database. For example, you might create a view called ORDER_ITEMS that joins related records in the ORDERS and ITEMS tables.

■ You can use a view to present derived data that is not actually stored in a table. For example, you might create a view of the ITEMS table with a column called TOTAL that calculates the line total for each record.

Figure 2-4 illustrates the CUST and CUST_USA views in the previous examples.

As the previous examples illustrate, views provide a flexible means to present the table data in a database. In fact, you can create a view of any data that you can represent with a SQL query. That's because a view is really just a query that Oracle stores in a database's data dictionary as a database object. When an application uses a view to do something, Oracle derives the data of the view based on the view's *defining query*. For example, when an application queries the CUST_USA view described in a

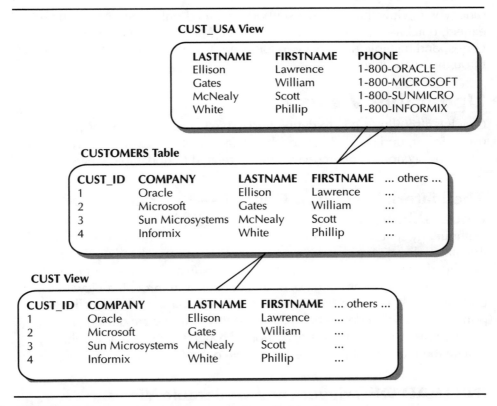

FIGURE 2-4. *A view is a representation of table data.*

previous example, Oracle processes the query against the data described by the view's defining query.

NOTE
The next chapter teaches you all about SQL queries.

The next few sections explain more about the specific types of views that Oracle8 supports.

→ Read-Only Views

One type of view that Oracle8 supports is a read-only view. As you might expect, database applications can use a *read-only view* to retrieve corresponding table data, but cannot insert, update, or delete table data through a read-only view.

→ Updatable Views

Oracle8 also allows you to define *updatable views* that an application can use to insert, update, and delete table data as well as query data. The following sections explain several topics related to updatable views.

The Materialized View Principle—Restrictions for Updatable Views

Without any special work, a view can be updatable if the server can uphold the materialized view principle when applications use the view. Briefly translated, the *materialized view principle* ensures that the server can correctly map an insert, update, or delete operation through a view to the underlying table data of the view. To comply with the materialized view principle, you must define an updatable view with certain attributes. Furthermore, Oracle restricts operations through the view that would violate the integrity of the underlying table or tables.

INSTEAD OF Triggers and Updatable Views

Even when a view's attributes violate the materialized view principle, you can still make the view updatable if you define the view with INSTEAD OF triggers. *INSTEAD OF triggers* are PL/SQL programs that you define with a view. These triggers explain what to do when INSERT, UPDATE, and DELETE statements target the view that would otherwise not be updatable. See Chapter 4 for more information about PL/SQL and triggers, and Chapter 5 for more information about views and INSTEAD OF triggers.

Updatable Views and Integrity Constraints

Oracle8 automatically enforces the integrity constraints of a table, no matter whether applications work directly with the table or indirectly with an updatable view of the table. Optionally, you can define an updatable view with a special type of CHECK integrity constraint. When you do so, Oracle allows applications to insert and update through the view only those rows that the view can also read. This special type of integrity constraint prevents table access through a view that is not authorized by the definition of the view itself. For example, if you defined the CUST_USA view (see earlier) with a view constraint, an application can use the view to insert new customers, but only customers that live in the USA.

Other Types of Views

Oracle8 allows you to create read-only and updatable views that support unique server functionality, including:

- Partition views
- Object views

See the sections "Objects and Views" in Chapter 5 and "Partition Extended Table Names" in Chapter 6 later in this book that explain more about using views.

Indexes—Improving the Performance of Table Access

The performance of an application is always critical. That's because the productivity of an application user directly relates to the amount of time that the user must sit idle while the application tries to complete work. With database applications, performance depends greatly on how fast an application can access table data. Typically, disk I/O is the primary performance determining factor for table access—the less disk I/O that's necessary to access table data, the better the dependent applications will perform. In general, it's best to try and minimize the amount of disk access that applications must perform when working with database tables.

The judicious use of table indexes is the principal method to reduce disk I/O and improve the performance of table access. Just like an index in a book, an *index* of a table column (or set of columns) allows Oracle to quickly find specific table records. When an application queries a table and uses an indexed column in its selection criteria, Oracle automatically uses the index to quickly find the target rows with minimal disk I/O. Without an index, Oracle has to read the entire table from disk to locate rows that match a selection criteria.

The presence of an index for a table is entirely optional and transparent to users and developers of database applications. For example:

■ Applications can access table data with or without associated indexes.

■ When an index is present and will help the performance of an application request, Oracle automatically uses the index; otherwise, Oracle ignores the index.

■ Oracle automatically updates an index to keep it in synch with its table.

Although indexes can dramatically improve the performance of application requests, it's unwise to index every column in a table. Indexes are meaningful only for the key columns that application requests specifically use to find rows of interest. Furthermore, index maintenance generates overhead—unnecessary indexes can actually slow down your system rather than improve its performance.

Oracle8 supports several different types of indexes to satisfy many types of application requirements. The following sections explain more about the various types of indexes that you can create for a table's columns.

B-Tree Indexes

The default and most common type of index for a table column is a B-tree index. A *B-tree index* is an ordered tree of index nodes, each of which

contains one or more index entries. Each *index entry* corresponds to a
row in the table, and contains:

- The indexed column value (or set of values) for the row

- The *ROWID*, or physical disk location, of the row

A B-tree index contains an entry for every row in the table, unless the
index entry for a row is null. Figure 2-5 illustrates a typical B-tree index.
    When using a B-tree index, Oracle descends the tree of index nodes
looking for index values that match the selection criteria of the query.
When it finds a match, Oracle uses the corresponding ROWID to locate
and read the associated table row data from disk.

Using B-Tree Indexes Appropriately

B-tree indexes are not appropriate for all types of applications and all types
of columns in a table. In general, B-tree indexes are the best choice for

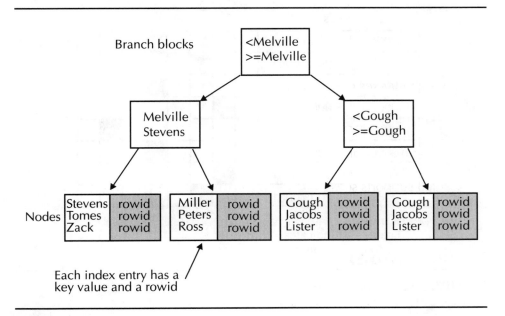

FIGURE 2-5.   *A B-tree index*

OLTP applications where data is constantly being inserted, updated, and deleted. In such environments, B-tree indexes work best for key columns that contain many distinct values relative to the total number of key values in the column. The primary and alternate keys in a table are perfect examples of columns that should have B-tree indexes. Conveniently, Oracle8 automatically creates B-tree indexes for all PRIMARY KEY and UNIQUE integrity constraints of a table.

Bitmap Indexes

Another Oracle8 indexing option for the columns in a table is a *bitmap index*. As Figure 2-6 illustrates, you can visualize a *bitmap index* of a column as a table.

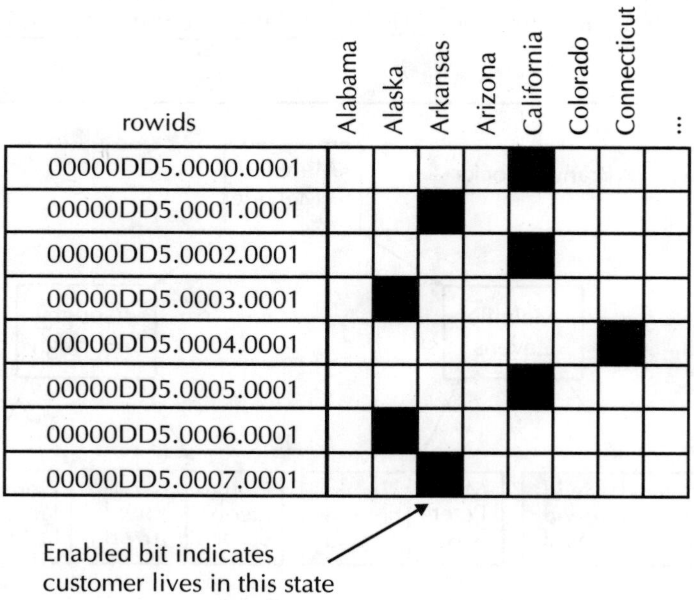

rowids	Alabama	Alaska	Arkansas	Arizona	California	Colorado	Connecticut	...
00000DD5.0000.0001					■			
00000DD5.0001.0001			■					
00000DD5.0002.0001					■			
00000DD5.0003.0001		■						
00000DD5.0004.0001							■	
00000DD5.0005.0001					■			
00000DD5.0006.0001		■						
00000DD5.0007.0001			■					

Enabled bit indicates customer lives in this state

FIGURE 2-6. *A bitmap index*

Figure 2-6 illustrates the following characteristics of a bitmap index:

- The columns in a bitmap index correspond to each distinct value in the indexed column—in this example, the 50 or so different U.S. state abbreviation codes.

- Each row in a bitmap index corresponds to a row in the table that is being indexed.

- When a row contains a specific indexed value, the bit for that value in the row is 1 and the bits for all other values in the same row are 0.

Using Bitmap Indexes Appropriately

Bitmap indexes are not suitable for many types of indexing needs for a couple of reasons:

- Bitmap indexes work best with columns that have just a few distinct values relative to the total number of rows in the table. The more distinct values that an indexed column contains, the more columns in its bitmap index, and the more space that is necessary to store the index.

- Because of the way that Oracle must lay out a bitmap index, bitmap indexes are useful typically only for DSS and data warehouse applications that query data. Bitmap indexes should not be created to support applications that frequently insert and update data.

Index-Organized Tables

When you create a B-tree or bitmap index for a table, Oracle creates a separate data structure to store the index's data. Another indexing option is to create a table "within" a B-tree index, or as an *index-organized table*. In an index-organized table, each index entry contains a key value and its corresponding row data. Index-organized tables must have a primary key, which serves as the index for the structure. Figure 2-7 illustrates the structure of an index-organized table.

In general, index-organized tables are appropriate only for applications that manage complex or unstructured data, and thus require some form of

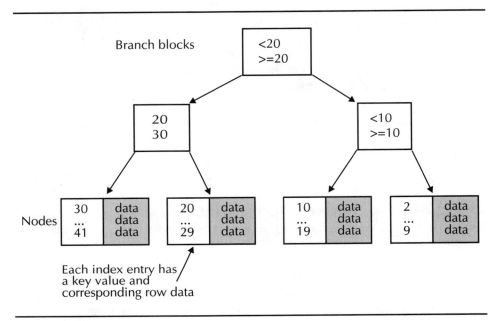

Branch blocks

FIGURE 2-7. *An index-organized table*

cooperative indexing. With *cooperative indexing*, the application must
be able to interpret the non-key values that are part of each index-entry.
Spatial data and online analytical processing (OLAP) applications are
examples of applications that manage complex data and can benefit from
the use of index-organized tables.

Other Indexing Options

Just as with views, Oracle8 allows you to create special types of indexes
that support some unique server features.

- partition indexes
- reverse key indexes

See "Partitioned Indexes" in Chapter 7 and "Reverse Key Indexes"
in Chapter 12 later in this book to learn more about these other Oracle8
index options.

Data Clusters—A Unique Way of Storing Table Data

Oracle8 also offers data clusters as an alternative to indexing, which can also decrease disk I/O for table access. A *data cluster* is a unique way of storing table data. In a data cluster, Oracle clusters the related rows of one or more tables together in the same data block. Figure 2-8 is an example of a data cluster.

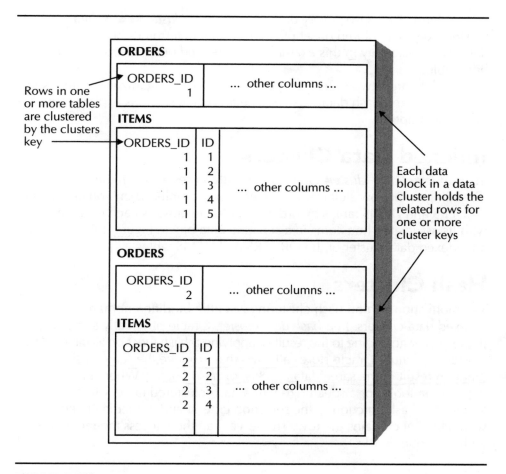

FIGURE 2-8. *A data cluster*

The motivation for using a data cluster is to store on disk the rows that an application commonly uses together. When the application requests the set of rows, Oracle can retrieve all the requested rows with perhaps one or just a few disk I/Os. For example, you might use a data cluster to "prejoin" the ORDERS and ITEMS table in a data warehouse. When a sales analysis application requests historical information about specific sales orders, Oracle can read the data for a specific order with only one disk I/O. In contrast, when related rows are stored unclustered in random data blocks across a disk, several disk I/Os are necessary to complete the application's request.

As Figure 2-8 shows, every data cluster has a *cluster key*. A data cluster's key is a column or set of columns that determines how to cluster data. The cluster key in this example is the related order ID column of both tables.

Oracle8 offers two different types of data cluster organizations: indexed data clusters and hash data clusters. The following sections explain more about each option.

Indexed Data Clusters

In an *indexed data cluster,* Oracle physically stores a row in the cluster according to the row's cluster key value. For example, when you cluster the ORDERS and ITEMS tables by order IDs, Oracle clusters each order along with its associated line items in a separate data block. Figure 2-8 illustrates an indexed data cluster of the ORDERS and ITEMS tables.

Hash Clusters

The motivation behind hash clustering is a little bit different than with indexed data clusters. In a *hash data cluster,* Oracle physically stores a row in the cluster according to the result of applying a *hash function* to the row's cluster key value. Oracle stores all rows that produce the same hash function result in the same data block(s) or *hash bucket.* When an application looks for a specific row in a hash-clustered table, Oracle applies the hash function to the selection criteria and immediately knows which bucket contains the row. The server can then access the target row with only one disk I/O.

Using Data Clusters Appropriately

As with the different types of indexes that Oracle8 offers, index and hash clusters have particular settings in which they work better than others:

- Indexed data clusters have been available for many releases of Oracle. In most cases, indexed data clusters produce only minimal gains in application performance. Consequently, developers typically opt to use indexes or hash clusters rather than indexed data clusters to improve application performance.

- Similar to bitmap indexes, a hash cluster has a rigid physical structure that does not work well when applications make extensive inserts and updates to table data.

- The previous example of a hash cluster shows how hash clusters can dramatically improve the performance of application queries that use exact match searches, or equality searches. In contrast, hash clusters perform poorly for queries that look for ranges of rows. Oracle can much better service range searches using B-tree indexes.

Sequences—Efficient Generation of Unique Values

An OLTP application, such as an airline reservation system, typically supports a large number of concurrent users. As each user's transaction inserts one or more new rows into various database tables, coordinating the generation of unique primary keys among multiple, concurrent transactions can be a significant challenge for the application.

Fortunately, Oracle8 has a feature that makes the generation of unique values a trivial matter. A *sequence* is a database object that generates a series of unique integers. When an application inserts a new row into a table, the application simply requests a database sequence to provide the next available value in the sequence for the new row's primary key value. What's more, the application can subsequently reuse a generated sequence number to coordinate the foreign key values in related child rows. Oracle manages sequence generation with an insignificant amount of overhead, allowing even the most demanding of OLTP applications to perform well.

As the previous example reveals, a sequence is appropriate only for tables that use simple, numerical columns as keys. When you create a sequence, you can customize it to suit an application's particular needs; for example, an Oracle sequence can ascend or descend by one or more integers, have a maximum or minimum value, and more.

Synonyms—Objects by a Different Name

When developers build a database application, it's prudent to avoid having application logic directly reference tables, views, and other database objects. Otherwise, applications must be updated and recompiled after an administrator makes a simple modification to an object such as a name or structural change.

To help make applications less dependent on database objects, you create synonyms for database objects. A *synonym* is a simple alias for a table, view, sequence, or other database object. Because a synonym is just an alternate name for an object, it requires no storage other than its definition in the data dictionary. When an application uses a synonym, Oracle forwards the request to the synonym's underlying base object.

Oracle allows you to create both public and private synonyms. A *public synonym* is an object alias that is available to every user in a database. A *private synonym* is a synonym within the schema of a specific user who has control over its use by others.

An Example Application Schema

This chapter has presented a number of Oracle8 concepts that relate to schemas and database objects. Figure 2-9 is a representation of the example SALES schema used throughout this book.

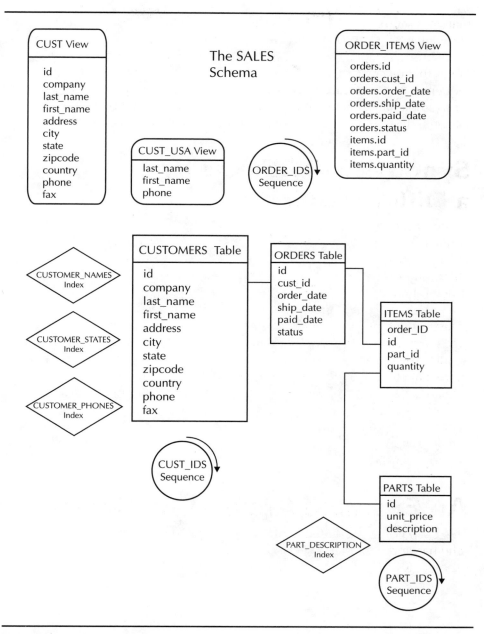

FIGURE 2-9.   *An example of a database schema*

CHAPTER
3

Using SQL and
Transactions

o get work done, applications must communicate with Oracle8 to enter and retrieve data, and do so in a way that protects the integrity of the database's data. This chapter introduces the basic concepts of how applications use SQL statements and encompassing transactions to interact with an Oracle8 database system.

SQL—Communicating with Oracle8

To work with a commercial relational database system such as Oracle8, applications must use *Structured Query Language (SQL)* commands. SQL (pronounced both "sequel" and "es-que-el") is a simple command language that allows database administrators, developers, and application users to:

- Retrieve, enter, update, and delete database data

- Create, alter, and drop database objects

   In fact, the only way that an application can interact with an Oracle database server is to issue a SQL command. Sophisticated graphical user interfaces might hide the complexities of SQL commands from users, but under the covers, an application always communicates with Oracle using SQL. The next few sections briefly introduce the different categories of SQL commands and the most commonly used commands in each category.

Queries

The most basic SQL statement is a query. A *query* is a SQL statement that uses the SELECT command to retrieve information from a database. For example, the following query retrieves all rows and columns from the ORDERS table in the SALES schema:

```
SELECT * FROM sales.orders;

ID          CUST_ID    ORDER_DATE SHIP_DATE PAID_DATE STATUS
----------  ---------- ---------- --------- --------- ------
         1           1 16-OCT-97  16-OCT-97 16-OCT-97 F
         2          10 16-OCT-97  16-OCT-97 16-OCT-97 B
         3          23 16-OCT-97  16-OCT-97 16-OCT-97 F
...
```

Column Lists and Selection Criteria

A query's *result set* is the set of columns and rows that the query requests from a database server. In the previous example:

- The wildcard character * indicates that the query should retrieve all columns from the table

- The absence of any selection criteria indicates that the query should retrieve all rows from the table

Alternatively, a query can request only specific columns and rows. For example:

```
SELECT id, order_date
  FROM sales.orders
  WHERE cust_id = 1;

ID          ORDER_DATE
---------- ----------
        1  16-OCT-97
       68  19-OCT-97
      130  23-OCT-97
...
```

This query requests only the ID and ORDER_DATE columns of orders placed by customer number 1. A *column list* identifies the columns in a query's result set, while a *WHERE clause* provides selection criteria for the rows in a query's result set. The following SQL statements show more complex examples of selection criteria in a query's WHERE clause.

```
SELECT * FROM sales.orders
  WHERE order_date = '16-10-97' AND status = 'F';

ID          CUST_ID     ORDER_DATE SHIP_DATE PAID_DATE STATUS
---------- ----------  ---------- --------- --------- ------
        1           1  16-OCT-97  16-OCT-97 16-OCT-97 F
        3          23  16-OCT-97  16-OCT-97 16-OCT-97 F
...

SELECT * FROM sales.orders
  WHERE cust_id = (
    SELECT id FROM sales.customers
      WHERE last_name = 'Ellison' OR last_name = 'White' );
```

```
ID          CUST_ID    ORDER_DATE SHIP_DATE PAID_DATE STATUS
----------  ---------- ---------- --------- --------- ------
        1           1 16-OCT-97  16-OCT-97 16-OCT-97 F
        2          10 16-OCT-97  16-OCT-97 16-OCT-97 B
...
```

The first example demonstrates how the Boolean operator AND can create a more complex condition to restrict the result set of a query. The second example demonstrates a subquery. A *subquery* is nested inside a WHERE clause to define selection criteria. Notice that the subquery in this example uses the Boolean operator OR to create a more complex condition that expands the result set of the subquery.

Joins

The previous examples are queries that target data from only one table. A query can also *join* information from multiple tables. For example, the following join query relates corresponding information from the child table ITEMS and its parent table PARTS.

```
SELECT i.id lineid, p.description, i.quantity, p.unitprice
  FROM sales.items i, sales.parts p
 WHERE i.order_id = 1732
   AND i.part_id = p.id;

LINEID      DESCRIPTION          QUANTITY   UNIT_PRICE
----------  -------------------- ---------- ----------
        1 Pentium 166 CPU              2       150.9
        2 Network Computer            1         500
...
```

This example introduces several SQL constructs:

■ The table list indicates the two tables in the join query, ITEMS and PARTS. For convenience in other parts of the query, the query also defines corresponding one-letter *aliases* for each table, I and P.

■ The column list prefixes each column name with the table alias for the corresponding table name.

■   The ITEMS and PARTS tables both have an ID column. For clarity,
the column list declares a *column alias* for the I.ID column to
remove ambiguity concerning the column's reference.

■   The second condition of the WHERE clause defines the join relation
of the two tables.

Sorting Query Output

A query can sort the rows in its result set in ascending or descending order.
For example:

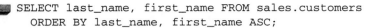

```
SELECT last_name, first_name FROM sales.customers
   ORDER BY last_name, first_name ASC;

LAST_NAME          FIRST_NAME
------------------ -------------------
Ellison            Lawrence
Gates              William
White              Phillip
...
```

This query outputs all customer records in ascending order of
customer names.

DML Statements

Data manipulation or *data modification language (DML)* commands are
SQL commands that insert, update, and delete table rows in an Oracle
database. DML commands include the INSERT, UPDATE, and DELETE
commands.

INSERT

Applications use the INSERT command to insert new rows into a table.
For example:

```
INSERT INTO sales.parts (id, unit_price, description)
   VALUES (45, 1000.00, 'Pentium 166 CPU');
```

This INSERT statement inserts a new part into the PARTS table. The VALUES clause specifies the field values for the preceding column list. An INSERT command can omit a column list when the VALUES clause includes a value for all columns in the target table in the default column order. Additionally, an INSERT statement can substitute a subquery for a VALUES clause to copy the rows from one table to another, as shown in the following example:

```
INSERT INTO archive.customers
   (SELECT * FROM sales.customers);
```

UPDATE
Applications use the UPDATE command to modify column values of rows in a table. For example:

```
UPDATE sales.parts
   SET unit_price = 250.00
   WHERE id = 492;
```

This example updates the price of a part in the PARTS table. Be careful—when an UPDATE statement omits selection criteria (in other words, a WHERE clause), the UPDATE statement updates all rows in the target table.

DELETE
To delete rows from a table, an application uses the DELETE command. For example:

```
DELETE FROM sales.customers
   WHERE last_name = 'Gates' AND first_name = 'William';
```

A DELETE statement should always include a WHERE clause to target specific rows in a table unless you want to delete all rows in the table.

DDL Statements
Data definition language (DDL) commands create, alter, and drop database objects. Most types of database objects have corresponding CREATE, ALTER, and DROP commands. The following sections preview some of the most commonly used DDL commands.

CREATE TABLE, ALTER TABLE

The following example of the CREATE TABLE command shows how to create the PARTS table used in previous examples in this chapter.

```
CREATE TABLE sales.parts
( id INTEGER PRIMARY KEY,
  unit_price NUMBER(10,2),
  description VARCHAR2(150));
```

The statement declares each column with an Oracle or ANSI/ISO datatype, and declares a PRIMARY KEY constraint for the ID column. The following example of the ALTER TABLE command alters the PARTS table.

```
ALTER TABLE sales.parts
  MODIFY (unit_price DEFAULT 0.00, description NOT NULL);
```

The statement declares a specific default value for the UNIT_PRICE column, and declares a NOT NULL constraint for the DESCRIPTION column.

CREATE VIEW

The following example of the CREATE VIEW command creates the CUST_USA view described in Chapter 2.

```
CREATE VIEW cust_usa AS
  SELECT last_name, first_name, phone
    FROM sales.customers
    WHERE country = 'USA'
  WITH CHECK OPTION;
```

Notice the view's defining query and that the view includes a CHECK constraint to limit the INSERT and UPDATE functionality of the view.

CREATE INDEX, ALTER INDEX, DROP INDEX

The following examples show how to use the CREATE INDEX, ALTER INDEX, and DROP INDEX commands.

```
CREATE INDEX sales.part_descriptions ON sales.parts(description);

ALTER INDEX sales.part_descriptions REBUILD;

DROP INDEX sales.part_descriptions;
```

The first example creates an index for the DESCRIPTION column in the PARTS table. The second and third examples rebuild and drop the same index, respectively.

CREATE SEQUENCE

The following example of the CREATE SEQUENCE command creates a sequence that applications can use to generate primary keys for the PARTS table's ID column.

```
CREATE SEQUENCE sales.parts_id
    START WITH 1
    INCREMENT BY 1
    NOMAXVALUE
    NOCYCLE;
```

These relatively simple examples of DDL commands illustrate several concepts that the previous chapter presents about database objects.

DCL Statements

An administrative application uses *data control language (DCL)* commands to control user access to an Oracle database. The three most commonly used DCL commands include the GRANT, REVOKE, and SET ROLE commands. See Chapter 6 for more information about and examples of these DCL commands.

Application Portability and the ANSI/ISO SQL Standard

The *ANSI/ISO SQL standard* defines a generic specification for the SQL language. Most commercial relational database systems, including Oracle8, support ANSI/ISO standard SQL. When a database supports the SQL standard and an application uses only standard SQL commands, the application is said to be *portable*. In other words, if you decide to substitute another database that supports the ANSI/ISO SQL standard, the application continues to function unmodified.

The ANSI/ISO SQL-92 standard has three different levels of compliance: Entry, Intermediate, and Full. Oracle8 complies with the SQL-92 Entry level, and has many features that conform to the Intermediate and Full levels. Oracle also has many features to comply with the SQL3 standard, including its new object-oriented database features which are discussed in Chapter 5.

Oracle8 also supports many extensions to the ANSI/ISO SQL-92 standard. Such extensions enhance the capabilities of Oracle. *SQL extensions* can be in the form of non-standard SQL commands or just non-standard options to standard SQL commands. However, understand that when an application makes use of proprietary Oracle8 SQL extensions, the application is no longer portable—most likely, you must modify and recompile the application before it will work with other database systems.

The Optimizer—Executing SQL Statements

To execute SQL statements optimally, Oracle8 has an internal system feature called the *optimizer*. When you issue a SQL statement, the Oracle optimizer determines one or more *execution plans* that it can use to execute the statement. After comparing the *costs* of execution for each plan, Oracle then executes the statement using the plan with the lowest relative cost, which typically executes the fastest. Consequently, you and all application users see better performance for SQL statement execution.

Optimizer Statistics

To determine the best execution plans for statements, Oracle examines statistics in the data dictionary about the data with which the statement works. To generate and keep the optimizer statistics for tables, indexes, and other data storage objects, you must *analyze* them using the SQL command ANALYZE or a tool that executes this command. When you analyze an object, Oracle generates statistics for the object and stores them in the data dictionary so that the statistics are available to the optimizer. For example, when you analyze a table, Oracle generates statistics for the number of rows in the table, the amount of physical storage space used to store the table, and more. Statistics can get out of date as applications insert, update, and delete information from tables and indexes. Therefore, it's important to regularly analyze application objects to make their statistics representative of the corresponding objects.

Optimizer Choices

Depending on the SQL statement, Oracle's optimizer might be able to find several different ways to execute a SQL statement. Simple statements are likely to have one or just a few execution plan options. More complicated SQL statements typically present more execution plan options.

For example, consider a CUSTOMERS table that has an index for the STATE column. When you issue a query to find all of the customers that live in the state of California, the optimizer can pick from two execution plans.

■ Oracle can execute the statement by performing a *full table scan*—that is, Oracle can read every row in the table and return only the records for customers who live in California.

■ Oracle can execute the statement using the index on the STATE column—that is, Oracle can quickly search the index for customers who live in California and then read and return only the requested customer records in the CUSTOMERS table.

At a glance, you might naively assume that using an available index is always optimal, and that Oracle's optimizer would always choose the second option to execute the example query. However, this might not always be the case. For example, consider what execution plan would be optimal if all or the large majority of your customers live in California. In this case, looking up customers in a state index to find just the California customers, only to find that all of the customers already live in California, would be a relative waste of time. To make intelligent choices, Oracle's optimizer uses the statistics in the data dictionary.

Hints and Optimizer Control

In certain circumstances, Oracle's optimizer might not be able to choose the optimal execution plan for a statement. In such cases, you can influence and control the optimizer's choices using hints. A *hint* is a specially formatted comment within a SQL statement that instructs Oracle's optimizer how to execute the statement. For example, the following statement includes a hint that tells Oracle to query the CUSTOMERS table using the STATE index.

```
SELECT --+INDEX(customers state)
  id, last_name, first_name
FROM customers
WHERE state = 'CA';
```

The INDEX hint is one of many hints that you can use when designing SQL statements. For example, Oracle has hints that let you force full table scans, index searches in ascending or descending order, hash cluster scans, and joins of tables using several different techniques.

Transactions—Getting Work Done

Applications typically perform work with a database system within the context of a transaction. A database *transaction* is a unit of work performed by one or more closely related SQL statements. For example, consider the SQL statements that a typical order-entry application uses to insert a new order and its associated line items into a database:

```
INSERT INTO sales.orders
   (id, cust_id, order_date, ship_date, paid_date, status)
   VALUES (sales.order_id.NEXTVAL, 391, SYSDATE, NULL, NULL, 'F');
INSERT INTO sales.items
   (order_id, id, part_id, quantity)
   VALUES (sales.order_id.CURRVAL, 1, 32, 2);
INSERT INTO sales.items
   (order_id, id, part_id, quantity)
   VALUES (sales.order_id.CURRVAL, 2, 11, 1);
```

The statements in this transaction insert a new order and two corresponding line items. To permanently *commit* the work of the transaction to the database, the application uses the SQL command COMMIT.

```
COMMIT WORK;
```

Alternatively, an application can undo or *roll back* the work of a transaction's SQL statements with the SQL command ROLLBACK.

```
ROLLBACK WORK;
```

When a database user starts a database application, Oracle implicitly starts a new transaction for the user's session. After an application commits or rolls back a transaction, Oracle again implicitly starts a new transaction for the application user's session.

All or Nothing

A fundamental principle to remember about transactions is that a transaction is a unit of work. That is, although a transaction might be made up of several SQL statements, they all commit or roll back as a single operation. For example, when an application commits a transaction, Oracle permanently records the changes made by *all* SQL statements in the transaction. If for some reason Oracle cannot commit the work of any statement in a transaction, Oracle automatically rolls back the effects of all statements in the transaction.

Types of Transactions

Oracle supports several types of transactions, including read-write, read-only, and discrete transactions. The following sections explain each type of transaction.

Read-Write Transactions

By default, when Oracle starts a new transaction for an application session, the transaction is read-write. A *read-write transaction* can include any type of SQL statement, including DML statements that query, insert, update, and delete table rows. To explicitly declare a transaction as a read-write transaction, an application can begin the transaction with a SET TRANSACTION command.

```
SET TRANSACTION READ WRITE;
```

Read-Only Transactions

A *read-only transaction* includes queries only. In other words, a read-only transaction does not modify the database in any way. Certain reporting applications might want to explicitly declare a transaction as read-only with the SET TRANSACTION command.

```
SET TRANSACTION READ ONLY;
```

When an application declares an explicit read-only transaction, Oracle guarantees *transaction-level read consistency* for the transaction. This means that the result sets of all queries in the transaction reflect the database's data as it existed at the beginning of the transaction, even as other transactions modify and commit work to the database. Reporting applications commonly use an explicit read-only transaction to encompass several queries and produce a report with consistent data.

For more information about read consistency, please read Chapter 9.

Discrete Transactions

In certain situations, applications can improve performance with *discrete transactions*. When an application declares a discrete transaction, Oracle defers many expensive internal system operations that modify and log the changes made by its SQL statements. By deferring and concentrating transaction changes until an application commits a discrete transaction, Oracle can reduce the overall processing overhead for the transaction. For demanding OLTP applications, the result is better system performance.

To declare a discrete transaction, an application starts the transaction with a call to the packaged procedure DBMS_TRANSACTION.BEGIN_ DISCRETE_TRANSACTION.

```
EXECUTE dbms_transaction.begin_discrete_transaction;
INSERT ... ;
INSERT ... ;
INSERT ... ;
COMMIT WORK ;
```

Oracle places many strict restrictions on when an application can use and cannot use discrete transactions. Because application developers must carefully consider these requirements and rigorously test discrete transactions, developers commonly avoid using discrete transactions. However, used prudently, discrete transactions can help improve performance for OLTP-type applications that overwhelm a server with numerous short, simple transactions.

NOTE
The next chapter discusses packages and stored procedures.

Designing Transactions

The previous sections discuss exactly what transactions are and the different types of transactions that an Oracle database application can use, but they do not discuss how to design transactions. The design of application transactions is very important because a transaction's design can directly affect database integrity and the performance of applications. To conclude this chapter, the following sections discuss several issues to consider when designing a database application's transactions.

A Unit of Work

Remember that a transaction is meant to encompass many closely related SQL statements that, together, perform a single unit of work. More specifically, a transaction should not encompass multiple units of work, nor should it encompass a partial unit of work. The following example demonstrates bad transaction design.

```
INSERT INTO sales.customers ... ;
INSERT INTO sales.parts ... ;
INSERT INTO sales.orders ... ;
INSERT INTO sales.items ... ;
INSERT INTO sales.items ... ;
COMMIT WORK ;
```

In this example, the bad transaction design encompasses three separate units of work.

1. The transaction inserts a new customer record.

2. The transaction inserts a new part record.

3. The transaction inserts the records for a new sales order.

Technically, each unit of work in the transaction has nothing to do with the others. When a transaction encompasses more than a single unit of work, Oracle must maintain internal system information on behalf of the transaction for a longer period of time. Quite possibly, this can detract from system performance, especially when many transactions burden Oracle with the same type of bad transaction design.

To contrast the previous type of bad transaction design, consider another example:

```
INSERT INTO sales.orders ... ;
COMMIT WORK ;
INSERT INTO sales.items ... ;
COMMIT WORK ;
INSERT INTO sales.items ... ;
COMMIT WORK ;
```

This example does the opposite of the previous example—there are three transactions to input the records for a single sales order. The overhead of many unnecessary small transaction commits can detract from server performance. More important, partial transactions can risk the integrity of a database's data. For example, consider what would happen if an application uses the above transaction design to insert a new sales order, but before the application can commit the insert of all line items for the new sales order, the user's session abnormally disconnects from the database server. At this point, the database contains a partial sales order, at least until the user reconnects to finish the sales order. In the interim, a shipping transaction might look at the partial sales order and not realize that it is working with incomplete information. As a result, the shipping department might unknowingly send a partial product shipment to a customer and mark it as complete. The irate customer calls days later demanding to know why she didn't receive the other ordered products. When the shipping clerk looks at the order in the database, he sees the missing line items although he cannot explain why the order did not contain the products, yet was marked as complete.

Constraint Checks

When designing a transaction, you might also consider the timing of when Oracle enforces integrity constraints. Oracle can enforce an integrity constraint at two different times:

- Oracle can enforce an integrity constraint immediately after an application submits a SQL statement to insert, update, or delete rows in a table. When a statement causes a data integrity violation, Oracle automatically rolls back the effects of the statement.

■ Oracle can defer the enforcement of an integrity constraint for the SQL statements in a transaction until an application commits the transaction. When any statement in the transaction causes a data integrity violation, Oracle automatically rolls back the entire transaction.

When you declare an individual integrity constraint, you can specify the enforcement timing that you prefer for the constraint—immediate or deferred. Base your choice on specific application requirements. Typical database applications should choose the default: to immediately check data integrity after the execution of each SQL statement. However, certain applications might need to update many tables such that integrity rules are temporarily violated until the end of the transaction.

CHAPTER
4

Programming
the Server

QL is nothing more than a data access language that allows applications to put data into and get data out of an Oracle database. In other words, SQL by itself is not a full-featured programming language that you can use to develop powerful database applications. To build a database application, you must use a procedural language that encompasses SQL to interact with an Oracle database. This chapter explains Oracle's own procedural language, PL/SQL, that you can use to program an Oracle Server.

- PL/SQL language basics

- Anonymous PL/SQL blocks

- Stored procedures, functions, and packages

- Database triggers

- Standard database utility packages

- Advanced queuing

- External function calls

NOTE
By no means is this chapter a complete guide to PL/SQL. However, this chapter does provide an intermediate-level overview of PL/SQL's capabilities so that you can get started programming an Oracle Server.

PL/SQL—Adding the Power of Procedural Flow to SQL

PL/SQL is a procedural programming language that's built into most Oracle products. Oracle8 Server supports PL/SQL version 3. With PL/SQL, you can build programs that combine PL/SQL procedural statements to control program flow with SQL statements that access an Oracle database to process information. For example, the following is a very simple PL/SQL program that updates a part's unit price given the part's ID number.

```
PROCEDURE update_part_unitprice (part_id IN INTEGER, new_price IN
NUMBER)
IS
 invalid_part EXCEPTION;
BEGIN
-- HERE'S AN UPDATE STATEMENT TO UPDATE A DATABASE RECORD
 UPDATE sales.parts
  SET unit_price = new_price
  WHERE id = part_id;
-- HERE'S AN ERROR-CHECKING STATEMENT
 IF SQL%NOTFOUND THEN
  RAISE invalid_part;
 END IF;
EXCEPTION
-- HERE'S AN ERROR-HANDLING ROUTINE
 WHEN invalid_part THEN
  raise_application_error(-20000, 'Invalid Part ID');
END update_part_unitprice;
```

The example program above is a procedure. Using PL/SQL, you can build many types of database access program units, including procedures, functions, and packages. Later sections of this chapter include many examples of PL/SQL programs. But before learning about full-blown PL/SQL programs, you need to understand the basic programmatic constructs that the PL/SQL language offers.

PL/SQL is a procedural language that's very similar to Ada. PL/SQL has statements that allow you declare variables and constants, control program flow, assign and manipulate data, and more.

Blocks

A PL/SQL program is structured using distinct *blocks* that group related declarations and statements. Each block in a PL/SQL program has a specific task and solves a particular problem. Consequently, you can organize a PL/SQL program so that it is easy to understand.

A PL/SQL block can include three sections: declarations, the main program body, and exception handlers.

■ The *declaration section* of a PL/SQL block is where the block declares all variables, constants, exceptions, etc., that are then accessible to all other parts of the block.

- The main program *body* contains the executable statements for the block. In other words, the body is where the PL/SQL block defines its functionality.

- The *exception handling section* contains the *exception handlers* (error handling routines) for the block. When a statement in the block's body *raises an exception* (detects an error), it transfers program control to a corresponding exception handler in the exception section for further processing.

PL/SQL programs are not limited to one block. To organize subtasks even further, a PL/SQL program can nest blocks within the body and exception sections of a block. In general, the declarations of a block are visible to everything in the block's body and exception-handling section, including all nested sub-blocks.

Program Comments

All blocks of a PL/SQL program should include *comments* that document program declarations and functionality. Comments clarify the purpose of specific programs and code segments.

PL/SQL supports two different styles for comments, as the following code segment shows.

```
-- PRECEDE A SINGLE-LINE COMMENT WITH A DOUBLE-HYPHEN.
/* DELIMIT A MULTI-LINE COMMENT WITH "/*" AS A PREFIX AND "*/" AS
A SUFFIX. A MULTI-LINE COMMENT CAN CONTAIN ANY NUMBER OF LINES. */
```

The examples in the remainder of this chapter often use comments to help explain the functionality of code listings.

Program Declarations

A block in a PL/SQL program can declare many types of constructs. The next few sections briefly explain how a PL/SQL program can declare the following:

- Variables and constants
- User-defined subtypes

■ User-defined composite types, including records, nested tables, and varying arrays

■ Cursors and cursor variables

Variables and Constants

The declaration section of a PL/SQL program can include *variable* and *constant* declarations. A program variable or constant can use any Oracle or ANSI/ISO datatype (see Chapter 2). For example, the following program segment declares a variable and a constant using the ANSI datatype INTEGER:

```
DECLARE
  emp_id INTEGER;
  standard_commission CONSTANT INTEGER := 500;
...
```

When a program declares a variable, the program can initialize the variable with a default value or an initial value. For example:

```
DECLARE
  counter INTEGER := 0;   -- example of initial value
  emp_commission INTEGER DEFAULT 0;   -- example of default value
```

In addition to supporting Oracle and ANSI/ISO datatypes, PL/SQL also supports the declaration of variables and constants using several other simple datatypes. Table 4-1 summarizes some additional PL/SQL scalar datatypes and related subtypes—a *subtype* is a constrained version of its base type.

NOTE
PL/SQL also supports NLS versions of the CHAR, VARCHAR2, and CLOB datatypes with the NCHAR, NVARCHAR2, and NCLOB datatypes, respectively.

User-Defined Subtypes

As Table 4-1 shows, PL/SQL supports many common subtypes of its base types. A block in a PL/SQL program can also declare *user-defined subtypes* to customize the acceptable domain of values for a variable or constant.

Datatype	Subtype	Description
BINARY_INTEGER	NATURAL, NATURALN, POSITIVE, POSITIVEN, SIGNTYPE	Stores signed integers. Uses library arithmetic. NATURAL and NATURALN store only non-negative integers; the latter disallows nulls. POSITIVE and POSITIVEN store only positive integers; the latter disallows nulls. SIGNTYPE stores only -1, 0, and 1.
NUMBER (*precision,scale*)	DEC, DECIMAL, DOUBLE PRECISION, FLOAT (*precision*), INTEGER, INT, NUMERIC, REAL, SMALLINT	Stores fixed or floating-point numbers. Uses library arithmetic.
PLS_INTEGER		Stores signed integers. Uses machine arithmetic for fast calculations.
CHAR (*size*)	CHARACTER (*size*)	Stores fixed-length character strings. Maximum size is 32767 bytes; however, database maximum CHAR is 2000 bytes.
VARCHAR2 (size)	VARCHAR (*size*), STRING	Stores variable-length character strings. Maximum size is 32767 bytes; however, database maximum CHAR is 4000 bytes.
DATE		Stores time-related information, including dates, hours, minutes, and seconds.
BOOLEAN		Stores logical values (TRUE, FALSE, and NULL).
CLOB		Stores large, single-byte character objects.
BLOB		Stores large binary objects.
BFILE		Stores file pointers to LOBs managed by file systems external to the database.

TABLE 4-1. *PL/SQL Scalar Datatypes and Related Subtypes*

Judicious use of user-defined subtypes can enhance the readability of a PL/SQL program. For example, the following program segment declares a user-defined subtype and corresponding variable for part descriptions.

```
DECLARE
 varchar2_50 VARCHAR2(50);
 SUBTYPE description IS Varchar2_50;
 current_description Description DEFAULT 'Unknown';
 ...
```

This example demonstrates that a program cannot define constrained subtypes directly. Instead, a program must first declare a constrained variable and then a subsequent subtype declaration in order to create the constrained subtype.

User-Defined Composite Types

PL/SQL allows a program to create user-defined composite types, and then declare variables and constants using the new types. A variable declared with a *composite type* has distinct components that a program can manipulate individually. For example, a program can update a particular field in a record variable without updating other fields. The following sections briefly introduce how a program can declare user-defined records, tables, and varying array composite datatypes. Later sections of this chapter explain how programs can manipulate objects declared with composite types.

RECORDS   A *record type* is a group of related fields, each of which has its own name and datatype. Typically, PL/SQL programs use a record type to create variables that match all or a subset of table columns. For example, the following code segment declares a user-defined record type to match the attributes of the PARTS table, and then declares a variable using the new type.

```
DECLARE
 TYPE part_record IS RECORD (
  id INTEGER,
  unit_price NUMBER(10,2),
  description VARCHAR2(200)
  );
 current_part Part_Record;
 ...
```

ID	UNIT_PRICE	DESCRIPTION
1	10.90	Pentium 166 CPU

FIGURE 4-1. *An example of a record variable*

Figure 4-1 illustrates the structure of the example CURRENT_PART variable after each field has been assigned a value.

A section later in this chapter shows how PL/SQL programs can manipulate record variables.

NESTED TABLES   A program can declare a *nested table type* to create variables that have one or more columns and an **unlimited** number of rows, just like tables in a database. For example, the following code segment declares a nested table type to match the PARTS table, and then declares a variable using the new type.

```
DECLARE
  TYPE part_record IS RECORD (
   id INTEGER,
   unit_price NUMBER(10,2),
   description VARCHAR2(200)
  );
  TYPE parts_table IS TABLE OF Part_Record;
  current_parts_table Parts_Table;
  ...
```

Figure 4-2 illustrates the structure of the example CURRENT_PARTS_-TABLE variable after it has been assigned three records.

A section later in this chapter shows how PL/SQL programs can work with nested tables.

VARYING ARRAYS   Similar to nested tables, a program can also declare a *varying array (varray) type* to create table-like variables that have one or more columns and a **limited** number of rows. For example, the following code segment declares a varray type to match the PARTS table, and then declares a variable that can contain up to three records.

ID	UNIT_PRICE	DESCRIPTION
1	150.90	Pentium 166 CPU
2	200.50	CD-ROM 8X Internal
3	500.00	Network Computer
...	...	...

Unlimited number of rows

FIGURE 4-2. *An example of a nested table variable*

```
DECLARE
  TYPE part_record IS RECORD (
   id INTEGER,
   unit_price NUMBER(10,2),
   description VARCHAR2(150)
  );
  TYPE parts_table IS VARRAY(3) OF Part_Record;
  current_parts_table Parts_Table;
  ...
```

Figure 4-3 illustrates the structure of the example CURRENT_PARTS _-TABLE variable after it has been assigned three records.

A section later in this chapter shows how PL/SQL programs can use varrays.

Attributes

A PL/SQL program can use the %TYPE and %ROWTYPE *attributes* to declare variables, constants, and even user-defined subtypes and composite types that match the properties of database columns and tables or other program constructs. Not only do attributes simplify the declaration of program constructs, but their use makes programs flexible to database modifications. For example, after an administrator modifies the PARTS table

ID	UNIT_PRICE	DESCRIPTION
1	150.90	Pentium 166 CPU
2	200.50	CD-ROM 8X Internal
3	500.00	Network Computer

Limited number of rows

FIGURE 4-3. *An example of a varray variable*

to add a new column, a record variable declared using the %ROWTYPE attribute automatically adjusts to account for the new column at runtime, without any modification of the program. The following sections explain the %TYPE and %ROWTYPE in more detail.

%TYPE   The declaration of a PL/SQL program construct can use the *%TYPE attribute* to capture the datatype of another program construct or column in a database table at runtime. For example, the following code segment uses the %TYPE attribute to reference the columns in the SALES.PARTS table when declaring the PART_RECORD type.

```
DECLARE
  TYPE part_record IS RECORD (
    id sales.parts.id%TYPE,
    unit_price sales.parts.unit_price%TYPE,
    description sales.parts.description%TYPE
  );
  current_part Part_Record;
```

%ROWTYPE   A PL/SQL program can use the *%ROWTYPE attribute* to easily declare record variables and other constructs at runtime. For example, the following code segment shows how use of the %ROWTYPE attribute can simplify the declaration of the CURRENT_PARTS_TABLE nested table.

```
DECLARE
  TYPE parts_table IS TABLE OF sales.parts%ROWTYPE;
  current_parts_table Parts_Table;
...
```

Cursors, Cursor Types, and Cursor Variables

A *cursor* is a work area for a SQL statement. Whenever an application submits an SQL statement to Oracle, the server opens at least one cursor to process the statement. For simple INSERT, UPDATE, and DELETE statements, Oracle automatically opens a cursor. Oracle also can automatically process SELECT statements that return just one row. However, database access programs frequently must process a query that returns a set of database records rather than just one row. To process the rows of a query that correspond to a multi-row result set, an application can explicitly declare a cursor with a name, and then reference the cursor to process rows one at a time. For example, the following PL/SQL code segment declares two cursors.

```
DECLARE
  CURSOR parts_cursor IS
    SELECT * FROM sales.parts;

  CURSOR customers_cursor (state_id CHAR) IS
    SELECT id, last_name, first_name, phone
      FROM sales.customers
      WHERE state = state_id;
...
```

PARTS_CURSOR is a simple cursor that corresponds to all columns and rows in the PARTS table. CUSTOMERS_CURSOR corresponds to a subset of the columns and rows in the CUSTOMERS table. The cursor selects only the ID, LAST_NAME, FIRST_NAME, and PHONE fields of selected customer records. The cursor uses a *cursor parameter*, STATE_ID, to define the cursor's record selection criteria at runtime.

After declaring a cursor, a PL/SQL program can open and fetch records from the cursor to process individual rows of database information, one at a time. Sections later in this chapter explain how a PL/SQL program can work with a cursor.

CURSOR TYPES AND VARIABLES   Cursors have several limitations. For example, a PL/SQL program *cannot* pass a cursor as a parameter to another program—a PL/SQL program can only open the cursor and process corresponding information within the program itself. To work around the functional limitations of cursors, a program can instead declare user-defined *cursor types* and corresponding *cursor variables.* For example, the following code segment declares two different cursor types and corresponding cursor variables.

```
DECLARE
-- STRONG, SPECIFIC CURSOR TYPE ...
  TYPE parts_type IS REF CURSOR RETURN sales.parts%ROWTYPE;
-- ... AND CORRESPONDING CURSOR VARIABLE
  parts_cursor1 Parts_Type;
  parts_cursor2 Parts_Type;
  parts_cursor3 Parts_Type;

-- WEAK, GENERIC CURSOR TYPE ...
  TYPE cursor_type IS REF CURSOR;
...
```

The first cursor type, PARTS_TYPE, is *strong*; that is, the cursor type's declaration includes a RETURN clause that specifies a *shape* or set of attributes for the cursor type. Therefore, a strong cursor type restricts the definition of subsequent cursor variables that use the type. Use strong cursor types when you want to explicitly restrict the shape of subsequently defined cursor variables.

Alternatively, the second cursor type, CURSOR_TYPE, is *weak* because it does not include a shape specification. The program can use the weak cursor type to declare a cursor variable with any shape. Use weak cursor types when you want more flexibility in subsequent cursor designs and do not care about restricting their shape.

After declaring a cursor variable, a program can open it and fetch corresponding database rows to process information. A program can also pass a cursor variable and its current state to another program for processing because a cursor variable in a PL/SQL program is similar to a pointer that other programming languages support. See the sections later in this chapter that discuss how a PL/SQL program can use cursors and cursor variables.

Program Functionality

Now that you have some idea about the types of constructs that a PL/SQL block can declare, it's time to learn the type of functionality that's possible within a PL/SQL body (and exception-handling section). The following sections briefly introduce some fundamental PL/SQL functionality.

Assignment Statements

Value assignment is one of the most common operations within any type of procedural program. The following examples demonstrate how a PL/SQL block can assign values to scalar, record, table, and varray variables. Notice that the statements use standard *dot notation* to reference specific fields (elements) in record variables and *subscripts* to reference specific *members* in a nested table or varray.

```
-- EXAMPLE SCALAR VARIABLE ASSIGNMENTS
DECLARE
 emp_id INTEGER;
 another_integer_variable INTEGER := 0;
 part_description VARCHAR2(200);
BEGIN
 emp_id := 1;
 emp_id := another_integer_variable;
 part_description := 'Network Computer';
...


-- EXAMPLE RECORD VARIABLE ASSIGNMENTS
DECLARE
 TYPE part_record IS RECORD (
  id INTEGER,
  unit_price NUMBER(10,2),
  description VARCHAR2(200)
 );
 current_part Part_Record;
 another_Part_Record_variable Part_Record;
BEGIN
 current_part.id := 1;
 current_part.description := 'Network Computer';
 current_part := another_Part_Record_variable;
...
```

```
-- EXAMPLE NESTED TABLE OR VARRAY VARIABLE ASSIGNMENTS
DECLARE
 TYPE part_record IS RECORD (
  id INTEGER,
  unit_price NUMBER(10,2),
  description VARCHAR2(200)
 );
 TYPE parts_table IS TABLE OF Part_Record;
 current_parts_table Parts_Table;
BEGIN
 current_parts_table(1).id := 1;
 current_parts_table(1).description := 'Network Computer';
 current_parts_table(1) := current_parts_table(2);
...
```

Unique Considerations for Nested Tables and Variable Arrays

When working with nested tables and varrays, there are several functional issues that you need to consider:

- Nested tables can have any number of rows. The size of a table can increase or decrease dynamically.

- Varrays have a constant number of rows and, therefore, restrict the possible number of rows.

- Nested tables can be *sparse*. A program can insert members into a nested table using non-consecutive subscripts and can remove individual members anywhere in the table.

- Varrays must remain *dense*. A program must insert members into a varray using consecutive subscripts.

INITIALIZING NESTED TABLES AND VARRAYS   To initialize a nested table or varray, a PL/SQL program uses the corresponding *constructor* function for the type. PL/SQL automatically provides a constructor function with the same name as its nested table or varray type. When a program calls a constructor function to initialize a table or varray, it can specify a comma-separated list of members. When initializing a table or varray of records, make sure to delimit each member specification by inner parentheses. For example, the following code segment shows how to initialize a nested table with three members when the program declares the table.

```
DECLARE
 TYPE parts_table IS TABLE OF sales.parts%ROWTYPE;
 current_parts_table Parts_Table := Parts_Table (
  (1, 150.90,'Pentium 166 CPU'),
  NULL,
  (3,500.00,'Network Computer')
 );
...
```

➤ Notice that you can initialize a null member of a nested table using the NULL keyword.

USING COLLECTION METHODS WITH NESTED TABLES AND VARRAYS   PL/SQL supports several different *collection methods* that programs can use to manipulate nested tables and varrays. Table 4-2 lists the collection methods that are available in PL/SQL.

Collection Method	Description
EXISTS (x)	Returns TRUE if the xth element in a nested table or varray exists. Otherwise, the method returns FALSE.
COUNT	Returns the number of elements currently in a nested table or varray.
LIMIT	For varrays, returns the maximum number of elements that the collection can contain.
FIRST	Returns the first member of the nested table or varray.
LAST	Returns the last member of the nested table or varray.
PRIOR (x)	Returns the member prior to the xth member of the nested table or varray.
NEXT (x)	Returns the member after to the xth member of the nested table or varray.
EXTEND (x, y)	Appends x copies of the yth element to a nested table or varray.
TRIM (x)	Trims x elements from the end of a nested table or varray.
DELETE	Deletes some or all of a nested table's or varray's elements.

TABLE 4-2.   *Collections Methods Available with PL/SQL*

To use a collection method, a PL/SQL statement names the collection (nested table or varray) with the collection method as a suffix using dot notation. The following PL/SQL statements use collection methods to perform work.

```
record_count := current_parts_table.COUNT;
current_parts_record := current_parts_table.FIRST;
current_parts_table.DELETE(3);
current_parts_table.DELETE(4,6);
current_parts_table.DELETE;
```

The DELETE collection method is available only for nested tables because varrays must remain dense. As the examples show, use of the DELETE collection method can vary. The first DELETE example deletes just the third member in CURRENT_PARTS_TABLE; the second example deletes the 4th, 5th, and 6th members in the table; the final example deletes all members in the table—be careful!

Control of Program Flow

Typical procedural programs have flow. That is, a program uses some sort of logic to control what and when the program executes given statements. PL/SQL programs can control program flow using conditional, iterative, and sequential logic. The following sections explain the different program flow control statements that PL/SQL offers.

CONDITIONAL CONTROL   An IF statement in a PL/SQL program evaluates a Boolean condition, and if the condition is TRUE executes one or more statements. The following pseudo-code examples show use of the IF command and its variations.

```
-- BASIC IF STATEMENT
IF condition THEN
 statement1;
 statement2;
 ...
END IF;

-- IF-ELSE STATEMENT
IF condition THEN
 statement1;
 statement2;
```

```
  ...
ELSE
  statement3;
  ...
END IF;

-- MORE COMPLEX IF-ELSIF-ELSE STATEMENT
IF condition THEN
  statement1;
  statement2;
  ...
ELSIF  -- NOT "ELSEIF"
  statement3;
  statement4;
  ...
ELSIF
  statement5;
  ...
ELSE
  statement6;
  statement7;
  ...
END IF;
```

Notice that a single IF statement can test just one or a number of conditions to determine how to control program flow.

ITERATIVE CONTROL   A PL/SQL program can use a loop to iterate the execution of a series of statements a certain number of times. The following pseudo-code examples demonstrate the use of basic, WHILE, and FOR loops.

```
-- BASIC LOOP THAT USES EXIT-WHEN
LOOP
  statement1;
  statement2;
  ...
  EXIT WHEN condition;
END LOOP;

-- WHILE LOOP
WHILE condition LOOP
  statement1;
  statement2;
```

```
  ...
END LOOP;

-- FOR LOOP WITH NESTED LOOP AND LABELS
<< outer_loop >>  -- loop label or name
FOR x IN y..z LOOP
 outer_statement1;
 << inner_loop >>
 LOOP
  inner_statement1;
  inner_statement2;
  EXIT outer_loop WHEN condition1;
  EXIT inner_loop WHEN condition2;
 END LOOP inner_loop;
 outer_statement3;
 ...
END LOOP outer_loop;
...
```

Every basic loop definition should use either an EXIT WHEN or EXIT statement to terminate the loop—otherwise the loop executes infinitely. Conversely, the definition of a WHILE or FOR loop requires that you describe how the loop terminates. The third example also shows how to nest loops, use loop labels to name loops, and reference specific loops by name in EXIT and END LOOP statements.

SEQUENTIAL CONTROL   Unlike conditional and iterative flow control, sequential control or branching is rarely necessary in PL/SQL programs; however, PL/SQL provides the GOTO command should the need arise. For example, the following code segment shows how to use a GOTO statement to branch to a program label that proceeds an executable statement in a PL/SQL program.

```
BEGIN
 ...
 IF ...  THEN
  GOTO section_1;
 END IF;
 ...
 << section_1 >>
 DELETE FROM sales.parts WHERE ... ;
 ...
```

Database Interaction

The primary reason for using PL/SQL is to create database access programs. A PL/SQL program can interact with an Oracle database only through the use of SQL. The following sections explain how a PL/SQL program can manipulate database information using standard SQL DML statements, cursors, and dynamic SQL.

STANDARD DML   A PL/SQL program can use any SQL DML statement to modify an Oracle database. For example, the UPDATE_PART_UNITPRICE procedure at the beginning of this chapter uses a simple UPDATE statement to modify a record in the PARTS table. PL/SQL programs can include any valid INSERT, UPDATE, or DELETE statement to modify the rows in a database table.

SELECT INTO ...   PL/SQL programs often use assignment statements to assign a specific database value or set of values to a program variable. To accomplish this, a PL/SQL program can use a SELECT INTO command. For example:

```
DECLARE
  current_part sales.parts%ROWTYPE;
BEGIN
  SELECT * INTO current_part
   FROM sales.parts
   WHERE id = 6;
...
```

If the result set of a SELECT INTO statement contains more than one row, Oracle returns an error. To process a query that returns more than one row, a PL/SQL program must use a cursor. The next section explains more about using cursors and cursor variables.

WORKING WITH CURSORS   To work with the rows that correspond to a multi-row cursor, a program must perform three steps: open the cursor, fetch the rows in the cursor, and then close the cursor. The following is a typical example of how a program might open a cursor, fetch individual rows of the cursor using a loop, and then close the cursor.

```
DECLARE
 CURSOR parts_cursor IS
  SELECT * FROM sales.parts;
 current_part sales.parts%ROWTYPE;
BEGIN
 OPEN parts_cursor;
 LOOP
  FETCH parts_cursor INTO current_part;
  ... other statements ...
 END LOOP;
 CLOSE parts_cursor;
 ...
```

Because cursors are designed to process queries with multiple row result sets, programs almost always process cursors using loops. To simplify the steps necessary to set up and process a cursor, a PL/SQL program can use a cursor FOR loop. A *cursor FOR loop* automatically declares a variable or record capable of receiving the rows in the cursor, opens the cursor, fetches rows from the cursor, and closes the cursor when the last row is fetched from the cursor. The following code segment shows how a cursor FOR loop can simplify the steps necessary to process a cursor.

```
DECLARE
 CURSOR parts_cursor IS
  SELECT * FROM sales.parts;
BEGIN
 FOR current_part IN parts_cursor LOOP
  ... other statements ...
 END LOOP;
 ...
```

When a program opens a cursor that has a cursor parameter, the program can indicate a value for each cursor parameter. For example, the following program defines the result set of the cursor to include all records for customers that live in California.

```
DECLARE
 CURSOR customers_cursor (state_id CHAR) IS
  SELECT * FROM sales.customers
   WHERE state = state_id;
BEGIN
```

```
FOR current_customer IN customers_cursor('CA') LOOP
 ... other statements ...
END LOOP;
...
```

A PL/SQL program can use several unique *cursor attributes*—%ISOPEN, %FOUND, %NOTFOUND, and %ROWCOUNT—to make decisions when processing cursors. For example, the following loop uses the %FOUND cursor attribute to determine when to terminate the loop.

```
WHILE parts_cursor%FOUND LOOP
 FETCH parts_cursor INTO current_part;
 ... other statements ...
END LOOP;
```

As a program fetches individual rows from a cursor's result set, there is the concept of the cursor's current row. Figure 4-4 illustrates the concept of a cursor's current row.

A PL/SQL program can take advantage of the special CURRENT OF syntax in an UPDATE or DELETE statement that needs to process the current row of a cursor.

```
BEGIN
 FOR current_customer IN customers_cursor('CA') LOOP
  IF ... THEN
   DELETE FROM sales.customers
    WHERE CURRENT OF customers_cursor;
  END IF;
 END LOOP;
...
```

ID	UNIT_PRICE	DESCRIPTION
1	150.90	Pentium 166 CPU
2	200.50	CD-ROM 8X Internal
3	500.00	Network Computer

Current row⟶ (row 2)

FIGURE 4-4. *The most recently fetched row from a cursor is the cursor's current row.*

WORKING WITH CURSOR VARIABLES Working with cursor variables is similar to working with cursors. However, there are a few notable differences:

- A cursor variable cannot use a cursor FOR loop construct.

- A program opens a cursor using an OPEN FOR statement. When using a strongly typed cursor type, the shape of the query that defines a cursor variable must match the shape of the cursor type.

The following code segment demonstrates the steps necessary to process a cursor variable.

```
DECLARE
  TYPE cursor_type IS REF CURSOR;
  customers_cursorv Cursor_Type;
BEGIN
  OPEN customers_cursorv FOR
    SELECT id, last_name, first_name, phone FROM sales.customers;
  WHILE customers_cursorv%FOUND LOOP
   IF ... THEN
   ... other statements ...
   END IF;
   ... other statements ...
  END LOOP;
  CLOSE customers_cursorv;
...
```

The above example shows that cursor variables have attributes just like cursors (for example, %FOUND), and that UPDATE and DELETE statements can use the CURRENT OF syntax in a WHERE clause to reference the current row in a cursor.

USING DYNAMIC SQL PL/SQL is a procedural language designed specifically to create fast performing database access programs for Oracle. With this goal in mind, a PL/SQL program statically binds all SQL when compiling the program. This process ensures that the SQL corresponds to referenced database objects, that the necessary database privileges are available to access the referenced objects, and more. Because SQL binding occurs during program compile time, it does not have to happen when an application executes the program. Consequently, the application can execute with less overhead at runtime.

While statically bound SQL maximizes the performance of PL/SQL programs, it also limits the type of SQL statements that a PL/SQL program can contain. For example, a PL/SQL program cannot accept SQL statements provided at runtime by the application, only those contained in the compiled program. PL/SQL programs also cannot execute SQL DDL statements due to binding requirements. Thus the need for dynamic SQL. With *dynamic SQL*, a PL/SQL program can build SQL statements at runtime, which means that you can create programs that are very flexible.

To perform dynamic SQL, a PL/SQL program uses a special database utility called the DBMS_SQL package. This utility package contains several procedures and functions that a program calls to open a cursor for a dynamic SQL statement, execute it, and then close the cursor. The exact type and number of steps necessary to perform dynamic SQL in a PL/SQL program vary, depending on the type of statement that you want to execute. For example, the following stored procedure uses the DBMS_SQL package to drop a table whose name is provided at runtime.

```
CREATE OR REPLACE PROCEDURE utilities.drop_table (
  schema_name IN OUT VARCHAR2,
  table_name IN OUT VARCHAR2
)
IS
  cursor_id INTEGER;
  return_value INTEGER;
  command_string VARCHAR2(250);
BEGIN
  command_string := 'DROP TABLE '|| schema_name||'.'||table_name;
  cursor_id := dbms_sql.open_cursor;
  dbms_sql.parse(cursor_id, command_string, dbms_sql.v7);
  return_value := dbms_sql.execute(cursor_id);
  dbms_sql.close_cursor(cursor_id);
END drop_table;
```

This program also illustrates how dynamic SQL allows a PL/SQL program to execute DDL. Other types of dynamic SQL statements, such as queries, require several more steps.

Program Exception Handling

A program is not complete unless it contains routines to process the errors that can occur during normal processing. Rather than embed error-handling routines into the body of a program, a PL/SQL program addresses error-handling requirements using exceptions and corresponding exception handlers. A PL/SQL program *raises* a named *exception* when it detects an error and then passes control to an associated *exception handler* routine that is separate from the main program body.

An exception is a named error condition. PL/SQL contains many *predefined exceptions* that correspond to common Oracle errors. For example:

- A program detects the NO_DATA_FOUND exception when a SELECT INTO statement has a result set with no rows, and the TOO_MANY_ROWS exception when a SELECT INTO statement has a result set with more than one row.

- A program detects the DUP_VAL_ON_INDEX exception when an INSERT or UPDATE statement duplicates a key value already in a table.

- A program detects the ZERO_DIVIDE exception when a statement attempts to divide a number by zero.

PL/SQL includes almost 20 predefined exceptions. A program does not have to perform checks for predefined exceptions. When a program encounters a predefined exception, it automatically transfers program control to the associated exception handler if one is available.

A program can also declare *user-defined exceptions* in the declarative section of a block. However, a program must perform explicit checks for a user-defined exception that then raise the exception. Optionally, a program can associate a specific Oracle error number with a user-defined exception. By doing so, the program automatically raises the user-defined exception should it cause the associated Oracle error.

An exception handler is a routine that takes control of a program should the program raise the associated exception. The exception handler section of a PL/SQL block includes handlers for all exceptions. The following example demonstrates the use of predefined and user-defined exceptions and corresponding exception handlers.

```
DECLARE
  invalid_part EXCEPTION;
  insufficient_privileges EXCEPTION;
  PRAGMA EXCEPTION_INIT (insufficient_privileges, -1031);
  err_num INTEGER;
  err_msg VARCHAR2(2000);
  part_num INTEGER;
BEGIN
  SELECT ... INTO ... FROM ... ;
  UPDATE sales.parts
   SET unit_price = 20.00
   WHERE id = 6;
  IF SQL%NOTFOUND THEN  -- CHECK FOR USER-DEFINED EXCEPTION
   RAISE invalid_part;
  END IF;
EXCEPTION
  WHEN no_data_found THEN
   raise_application_error(-20001, 'No rows found');
  WHEN too_many_rows THEN
   raise_application_error(-20002, 'Too many rows found');
  WHEN invalid_part THEN
   raise_application_error(-20003, 'Invalid Part ID');
  WHEN insufficient_privileges THEN
   raise_application_error(-20004, 'Insufficient privileges to update table');
  WHEN OTHERS THEN
   err_num := SQLCODE;
   err_msg := SUBSTR(SQLERRM, 1, 100);
   raise_application_error(-20000, err_num ||' '||err_msg);
...
```

The above example introduces several interesting points:

- A PL/SQL program can use the RAISE_APPLICATION_ERROR procedure to return a user-defined error number and message to the calling environment. All user-defined error messages must be in the range -20000 to -20999.

- A PL/SQL program can use the WHEN OTHERS syntax to create a generic exception handler for all exceptions that do not have a specific handler.

- A PL/SQL program can use the special SQLCODE and SQLERRM functions to return the most recent Oracle error number and message.

Types of PL/SQL Programs

Now that you understand the basics of the PL/SQL language, it's time to learn what types of programs you can create with PL/SQL. The following sections briefly explain how to write anonymous PL/SQL blocks, procedures, functions, and packages.

Anonymous PL/SQL Blocks

An *anonymous block* is a PL/SQL block that appears within your application. An anonymous PL/SQL block has no name and is not stored in the database. The application simply sends the block of code to the database server for processing at runtime. Once the server executes an anonymous block, the block ceases to exist.

The previous examples in this chapter are all anonymous PL/SQL blocks. An anonymous PL/SQL block begins its declarative section with the keyword DECLARE and ends with the keyword END.

Stored Procedures and Functions

A *subprogram* is a named PL/SQL program that can take parameters and be called by an application. You can store compiled bits of application logic inside an Oracle database using stored subprograms. An Oracle database can store two types of subprograms as schema objects:

- A stored procedure is a PL/SQL subprogram that performs an operation.

- A stored function is a PL/SQL subprogram that computes a value and returns it to the calling environment.

To create a stored procedure or function in an Oracle database, use the CREATE PROCEDURE or CREATE FUNCTION command; development tools such as Oracle Procedure Builder provide a user-friendly interface to the functionality of these SQL commands.

Parameters

When you create a procedure or function, <u>you can pass values into and out of the subprogram using *parameters*</u>. Typically, a calling program passes a variable as a parameter to a procedure or function.

For each parameter, you must specify a PL/SQL datatype in an unconstrained form. Furthermore, you should indicate the mode of each parameter as IN, OUT, or IN OUT:

■ An IN parameter passes a value into a subprogram, but a subprogram cannot change the value of the external variable that corresponds to an IN parameter.

■ An OUT parameter cannot pass a value into a subprogram, but a subprogram can manipulate an OUT parameter to change the value of the corresponding variable in the outside calling environment.

■ An IN OUT parameter combines the capabilities of IN and OUT parameters.

A Function's Return Value

<u>A function differs from a procedure in that it returns a value to its calling environment.</u> The specification of a function declares the type of the return value. The body of a function must include one or more RETURN statements to return a value to the calling environment. The following is an example of a simple stored function.

```
CREATE OR REPLACE FUNCTION sales.get_customer_id (
  last IN VARCHAR2,
  first IN VARCHAR2
  )
RETURN INTEGER IS
  cust_id INTEGER;
BEGIN
  SELECT id INTO cust_id
    FROM sales.customers
    WHERE last_name = last
    AND first_name = first;
  RETURN cust_id;
EXCEPTION
  WHEN OTHERS THEN
    RETURN NULL;
  END get_customer_id;
```

Notice that both a function's body and exception section can include RETURN statements.

Calling Procedures and Functions

Calling a database procedure or function is dependent on the calling environment. In general:

- An application calls a procedure by reference, providing arguments for all procedure parameters.

- An application calls a function by reference in an assignment statement. A SQL statement can also reference a user-defined function in a WHERE clause.

The following example demonstrates how to call the GET_CUSTOMER _ID function from an anonymous block.

```
DECLARE
  cur_cust_id INTEGER;
  cur_cust_last VARCHAR2(100);
  cur_cust_first VARCHAR2(100);
BEGIN
  ...
  cur_cust_id := sales.get_customer_id (cur_cust_last,
cur_cust_first);
  ...
```

The following shows how to call the same GET_CUSTOMER_ID function in the WHERE clause of a SQL statement.

```
DELETE FROM sales.orders
  WHERE cust_id = sales.get_customer_id ('Ellison','Lawrence');
```

Packages

A package is a group of procedures, functions, and other PL/SQL constructs, all stored together in a database as a unit. Packages are especially useful for organizing a number of PL/SQL procedures and functions that relate to a particular database application.

A package has two parts: a specification and a body.

■ A *package specification* defines the interface to the package. In a package specification, you declare all package variables, constants, cursors, procedures, functions, and other constructs that you want to make available to programs outside the package. In other words, everything that you declare in a package's specification is *public*.

■ A *package body* defines all public procedures and functions declared in the package specification. Additionally, a package body can include other construct definitions not in the specification; such package constructs are *private* (available only to programs within the package).

All variables, constants, and cursors declared in either a package specification or body are considered *global*. Unlike private variables, constants, and cursors declared within specific procedures and functions, global constructs are available to all package procedures and functions and have a state that persists independent of any particular package subprogram on a per-session basis.

The following is an example of a package that groups several procedures associated with part management.

```
CREATE OR REPLACE PACKAGE sales.part_mgmt IS
----------------------------------------------------------
-- GLOBAL TYPES AND VARIABLES
 TYPE parts_type IS REF CURSOR RETURN sales.parts%ROWTYPE;
 current_part sales.parts%ROWTYPE;
----------------------------------------------------------
-- PROCEDURES AND FUNCTIONS
-- insert_part INSERTS A NEW PART INTO THE PARTS TABLE
-- update_part_unitprice UPDATES A PART'S PRICE
-- update_part_description UPDATES A PART'S DESCRIPTION
-- delete_part DELETES A PART
-- get_part_id RETURNS A PART'S ID NUMBER
----------------------------------------------------------
 PROCEDURE insert_part ( part_record sales.parts%ROWTYPE);
 PROCEDURE update_part_unitprice (part_id IN INTEGER, new_price IN NUMBER);
 PROCEDURE update_part_description (part_id IN INTEGER, new_desc IN NUMBER);
 PROCEDURE delete_part (part_id IN INTEGER);
 FUNCTION get_part_id (part_desc IN VARCHAR2) RETURN INTEGER;
END part_mgmt;

CREATE OR REPLACE PACKAGE BODY sales.part_mgmt IS
```

```
----------------------------------------------------------
 PROCEDURE insert_part (part_record sales.parts%ROWTYPE) IS
  dup_primary_key EXCEPTION;
  PRAGMA EXCEPTION_INIT (dup_primary_key, -1);
 BEGIN
  INSERT INTO sales.parts
    VALUES (part_record.id, part_record.unit_price, part_record.description);
 EXCEPTION
  WHEN dup_primary_key THEN
    raise_application_error (-20001, 'Duplicate part ID');
  WHEN OTHERS THEN
    raise_application_error (-20000, 'Undefined exception');
 END insert_part;
---------------------------------------------------------
... other package procedure and function definitions ...
END part_mgmt;
```

Using Package Objects

Similar to stored procedures and functions, referencing package objects is dependent on the calling environment. However, applications generally reference a package's public objects using standard dot notation. The following anonymous PL/SQL block demonstrates references to packaged objects.

```
DECLARE
BEGIN
-- THIS STATEMENT INITIALIZES A GLOBAL PACKAGE VARIABLE
 SELECT * INTO sales.part_mgmt.current_part
  FROM sales.parts
  WHERE id = 3;
-- THIS STATEMENT CALLS THE INSERT_PART PACKAGED PROCEDURE
 sales.part_mgmt.insert_part(3, 500.00, 'Network Computer');
  ...
```

DBMS Utility Packages

Oracle includes several prebuilt utility packages that provide additional functionality not available with SQL or PL/SQL. Table 4-3 lists several of the prebuilt packages available with Oracle8.

Package Name	Description
DBMS_ALERT	Procedures and functions that allow applications to name and signal alert conditions without polling
DBMS_AQ DBMS_AQADM	Procedures and functions to queue the execution of transactions and administer queuing mechanisms
DBMS_DDL DBMS_UTILITY	Procedures that provide access to a limited number of DDL statements inside PL/SQL programs
DBMS_DESCRIBE	Procedures that describe the API for stored procedures and functions
DBMS_JOB	Procedures and functions to manage a database's job queuing mechanisms
DBMS_LOB	Procedures and functions to manipulate BLOBs, CLOBs, NCLOBs, and BFILEs
DBMS_LOCK	Procedures and functions that allow applications to coordinate access to shared resources
DBMS_OUTPUT	Procedures and functions that allow a PL/SQL program to generate terminal output
DBMS_PIPE	Procedures and functions that allow database sessions to communicate using pipes (communication channels)
DBMS_ROWID	Procedures and functions that allow applications to easily interpret a base-64 character external ROWID
DBMS_SESSION	Procedures and functions to control an application user's session.
DBMS_SQL	Procedures and functions to perform dynamic SQL from within a PL/SQL program
DBMS_TRANSACTION	Procedures to perform a limited amount of transaction control
UTL_FILE	Procedures and functions that allow a PL/SQL program to read and write text files to the server's file system

TABLE 4-3. *Prebuilt Packages Available with ORACLE8*

Database Triggers

A *database trigger* is a stored procedure that you associate with a table. In general, when applications target the table with a SQL DML statement that meets the trigger's execution conditions, Oracle automatically *fires* (executes) the trigger to perform work. Therefore, you can use triggers to customize an Oracle Server's reaction to application events. For example, the following trigger automatically logs changes made to the PARTS table.

```
CREATE OR REPLACE TRIGGER sales.parts_log
AFTER INSERT OR UPDATE OR DELETE ON sales.parts
DECLARE
 stmt_type CHAR(1);
BEGIN
 IF INSERTING
  THEN stmt_type := 'I';
 ELSIF UPDATING
  THEN stmt_type := 'U';
 ELSE
  stmt_type := 'D';
 END IF;
 INSERT INTO sales.part_change_log
  VALUES (stmt_type, USER);
END parts_log;
```

A trigger definition includes the following unique parts:

- A trigger's definition includes a list of *trigger statements*, including INSERT, UPDATE, and/or DELETE, that fire the trigger. A trigger is associated with one and only one table.

- A trigger can be set to fire before or after the trigger statement to provide specific application logic.

Additionally, a trigger's definition indicates whether the trigger is a statement trigger or a row trigger. A *statement trigger* fires only once, no matter how many rows the trigger statement affects. The previous definition of the PARTS_LOG trigger is an example of a statement trigger. Conversely, a *row trigger* fires once for each row that the trigger statement affects. The following rewrite of the PARTS_LOG trigger is an example of a row trigger.

```
CREATE OR REPLACE TRIGGER sales.parts_log
BEFORE INSERT OR UPDATE OR DELETE ON sales.parts
FOR EACH ROW
DECLARE
 stmt_type CHAR(1);
BEGIN
 IF INSERTING THEN
  stmt_type := 'I';
 ELSIF UPDATING THEN
  stmt_type := 'U';
 ELSE
  stmt_type := 'D';
 END IF;
 INSERT INTO sales.part_change_log
  VALUES (
    :new.id, :old.id,
    :new.unit_price, :old.unit_price,
    :new.description, :old.description,
    stmt_type,
    USER
  );
END parts_log;
```

NOTE

Optionally a row trigger can include a trigger restriction—a Boolean condition that determines when to fire the trigger.

Carefully review the two previous examples and you'll notice that PL/SQL provides the following unique language elements for database triggers:

■ When a trigger allows different types of statements to fire the trigger, the *INSERTING, UPDATING,* and *DELETING predicates* allow conditional statements to identify the type of trigger statement.

■ *Correlation values* allow a row trigger to access new and old field values of the current row. When a trigger statement is an INSERT statement, all old field values are null. Similarly, when a trigger statement is a DELETE statement, all new field values are null.

External Procedures

Rather than perform all work using PL/SQL and SQL statements, a PL/SQL program can make use of external procedures within external shared program libraries to get things done. This allows PL/SQL programs to take full advantage of existing code without having to rewrite it as PL/SQL, and perform work using the most efficient routines available. For example, why waste time writing a complex PL/SQL procedure that accesses a non-Oracle data source when it would be simple to create a tiny PL/SQL program that calls a readily available function within an ODBC (Open Database Connectivity Driver) to do the job?

To use an external shared library of procedures and functions, you must perform the following steps:

1. Write or make available the compiled shared program library. The library must be written or have a "wrapper" that was written using the C programming language. Dynamic link libraries (DLLs) in the Microsoft Windows operating systems are good examples of such libraries.

2. Use the SQL command CREATE LIBRARY to declare a name for the shared program library.

3. Write simple PL/SQL procedures or functions that serve to call corresponding procedures and functions in the external shared program library.

After you set up an external procedure, PL/SQL programs can call the procedure to perform work. Oracle safely executes an external procedure in its own address space on the server, separate from the address space that runs Oracle. This way, if an external procedure misbehaves in any way, it cannot crash the server.

The following SQL command script shows how to build an external procedure that executes the SQLExecDirect function in an ODBC driver on a Microsoft Windows PC.

```
CREATE LIBRARY external.odbc as 'c:\windows\system\odbc.dll';

CREATE OR REPLACE FUNCTION external.sql_exec_direct (
-- EXECUTE ANY SQL STATEMENT USING ODBC
```

```
    sql_handle BINARY_INTEGER,
    sql_statement VARCHAR2(2000),
    sql_length INTEGER )
RETURN VARCHAR2 AS EXTERNAL
    LIBRARY external.odbc
    NAME SQLExecDirect
    LANGUAGE C;
```

The following anonymous PL/SQL block calls the new
SQL_EXEC_DIRECT function.

```
DECLARE
 return_code VARCHAR2(2000);
 stmt VARCHAR2(2000) := 'DELETE FROM access.customers';
BEGIN
 return_code := external.sql_exec_direct(1, stmt, LENGTH(stmt));
 ...
```

Although this example is simple, it provides you with the basics of
getting started using external procedures with PL/SQL.

Summary

This chapter has provided you with a great overview of the extended
capabilities that PL/SQL offers to create powerful database access programs.
You've learned about the basics of the language itself, as well as how to
create PL/SQL programs, using stored procedures, functions, packages, and
subprograms that call procedures external to Oracle itself.

CHAPTER
5

Extending Oracle
with Objects

he previous chapters of this book explain the basic relational database features of Oracle8, including how you can use SQL and PL/SQL to work with relational database objects such as tables and views. In this chapter, you'll learn how to use Oracle8's object-oriented database features to build next-generation database systems that take advantage of the object-oriented development paradigm. You'll also learn about other Oracle8 features that let you integrate existing relational databases with newer object-oriented databases so that applications can operate with both types of systems seamlessly. This chapter covers the following topics:

- The basics of object-oriented technology, including classes, instances, subclasses, inheritance, polymorphism, and encapsulation

- Objects and object types

- Object attributes and methods

- Object views

Oriented Toward Objects

Have you ever thought about how a standard light bulb works? I'm not 100% sure, but I know that there are positive and negative electrical feeds, a glass bulb that encapsulates what I think is an air-free cavity, a lighting filament, and probably a few other things that I have never seen. What I do know for sure is that when I screw a light bulb into a socket and then turn on the lamp, the room fills with light. Simple, right? I don't concern myself with how the light bulb works, just that it works after I screw it into a socket and flip on a switch.

The goal of object-oriented programming is rather analogous to my ability to successfully use a light bulb. For the same reason people shouldn't have to obtain a Ph.D. in electrical engineering to use a light bulb, programmers should not have to program the low-level internal system calls necessary to create a simple window or a scroll bar when designing every new GUI application interface. And in the world of database applications, all developers should not have to be relational database modeling experts or SQL gurus just to write queries that access database information. The object-oriented approach to software development is advantageous because it can reduce the effort necessary to build applications. An object is a reusable application component that developers simply need to know how to use, not how it works.

Oracle8 and Object-Oriented Databases

To support object-oriented database application development, Oracle8 lets you create and use object types in your database designs. Implemented to closely follow the ANSI/ISO SQL3 standard, object types let you build hybrid object-relational databases and make application development easier. For example, you might find something similar to the following object type in a typical order-entry database:

```
CREATE OR REPLACE TYPE sales.part_type AS OBJECT (
  id INTEGER,
  description VARCHAR2(50),
  on_hand INTEGER,
  reorder_point INTEGER,
  MEMBER FUNCTION part_id (descr IN VARCHAR2) RETURN INTEGER,
  MEMBER FUNCTION parts_on_hand (part_id IN INTEGER) RETURN INTEGER,
  MEMBER PROCEDURE order_part (part_id IN INTEGER, quantity IN INTEGER),
  MEMBER PROCEDURE return_part (part_id IN INTEGER, quantity IN INTEGER)
);
```

This example of a basic object type quickly illustrates two of the primary reasons for using object types. First, object types let you define complex datatypes that more closely resemble real-world things. For example, PART_TYPE represents the common representation of a part in a typical order-entry system. Second, object types let you tightly couple data and associated operations. More specifically, an object type can include an application interface that describes what an application can do with objects of the type. For example, PART_TYPE has methods to:

- Reveal a part's ID number when you give it the part's description

- Reveal the current inventory level of a part when you give it the part's ID number

- Decrease the inventory level of a part when placing an order for the part

- Increase the inventory level of a part when a customer returns an order for the part

In summary, because PART_TYPE has a well-defined API, developers don't have to know much about parts to build applications that work with them. Furthermore, object types let you centralize application standards in an Oracle database and then reuse them to make application development more efficient and consistent.

These are just a few of the benefits of using objects in an Oracle database. Before learning more about how to create an Oracle database that uses objects, you must first understand some basic terminology related to object-oriented database extensions.

Object-Oriented Database Terms and Concepts

If you are new to object-oriented programming and database design, there are many general terms and terms specific to Oracle that you need to learn before you begin to understand how to work with objects. The following sections explain several concepts related to object-oriented databases.

Object Types, Classes, and Objects

In simple terms, an *object* is a collection of related data. For example, an object in an Oracle database typically represents a real-world thing such as a person, place, or thing. More specifically, an object is a simpler term for a specific *instance* of a *class* or *object type*. For example, consider the PART_TYPE object type in Figure 5-1. Instances of the PART_TYPE object type would be parts in a typical order-entry application. (In relational terms, you might think of objects as rows in a table.)

Attributes and Methods

An object type's *attributes* describe the data elements in corresponding objects. For example, every part has an ID, a description, a current inventory quantity (parts on hand), and a reordering threshold. (In relational terms, you might think of object type attributes as column definitions in a table.)

An object type's *methods* (or *predefined behaviors*) *encapsulate* or describe the interface that applications use to work with objects of the type. As a result, application developers do not need to know the details about objects to manipulate them; they simply code applications to access object data using the methods that are available for the type. For example, an application that works with parts can order a quantity of a part and

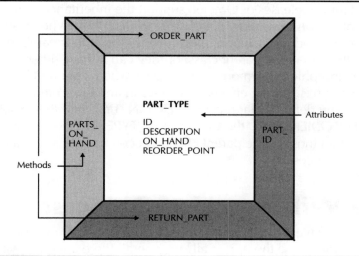

FIGURE 5-1.   *An object type (a class) has attributes to describe the corresponding object, as well as methods that allow applications to work with objects of the class.*

automatically decrease its level in inventory, return a quantity of a part back into inventory, and so on, all by using the methods associated with the PART_TYPE object type. (In relational terms, you might think of an object type's methods as the package of procedures and functions that provide an interface to work with a table's data.)

Subclasses, Inheritance, and Polymorphism

A *subclass* is a specialized class of an object type. In traditional object-oriented systems, a subclass *inherits* the attributes and methods of its parent class, and can have additional attributes and methods that are specific to the subclass. However, Oracle8 does **not** support inheritance of either attributes or methods.

NOTE
A subclass never inherits the data of its parent class—remember, a class is simply a definition of attributes and methods, not data. Instances or objects of an object type are data.

Should future releases of Oracle8 support the inheritance of methods, the concept of *polymorphism* would also be important. When a subclass inherits the methods of its parent class, inherited methods can behave exactly as they do in the parent class, or they can behave differently (they can be polymorphic). Polymorphism happens when a method behaves differently and has varying effects for classes in an object hierarchy. For example, if you define a class named PERSON_TYPE and then a subclass named CUSTOMER_TYPE, the CUSTOMER_TYPE's methods might behave differently than those in the parent class to account for different attributes and other variances.

How Will You Use Objects?

Now that you have a basic understanding of objects and object types, how will you decide to use them, if at all? In general, there are three ways to use object types in Oracle database designs:

- To implement user-defined datatypes that enhance the creation of relational database models

- To created nested tables inside relational database tables

- To create object tables that implement an object-oriented database design rather than a relational database design

As you can see, there are varying degrees to which you can commit to Oracle8's object-oriented database extensions—you can use object types simply to enhance a relational database design or take the leap and implement tables defined by object types. As with any important decision, consider the specific requirements that you face and determine the best choice for your system. Later sections of this chapter show you how to accomplish each type of implementation.

Do I Have to Use Object Types?

Another important choice not mentioned in the previous section is that you can ignore object types completely and stick with pure relational database designs. In addition to the fact that many respected relational database purists emotionally argue that objects are not meant for the database side of an application, there are several practical reasons to avoid using object types in an Oracle database:

- You might not have the time or nerve to convert existing applications to take advantage of new object-oriented database extensions.

- You might want to wait until Oracle8's object technology matures with subsequent releases and becomes more robust to offer such features as subclass inheritance, polymorphism, and type versioning—until then, you might choose to use object types only in prototype systems.

- Several other Oracle8 features restrict or prohibit the use of object types in database designs. For example, if you plan to use Oracle8's advanced replication feature with 8.0.3, you should know that you cannot replicate tables that use object types.

Whatever your reasons, it's entirely up to you whether you use object types, to some degree or not at all.

Working With Object Types

Now you are ready to learn the basics of creating and using objects in an Oracle database. The following sections explain how to create object types in a database, how to build methods for object types, and how to use object types to build tables and other structures in a database.

Designing Object Types

Before you start creating object types in a database, it's a good idea to understand what you want to achieve by using them. In general, you will create an object type to build a complex, user-defined datatype that more closely matches a real-world thing. Then you and other developers can use this object type to declare and work with tables and other database objects more easily.

For example, suppose you notice that the specification of an "address" varies across a business's database applications. Some implementations of an address are better than others—for example, poor implementations might not allow enough room for an unusually long street address or might not offer a field for a country specification. One way to ensure the consistency of addresses throughout database applications is to write and distribute standard development guidelines to all corporate developers. However, that would require the developers to read, understand, and most importantly, adhere to the guidelines. An easier way to ensure consistent addresses in your system is to create a new ADDRESS_TYPE that developers can use in their database designs.

A more advanced use of an object type is to create a nested table type that you can use to embed the data of what would otherwise be a child table into its parent table. For example, rather than create distinct ORDERS and ITEMS tables, you can create an ITEM_TYPE that you then nest in the ORDERS table. Using this design, each ORDER record can have a nested table of associated ITEMS. Rather than performing a join to retrieve an order and its line items, a simple query gets all of the nested table's information at once. Nested tables hide the relationship of two tables (in other words, the data model) from applications and put it with the data itself and can reduce the complexity of subsequent application development.

Creating Object Types

When you want to create a new object type, you can declare two separate parts—the type's specification and body:

- Similar to PL/SQL packages, an object type's *specification* is the public interface that developers use to work with the type when building applications. To create an object type's specification, you use the SQL command CREATE TYPE.

- An object type's *body* is the private implementation of the type's methods; it's only necessary to create a body for an object type when the type's specification declares one or more methods. To create an object type's body, you use the SQL command CREATE TYPE BODY.

Examples of Creating and Using Object Types

The following examples demonstrate some common object types and how you might use them in your database designs. The examples illustrate the varying degrees to which you can use object types in an Oracle database—from augmenting a relational database design to building an object database.

Creating Custom Datatypes with Object Types

The most straightforward use of object types is for the creation of custom datatypes that you can then use to build relational database objects more easily. For example, the following statement creates a new ADDRESS_TYPE:

```
CREATE OR REPLACE TYPE pub.address_type AS OBJECT (
  street1 VARCHAR2(50),
  street2 VARCHAR2(50),
  city VARCHAR2(50),
  state VARCHAR2(25),
  zipcode VARCHAR2(10),
  country VARCHAR2(50));
```

NOTE
When you create object types that must be available to everyone in the system, it's a good idea to first create a schema to contain "public" object types (for example, PUB). Then create object types in the schema and grant the necessary privileges for each object type.

Because the specification of the ADDRESS_TYPE does not include any method specifications, a body is not necessary for the type.

NOTE
When an object type specification includes neither attributes nor method specifications, the object type is an incomplete object type. Sometimes it's necessary to declare incomplete object types before you know what you want them to look like so that you can build other dependent objects.

When developers need to declare an address in a relational database table, they can use the ADDRESS_TYPE and automatically comply with corporate guidelines.

```
CREATE TABLE sales.customers (
  id INTEGER PRIMARY KEY,
  last_name VARCHAR2(50),
  first_name VARCHAR2(50),
  company_name VARCHAR2(50),
  address pub.Address_Type,
  ...
```

Likewise, when a developer must declare address parameters for a stored procedure, it's easy with the new ADDRESS_TYPE:

```
CREATE OR REPLACE PROCEDURE sales.new_customer (
  custid IN INTEGER,
  last IN VARCHAR2,
  first IN VARCHAR2,
  address IN pub.Address_Type)
BEGIN
  ...
```

To work with a column in a relational table that is declared using an object type, DML statements must reference column attributes with some special syntax. For example, to query the CUSTOMERS table that uses the custom datatype ADDRESS_TYPE, a SELECT statement must use an extended form of standard dot notation to reference specific attributes in the ADDRESS column:

```
SELECT
  id, last_name, first_name,
  address.street1, address.street2, address.city,
  address.state, address.zipcode, address.country
FROM sales.customers;
```

The results of the query might look like the following:

```
ID LAST_NAME                FIRST_NAME            ADDRESS.STREET1     ...
-- ----------------------   --------------------  ----------------    ...
 1 Ellison                  Lawrence              500 Oracle Parkway  ...
```

Similarly, to update a specific attribute of a column that's declared with an object type, you must use extended dot notation to reference the attribute:

```
UPDATE sales.customers
  SET address.zipcode = '94065'
  WHERE id = 1;
```

Inserting a row into a table that uses an object type to declare a column is slightly different. To accomplish this, you must use the object type's *constructor method*, which Oracle automatically creates for every object type so that you can build new objects of the type. An object type's constructor automatically takes the same name as the type itself. For example, the following INSERT statement inserts a customer into the CUSTOMERS table using the constructor method for the ADDRESS_TYPE:

```
INSERT INTO sales.customers VALUES (
  1,'Ellison','Lawrence','Oracle Corporation',
  pub.Address_Type(
    '500 Oracle Parkway', 'Box 659510',
    'Redwood Shores','CA','95045','USA'));
```

This example of the user-defined datatype ADDRESS_TYPE shows how you can use object types with Oracle8 merely to simplify the development of a relational database without moving completely to an object-oriented database design. Let's continue with a more advanced use of object types—how to create and use nested tables.

Creating Nested Tables

In this example, you'll see how to nest one table inside another using an object type. When you nest a child table inside its parent table, Oracle automatically manages the built-in relationships among each row of the parent table and the associated nested table rows. Nested tables remove the complexity of relational joins from applications and can make some areas of subsequent application development easier.

Nested tables are appropriate for master-detail relationships in which detail rows store unique information. For example, consider the typical ORDERS and ITEMS tables in a relational order-entry database. Each line item is a unique collection of data that corresponds to a particular order. This is the kind of master-detail relationship that is the perfect candidate for a nested table. The following example creates a simplified ITEM_TYPE (no reference to the part ID is included) and corresponding ITEM_LIST_TYPE that you can then use to nest a typical ITEMS table inside a typical ORDERS table.

```
CREATE OR REPLACE TYPE sales.item_type AS OBJECT (
  item_id INTEGER,
  quantity INTEGER );

CREATE OR REPLACE TYPE sales.item_list AS TABLE OF sales.Item_Type;

CREATE TABLE sales.orders (
  id INTEGER PRIMARY KEY,
  order_date DATE,
  ship_date DATE,
  line_items sales.Item_List )
  NESTED TABLE line_items STORE AS items;
```

NOTE
To simplify the example and focus on nested tables, the ITEM_TYPE does not contain an attribute for a part number nor does the ORDERS table contain a column for a customer ID. See the examples later in this chapter that show a more complete schema example for object tables that use references.

When you nest a table inside another table, Oracle stores the data within one physical data segment (see Chapter 7), but creates two logical tables in the data dictionary. In the previous example, Oracle creates the ORDERS table and the associated nested table ITEMS as one data segment, but two separate tables.

As you might expect, manipulating nested tables requires that you use some special DML syntax. For example, an application can insert a new order and corresponding items into the new ORDERS table using a single INSERT statement with constructors to insert ITEMS into the nested table.

```
INSERT INTO sales.orders VALUES (
  1, SYSDATE, NULL,
  sales.Item_List(
  sales.Item_Type(1, 22),
  sales.Item_Type(2,  100) ) );
```

To work with individual rows in a nested table, SQL statements must always access the master table using a *flattened subquery*, which is denoted by the special SQL expression THE. If you are a relational expert, a THE expression might seem a little strange at first. However, if you read SQL statements that contain flattened subqueries as they sound, the use of a THE expression becomes much more intuitive. For example, the following statement inserts another line item into an existing order using a flattened subquery. The pseudo-code in the comment makes the use of the THE expression obvious.

```
-- insert a new line item into "the" line items for order #1
INSERT INTO THE(SELECT line_items FROM sales.orders WHERE id = 1)
 VALUES (3, 200);
```

Additionally, to retrieve rows from a nested table, you must use a flattened subquery.

```
-- select the ID and quantity of "the" line items for order #1
SELECT item_id, quantity
 FROM THE (SELECT line_items FROM sales.orders WHERE id = 1)
 ORDER BY item_id;

ITEM_ID    QUANTITY
---------- ----------
        1         22
        2        100
        3        200
```

To delete rows in a nested table, you also must use a flattened subquery. For example, the following statement deletes the third line item in the ORDERS table.

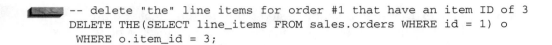

```
-- delete "the" line items for order #1 that have an item ID of 3
DELETE THE(SELECT line_items FROM sales.orders WHERE id = 1) o
 WHERE o.item_id = 3;
```

Creating Object Tables

All of the previous examples in this chapter show you how to use object types simply to enhance the creation of relational database objects, such as tables and stored procedures. When you want to go all the way to an object-oriented database design, you can use object types to create object tables. An *object table* is a database table that you define using an object type only, not relational columns, etc. When you create an object table, the table's columns correspond to the attributes of the object type that you use to create the table.

The rows in an object table are objects of the table's type. Each object in an object table has a unique *object identifier (OID)*, which Oracle automatically indexes and guarantees to be unique among all other OIDs. Oracle uses OIDs of object tables to define the relationships among various object tables in a database. For example, the following statements show you how to implement a typical order-entry schema using object types and object tables:

```
-- statements to create a CUSTOMERS object table
CREATE OR REPLACE TYPE sales.customer_type AS OBJECT (
  id INTEGER,
  last_name VARCHAR2(50),
  first_name VARCHAR2(50),
  company_name VARCHAR2(50),
  address pub.Address_Type);

CREATE TABLE sales.customers OF sales.Customer_Type
  (id PRIMARY KEY);

-- statements to create a PARTS object table
CREATE OR REPLACE TYPE sales.part_type AS OBJECT (
  id INTEGER,
  description VARCHAR2(50),
  unit_price NUMBER(10,2),
  on_hand INTEGER,
  reorder_point INTEGER);

CREATE TABLE sales.parts OF sales.Part_Type
  (id PRIMARY KEY);
```

```
-- statements to create an ORDERS object table
-- with a nested ITEMS table
CREATE OR REPLACE TYPE sales.item_type AS OBJECT (
 item_id INTEGER,
 part REF sales.Part_Type,
 quantity INTEGER);

CREATE OR REPLACE TYPE sales.item_list AS TABLE OF sales.Item_Type;

CREATE OR REPLACE TYPE sales.order_type AS OBJECT (
 id INTEGER,
 customer REF sales.Customer_Type,
 order_date DATE,
 ship_date DATE,
 line_items sales.Item_List );

CREATE TABLE sales.orders OF sales.Order_Type
 (id PRIMARY KEY)
 NESTED TABLE line_items STORE AS items;
```

Look closely at the definition of ITEM_TYPE and ORDER_TYPE and you'll see that the examples introduce the concept of an object reference—the PART attribute references objects of type PART_TYPE and the CUSTOMER attribute references objects of type CUSTOMER_TYPE. Similar to a foreign key in a relational database table, an *object reference* is an attribute of one object that points to another object somewhere in the database using an OID.

Now let's see how to work with object tables using standard SQL DML commands. First, the following statements demonstrate how to use the constructor methods to insert some data into the PARTS and CUSTOMERS tables:

```
INSERT INTO sales.parts
 VALUES (sales.Part_Type(1,'Pentium 200 CPU', 250.00, 1000, 300));

INSERT INTO sales.customers
 VALUES (sales.Customer_Type(1,'Ellison','Lawrence','Oracle Corporation',
  pub.Address_Type('500 Oracle Parkway', 'Box 659510',
  'Redwood Shores','CA','95045','USA')));
```

When an object table contains an attribute that is an object reference, DML involving the attribute requires the use of some special syntax. Most notably, SQL and PL/SQL statements must use the *REF function* to work with object references. REF is a SQL function that returns a reference or pointer to the OID of a specific object. The following INSERT statement uses a subquery to build the values list for the new object; the subquery also determines the OID of the customer for the new order:

```
INSERT INTO sales.orders
  SELECT 1, REF(c), SYSDATE, NULL, sales.Item_List()
   FROM sales.customers c
   WHERE id = 1;
```

To complete the order's line items, you must use INSERT statements with flattened subqueries, as the following examples demonstrate:

```
INSERT INTO THE(SELECT o.line_items FROM orders o WHERE o.id = 1)
  SELECT 1, REF(p), 20 FROM parts p
   WHERE id = 2;

INSERT INTO THE(SELECT o.line_items FROM orders o WHERE o.id = 1)
  SELECT 2, REF(p), 10 FROM parts p
   WHERE id = 11;

...
```

The following PL/SQL block demonstrates how a database application might use program variables to reference OIDs within SELECT, INSERT, and UPDATE statements. Read the comments in the code to learn exactly what is happening:

```
DECLARE
  -- declare variables to hold OID references
  custoid REF sales.Customer_Type;
  partoid REF sales.Part_Type;
BEGIN
  -- assign Larry Ellison's OID to CUSTOID
  SELECT REF(c) INTO custoid FROM sales.customers c
   WHERE c.last_name = 'Ellison'
   AND c.first_name = 'Lawrence';

  -- assign Pentium 200's OID to PARTOID
  SELECT REF(p) INTO partoid FROM sales.parts p
   WHERE p.description = 'Pentium 200 CPU';
```

```
-- insert a new order for CUSTOID
-- the order has one line item for PARTOID
-- assign the new order's OID to ORDOID
 INSERT INTO sales.orders
  VALUES (sales.Order_Type (1, custoid, SYSDATE, NULL,
    sales.Item_List(sales.Item_Type(1, partoid, 50) ) ) );
EXCEPTION
 WHEN NO_DATA_FOUND THEN
  raise_application_error(-20000,'No data found');
END;
```

At this point, you might think that the steps necessary to input data into object tables are not as intuitive as the corresponding relational SQL syntax. However, try to remember that it usually takes some practice to get used to anything new.

The benefits of object tables, OIDs, and object references quickly become evident when you want to combine information from related object tables. Rather than build complicated join queries as is necessary with relational models, you can use extended dot notation for attributes of object tables that are object references. Oracle8 automatically navigates object references to make SQL coding more straightforward. For example, the following object query returns related information from the ORDERS and CUSTOMERS object tables:

```
SELECT o.id, o.customer.company_name
  FROM sales.orders o;

ID          CUSTOMER.COMPANY_NAME
---------- -------------------------
         1 Oracle Corporation
```

In contrast, in a relational system, a developer would need to understand the relationship between the ORDERS and CUSTOMERS tables, and then code that relationship into every query that joins information from the two related tables, such as:

```
SELECT o.id, c.company_name
  FROM sales.orders o, sales.customers c
  WHERE o.cust_id = c.id;
```

Back to our system of object tables, the following query retrieves information from the nested ITEMS table and related PARTS object table:

```
SELECT o.item_id, o.part.description, o.quantity
  FROM THE(SELECT line_items FROM sales.orders WHERE id = 1) o;

ITEM_ID    PART.DESCRIPTION       QUANTITY
---------- ---------------------- ----------
         1 Pentium 200 CPU              50
```

Although the previous examples are relatively simple, you should now have a general understanding of why it is advantageous to use object tables and how to build and then use them when developing database applications.

Oh, What a Tangled Web We Weave— Beware of Dependencies!

The previous examples show how you can use object types to build database objects such as tables and stored procedures. When you do so, understand that you establish a tree of dependencies among database objects and object types that must remain intact. In fact, Oracle keeps track of dependencies and will not let you pull the rug out from under anything. You can query the data dictionary at any time to display the dependencies of objects. For example, the following query, executed while connected as the user SALES, reveals the dependencies of the SALES.CUSTOMERS table on PUB.ADDRESS_TYPE and SALES.CUSTOMER_TYPE:

```
SELECT * FROM user_dependencies
  ORDER BY name, type;

NAME       TYPE    REFERENCED_OWNER REFERENCED_NAME  REFERENCED_TYPE
---------- ------  ---------------- ---------------- ----------------
CUSTOMERS  TABLE   PUB              ADDRESS_TYPE     TYPE
CUSTOMERS  TABLE   SALES            CUSTOMER_TYPE    TYPE
...
```

Dependencies are OK when you never need to change things. In the real world, however, changes are inevitable. That's when the dependencies that object types establish can become a nightmare. For example, suppose that you want to expand CUSTOMER_TYPE with a new attribute for PHOTO. Because the CUSTOMERS table depends on CUSTOMER_TYPE, you cannot change the definition of CUSTOMER_TYPE without first dropping the CUSTOMERS table. In conclusion, carefully plan the object types for your database so that you get things right the first time. Then keep your fingers crossed and hope that things do not change once you have everything up and running.

More About Methods

When you specify methods in an object type specification, you implement the methods by creating a corresponding body for the object type. Using the SQL command CREATE TYPE BODY, you implement methods for an object type using Oracle's PL/SQL. A *method* is nothing more than a PL/SQL procedure or function that is stored with an object type and meant to encapsulate an object type.

NOTE
With the initial release of Oracle8, methods do not truly "encapsulate" object types. That's because applications can use object SQL to access objects of a type rather than corresponding object type methods.

An object type can have different types of methods, including a constructor method, member methods, and a map method or an order method. The following sections explain more about each type of method.

An Object Type's Constructor Method
The previous examples in this chapter have already introduced an object type's constructor method. Oracle automatically creates a constructor method for an object type so that you can instantiate new objects of the type. By default, a type's constructor takes the same name as the type itself and has parameters that match the attributes of the object type. See the previous sections for examples of using an object type's constructor method.

An Object Type's Member Methods
Every object type can have one or more member methods. An object type *member method* is nothing more than a stored procedure or function that is tied to the object type itself. An object type's member methods typically manipulate the attributes of the object type in some way. To prevent

unwanted side effects, object type methods cannot insert, update, or delete information in database tables.

The first step necessary to create member methods with an object type is to specify them as part of the object type specification. For example, the following statements create an alternative declaration of ORDER_TYPE with a member method and a corresponding ORDERS table:

```
CREATE OR REPLACE TYPE sales.order_type AS OBJECT (
  id INTEGER,
  customer REF sales.Customer_Type,
  order_date DATE,
  ship_date DATE,
  line_items sales.Item_List,
  MEMBER FUNCTION order_total RETURN NUMBER,
  PRAGMA RESTRICT_REFERENCES(order_total, WNDS, WNPS) );

CREATE TABLE sales.orders OF sales.Order_Type
  (id PRIMARY KEY)
  NESTED TABLE line_items STORE AS items;
```

Notice that the specification of an object type's member methods is similar to that of the specification of a PL/SQL package's procedures and functions, as follows:

- Each method can have one or more parameters (none are shown in this example).

- A member function must declare the type of a single return value.

- Each method must have a *pragma compiler directive* (in the form of a PRAGMA RESTRICT_REFERENCES specification) that constrains the operations that the method can perform. In this example, the ORDER_TOTAL method can "write no database state" (WNDS) and "write no package state" (WNPS). Other options include "read no database state" (RNDS) and "read no package state" (RNPS).

Additionally, each member method has an implicit first parameter called SELF that has the same type as the object type itself—for example, the ORDER_TOTAL has an implicit first parameter SELF that is of the type ORDER_TYPE. (The next example shows you how to use the SELF parameter.)

You implement an object type's member methods in the body of the object type. For example, the following statement implements the ORDER_TOTAL methods in the body for the object type ORDER_TYPE.

```
CREATE OR REPLACE TYPE BODY sales.order_type (
MEMBER FUNCTION order_total RETURN NUMBER IS
 return_value NUMBER;
BEGIN
 SELECT SUM(l.quantity * l.part.unit_price) INTO return_value
   FROM THE(SELECT o.line_items FROM sales.orders o WHERE o.id = SELF.id) l;
 RETURN return_value;
END order_total;
);
```

To use the member function, a SQL statement can simply reference the method. For example, the following query reveals order number 1's total value:

```
SELECT o.order_total() FROM sales.orders o WHERE id = 1;

O.ORDER_TOTAL
-------------
         5000
```

Notice how the ORDER_TOTAL method greatly simplifies the process of determining the order's total line item value. A comparable relational query might look similar to the following:

```
SELECT SUM(i.quantity * p.unit_price)
  FROM sales.items i, sales.parts p
  WHERE i.order_id = 1
  AND i.part_id = p.id;
```

Order and Map Methods—Ordering and Comparing Objects of the Same Type

Oracle can easily order and compare the data in columns that use standard datatypes such as NUMBER, DATE, and CHAR. For example, the number 100 comes before 101 when sorting a NUMBER column in ascending order because 100 is less than 101. The same kind of ordering is typically necessary to support user-defined object types. For example, Oracle cannot order customer records by address unless you explain to Oracle how it can compare two addresses.

```
SELECT c.company_name, c.address.zipcode FROM sales.customers c
 ORDER BY c.address;

ORA-22950: cannot ORDER objects without MAP or ORDER method
```

As the previous error message indicates, you must create an object type with either a *map* or an *order* method (but not both) to be able to order and compare objects of the type. Oracle uses an object type's map or order method to determine the outcome of:

■ Equality, less-than, and greater-than relations

■ BETWEEN and IN predicates

■ ORDER BY, GROUP BY, and DISTINCT clauses

■ UNIQUE and PRIMARY KEY constraints

NOTE
If you decide to declare an object type without a map or order method, Oracle can perform only equality and inequality comparisons for two objects of the same type. Two objects are equal only when all attributes in each object are identical.

First, let's examine map methods. The following declaration of the ADDRESS_TYPE includes a map method.

```
CREATE OR REPLACE TYPE pub.address_type AS OBJECT (
  street1 VARCHAR2(50),
  street2 VARCHAR2(50),
  city VARCHAR2(50),
  state VARCHAR2(25),
  zipcode VARCHAR2(10),
  country VARCHAR2(50),
  MAP MEMBER FUNCTION address_map RETURN VARCHAR2
);

CREATE OR REPLACE TYPE BODY address_type (
MAP MEMBER FUNCTION address_map RETURN VARCHAR2 IS
BEGIN
 RETURN zipcode || city || street1;
END address_map;
);
```

A type's map method does not take any input parameters and it returns a scalar datatype such as NUMBER, VARCHAR2, or DATE. Now, when a query asks to order records by the addresses in a table, Oracle implicitly uses the ADDRESS_TYPE's map method to order the return set by addresses.

```
SELECT c.company_name, c.address.zipcode FROM sales.customers c
  ORDER BY c.address;

COMPANY_NAME                     ADDRESS.ZIPCODE
------------------------         ----------------
Oracle Corporation               95045
Microsoft                        98052
...
```

NOTE
If you decide at a later time to change the implementation of ADDRESS_TYPE's map method, you simply replace the type's body and your new ordering mechanism is in place, without having to recompile applications that depend on it.

An alternative to a map method is an *order method*. An order method takes a bit more work to create and performs much less efficiently than a map method. The following declaration of the ADDRESS_TYPE demonstrates the use of an order method rather than a map method, but accomplishes the same goal.

```
CREATE OR REPLACE TYPE pub.address_type AS OBJECT (
  street1 VARCHAR2(50),
  street2 VARCHAR2(50),
  city VARCHAR2(50),
  state VARCHAR2(25),
  zipcode VARCHAR2(10),
  country VARCHAR2(50),
  ORDER MEMBER FUNCTION address_map (other address_type)
   RETURN INTEGER
);
```

```
CREATE OR REPLACE TYPE BODY pub.address_type (
ORDER MEMBER FUNCTION address_map (other address_type)
  RETURN INTEGER IS
 self_address VARCHAR2(150) := self.zipcode||self.city||self.street1;
 other_address VARCHAR2(150) := other.zipcode||other.city||other.street1;
BEGIN
 IF self_address < other_address THEN
  RETURN -1;
 ELSIF self_address > other_address THEN
  RETURN 1;
 ELSE
  RETURN 0;
 END IF;
END address_map;
);
```

An order method takes two input parameters—the implicit SELF parameter and another parameter of the object type itself. The return value of the method must be the integer -1, 1, or 0. You must code the order method to return the following:

- ■ -1 when SELF < the other input parameter
- ■ 1 when SELF > the other input parameter
- ■ 0 when SELF = the other input parameter

Just as with a map method, when a query asks to order records by the addresses in a table, Oracle implicitly uses the ADDRESS_TYPE's order method to order the return set by addresses.

```
SELECT c.company_name, c.address.zipcode FROM sales.customers c
 ORDER BY c.address;

COMPANY_NAME                  ADDRESS.ZIPCODE
----------------------------  -----------------
Oracle Corporation            95045
Microsoft                     98052
...
```

Objects and Views

As explained in Chapter 2, a view is a database object that you might create for several reasons. For example, you can use a view to derive new data, simplify access to a table or set of tables, present table data in a different way, or increase the security of specific columns and rows in a table. In Oracle8, views fully support object-extensions: you can create views of object tables as well as views of relational tables that use object types to declare complex columns. Additionally, by using some special types of triggers, any type of view can be updatable. The following sections explain more about using views in an object-relational Oracle8 database.

Object Views of Object Tables

If you decide to implement object tables in your Oracle8 database, you can create an *object view* of any object table that you like. However, you must have an object type to describe the shape of the view. First, let's look at an extremely simple example of an object view. The following view of the CUSTOMERS object table uses the existing CUSTOMER_TYPE to describe its shape.

```
CREATE OR REPLACE VIEW sales.cust OF sales.customer_type AS
  SELECT * FROM sales.customers;
```

The declaration of the CUST view is straightforward because there already is an object type available that describes the shape of the new view. When you create an object view of an object table, each row in the view is an object. When you base an object view on a single object table, it's clear to Oracle that the OID of an object in view is the OID of the corresponding row in the view's base table. The OIDs in an object view can be referenced when you add objects to other tables or views in the database.

Now let's look at a slightly more complicated example of an object view. Suppose that you want to create a view that summarizes the number of orders placed by each company. To create an object view that accomplishes your goals, you must first create a new type that describes the shape of the proposed view.

```
CREATE OR REPLACE TYPE sales.customer_order_type AS OBJECT (
  order_count INTEGER,
  company VARCHAR2(50) );
```

With the new type in place, you can now create the CUSTOMER_ORDERS view as follows:

```
CREATE OR REPLACE VIEW sales.customer_orders OF
sales.customer_order_type
 WITH OBJECT OID (company) AS
 SELECT COUNT(o.id), o.customer.company_name
  FROM sales.orders o
  GROUP BY o.customer.company_name;
```

Notice that the defining query of the view groups rows in the ORDERS table by customer company names. Consequently, it is unclear how to uniquely identify the objects that the view represents. In this case, it is necessary to specify the WITH OBJECT OID clause to clearly indicate what attributes of the view type Oracle can use to uniquely identify the OIDs of the object view. In the CUSTOMER_ORDERS view, the clear choice is the COMPANY attribute of the CUSTOMER_ORDER_TYPE.

A result set from the new CUSTOMER_ORDERS view would look similar to:

```
SELECT * FROM customer_orders;

ORDER_COUNT  COMPANY
-----------  --------------------------------------------------
         31 Oracle Corporation
...
```

Views of Relational Tables

No doubt, many of you reading this book are currently using the Oracle7 relational database management system. So let's assume that, after reading the previous sections in this chapter, you decide that Oracle8's new object-oriented database features are the best things since sliced bread. But how do you migrate from Oracle7 and the relational world that you operate in right now? Do you have to scrap all of your previous databases and applications just to reap the benefits of object-oriented database designs? Fortunately, the answer is a resounding NO. Oracle8 lets you define views on top of both relational and object tables so that you can smoothly transition from a pure relational environment to an object-oriented system. Using views, you can keep all of your data in either relational schemas, migrate to new object schemas, or have a mix of both. In any case, applications will never know the difference.

Views That Establish Object Abstractions for Relational Data

In most cases, migrating from an existing relational system to an object-relational system is not a one-step process. As you build new information systems, you might want to design new applications to take advantage of Oracle8's object-oriented database features, but leave existing relational database applications in place. In other words, both the new object-oriented applications and the existing relational applications must coexist and work with the same set of data that is in relational tables. Using views, you can achieve this goal. To demonstrate how this works, first consider the traditional CUSTOMERS table in a relational format:

```
CREATE TABLE sales.customers (
  id INTEGER PRIMARY KEY,
  last_name VARCHAR2(50),
  first_name VARCHAR2(50),
  company_name VARCHAR2(50),
  street1 VARCHAR2(50),
  street2 VARCHAR2(50),
  city VARCHAR2(50),
  state VARCHAR2(25),
  zipcode VARCHAR2(10),
  country VARCHAR2(50));
```

The following statements illustrate how a traditional RDBMS application works with the CUSTOMERS table:

```
INSERT INTO sales.customers
  VALUES (1,'Ellison','Lawrence','Oracle Corporation',
   '500 Oracle Parkway','Box 659511','Redwood Shores',
   'CA','95045','USA');

UPDATE sales.customers
  SET street2 = 'Box 659510'
  WHERE id = 1;
```

On the other hand, an object-oriented database application expects to work with a CUSTOMERS table that uses the ADDRESS_TYPE. The following statements illustrate how an object-oriented database application works with an object-oriented CUSTOMERS table:

```
INSERT INTO sales.customers
  VALUES (sales.Customer_Type(1,'Ellison','Lawrence','Oracle Corporation',
    pub.Address_Type('500 Oracle Parkway', 'Box 659511',
    'Redwood Shores','CA','95045','USA')));

SELECT c.address.street1, c.address.street2, c.address.city
  FROM sales.customers c;

UPDATE sales.customers c
  SET c.address.street2 = 'Box 659510'
  WHERE c.id = 1;
```

To enable the object-oriented database application to work with the relational CUSTOMERS table, you can create a view that establishes the necessary object abstractions. For example, consider the following definition of the CUST view:

```
CREATE OR REPLACE VIEW cust (id, last, first, company, address) AS
  SELECT id, last_name, first_name, company_name,
    pub.address_type(street1, street2, city, state, zipcode, country)
  FROM customers;
```

Now, the application can issue object-oriented queries against the view to retrieve information from the underlying relational table:

```
SELECT c.id, c.address.zipcode
  FROM sales.cust c;

ID         ADDRESS.ZIPCODE
---------- ----------------
         1 95045
...
```

Object Views of Relational Tables with OIDs

Oracle8 also allows you to create object views of relational tables. Just as with object views of object tables, you must have an object type that defines the shape of the view that you want to create. For example, the following statement creates an object view of the relational database table CUSTOMERS (see previous section for its definition) using the CUSTOMER_TYPE:

```
CREATE OR REPLACE TYPE sales.customer_type AS OBJECT (
  id INTEGER,
  last_name VARCHAR2(50),
  first_name VARCHAR2(50),
  company_name VARCHAR2(50),
  address pub.Address_Type);

CREATE OR REPLACE VIEW sales.cust OF sales.customer_type
  WITH OBJECT OID (id) AS
  SELECT id, last_name, first_name, company_name,
   pub.address_type(street1, street2, city, state, zipcode, country)
  FROM sales.customers;
```

Notice that because the base table of the object view is a relational database table, you must use the WITH OBJECT OID clause to indicate what attributes of the view type Oracle can use to uniquely identify the OIDs of the object view.

Now let's finish adding object abstractions for the remainder of the tables in our relational schema. The following statements establish object abstractions for the relational PARTS, ORDERS, and ITEMS tables:

```
CREATE OR REPLACE VIEW sales.part OF sales.Part_Type
  WITH OBJECT OID(id) AS
  SELECT * FROM sales.parts;

CREATE OR REPLACE VIEW sales.ord OF sales.Order_Type
  WITH OBJECT OID (id) AS
  SELECT id, MAKE_REF(sales.cust, cust_id), order_date, ship_date,
   CAST(MULTISET(SELECT id, MAKE_REF(sales.part, id), quantity
    FROM sales.items l
    WHERE l.order_id = o.id)
    AS sales.Item_List)
   FROM sales.orders o;
```

NOTE

This example introduces two new object SQL extensions. A CAST expression sets the results of a query to a nested table type that you specify. In the example, the CAST expression "casts" the subquery of the relational ITEMS table to the ITEMS_LIST nested table type. A MAKE_REF expression establishes a reference to an OID. For example, the first MAKE_REF expression creates an OID reference to a customer's OID in the CUST view.

With these views in place, an object-oriented application can use object SQL to query data that is actually stored in relational tables. For example, the following object SQL query retrieves information from the relational ORDERS and ITEMS tables:

```
SELECT o.id, o.customer.company_name
 FROM sales.orders o;

ID          CUSTOMER.COMPANY_NAME
----------  -------------------------
         1 Oracle Corporation
```

The queries that define object views of relational tables are often quite complicated and include references to many tables. Consequently, many object views of relational tables are not updatable unless you use the special types of triggers discussed in the next section.

Views and INSTEAD OF Triggers

In previous versions of Oracle, only views that meet the materialized view principle are updatable (see Chapter 2, "Basic Relational Database Structures"). With Oracle8, any view is updatable when you create INSTEAD OF triggers for the view. An *INSTEAD OF trigger* is a special type of database trigger that you create for a view. An INSTEAD OF trigger tells Oracle how to apply a DML operation performed on the view. For example, the following INSTEAD OF trigger specifies what to do when an application issues an INSERT statement against the ORD view (see the previous section):

```
CREATE OR REPLACE TRIGGER ord_insert_trigger
INSTEAD OF INSERT ON sales.ord
DECLARE
  item_var sales.Item_List;
  i INTEGER;
  cust_var sales.Customer_Type;
  part_var sales.Part_Type;
  part_var_ref REF sales.Part_Type;
BEGIN
  item_var := :new.line_items;
  SELECT DEREF(:new.customer) INTO cust_var FROM dual;
  INSERT INTO sales.orders
   VALUES (:new.id, cust_var.id, :new.order_date, :new.ship_date);
 FOR I IN 1 .. item_var.count LOOP
   part_var_ref := item_var(i).part;
   SELECT DEREF(part_var_ref) INTO part_var FROM dual;
   INSERT INTO sales.items
     VALUES (:new.id, part_var.id, item_var(i).item_id, item_var(i).quantity);
 END LOOP;
END;
```

NOTE
This example introduces a new object SQL extension, the DEREF function. A DEREF function returns the data value of a referenced object. For example, the first DEREF function returns the attribute values for the referenced customer object.

With the ORD view in place, an application can insert new objects into the underlying ORDERS and ITEMS relational tables using object SQL statements. For example, the following INSERT statement inserts a new order:

```
INSERT INTO sales.ord
  SELECT 1, REF(c), SYSDATE, NULL, sales.Item_List()
   FROM sales.cust c
   WHERE id = 1;
```

NOTE

The INSTEAD OF trigger in this example specifies what to do with INSERT statements issued against the ORD view. You can also create INSTEAD OF triggers for UPDATE and DELETE operations.

Although INSTEAD OF triggers are particularly useful for creating updatable object views that have complex defining queries, keep in mind that Oracle8 lets you use INSTEAD OF triggers with any type of view—object views or regular views on relational tables.

Summary

This chapter has explained the most important features of Oracle's new object-oriented database features, including object types, attributes and methods, and object views. Using objects, you can raise the level of abstraction in your database and make it easier for developers to work with application data.

PART

III

Oracle8 Database Structure

CHAPTER
6

Controlling Database Access

ith any multi-user computer system, security is a particularly important issue to address. Oracle database systems are certainly no exception. Without adequate security controls, malicious users might invade an Oracle database, view confidential information, and make unauthorized changes to database information. This chapter explains the various security features of Oracle8 that you can use to control user access to database resources.

- User management and authentication
- Privilege management and roles
- Database resource limits
- User password management
- Database auditing
- Trusted Oracle

User Management

The first line of defense against unwanted database access is controlling who can access the system in the first place. To connect to an Oracle database, a user must have a *username* in the database. You can create database usernames using the SQL command CREATE USER.

User Authentication

For each database user, you must indicate how you want Oracle to *authenticate* use of the new account. When someone attempts to connect to a database with a username, Oracle authenticates that the person utilizing the username is authorized to use the account. Oracle can authenticate users via three different techniques: password authentication, operating system authentication, and global user authentication.

Password Authentication

Oracle can authenticate a username with *a password*. When a user starts an application, the application prompts for a username and associated password. Oracle then authenticates the connection request using the user account information managed by the database. Password authentication is common in Oracle client/server environments when users connect to an Oracle database server using client PCs or NCs.

When you decide to use password authentication, it's a good idea to have a policy in place that ensures passwords have a certain degree of complexity and that users routinely change them. For more information about managing user passwords, see the section "User Account Management" later in this chapter.

Operating System Authentication

Oracle can authenticate a username using the *operating system* of the computer that's running the database server. When a user starts an application, the application does not request connection information from the user. Instead, the application forwards to Oracle the operating system account information of the user. Oracle then authenticates the connection request by making sure that the operating system user is registered as a user in the database. Operating system authentication is common in Oracle host-based environments when users connect to Oracle using terminals that are directly connected to the database server.

Global User Authentication

Oracle can authenticate a *global username* using an external network service. When a user starts an application and makes a connection request, Oracle authenticates the request with user information managed by an external security service. Oracle8 includes its own security service, *Oracle Security Server*, that you can use to manage global database users. Global user authentication is common in network environments where users require access to several Oracle databases, and the network is not necessarily secure.

A User's Default Tablespace

A tablespace is a logical storage division of a database that organizes the physical storage of database information. For each database user, you can set a *default tablespace*. When the user creates a new database object, such as a table or index, and does not explicitly indicate a tablespace for the object, Oracle stores the new database object in the user's default tablespace. Unless you specify otherwise, a user's default tablespace is the SYSTEM tablespace.

A User's Temporary Tablespace

Often, SQL statements require temporary work space to complete. For example, a query that joins and sorts a large amount of data might require temporary work space to build the result set. When necessary, Oracle allocates temporary work space for a user's SQL statements in the user's *temporary tablespace*. Unless you specify otherwise, a user's temporary tablespace is the SYSTEM tablespace.

Locked and Unlocked User Accounts

Oracle lets you *lock* and *unlock* a user account at any time so that you can control database access through the account. A user cannot connect to Oracle after you lock the user's account. To subsequently allow a user access through an account, you must unlock the account. Why would you want to lock and unlock user accounts?

- You might want to lock a user's account when the user takes a temporary leave of absence from work, but plans on returning in the future.

- When a person leaves your company, you might want to lock the user's account rather than drop the account, especially when the user's schema contains database objects that you want to preserve.

- You typically lock a user account that functions only as a schema to logically store all of an application's database objects.

When you create a new database user, Oracle creates the new account unlocked by default.

NOTE
Later in this chapter, you'll see how Oracle lets you lock user accounts automatically after a user's password expires or following a consecutive number of failed connection attempts.

Privilege Management

After you create the users for an Oracle database system, they cannot connect to the database server or do anything of consequence unless they have the *privileges* to perform specific database operations. For example, a database user cannot:

- connect to an Oracle database unless the user has the CREATE SESSION system privilege

- create a table in his corresponding schema unless the user has the CREATE TABLE system privilege

- delete rows from a table in a different schema unless the user has the DELETE object privilege for the table

This short list reveals just some of the different privileges that you can use to control access to operations and data within an Oracle database. The following sections explain more about the different types of database privileges, as well as how to grant them to and revoke them from users.

Types of Database Privileges

If you read the list in the previous section closely, you'll notice that there are two different kinds of privileges that control access to an Oracle database: system privileges and object privileges.

System Privileges

A *system privilege* is a powerful privilege that gives a user the ability to perform some type of system-wide operation. For example, the following examples are just a few of almost 100 system privileges in Oracle8:

- A user with the CREATE SESSION system privilege can connect to the database server and establish a database session.

- A user with the CREATE TABLE system privilege can create a table in her own schema.

- A user with the CREATE ANY TABLE system privilege can create a table in any schema of the database.

- A user with the CREATE ANY TYPE system privilege can create types and associated type bodies in any schema of the database.

- A user with the SELECT ANY TABLE system privilege can query any table in the database.

- A user with the EXECUTE ANY PROCEDURE system privilege can execute any stored procedure, stored function, or packaged component in the database.

- A user with the EXECUTE ANY TYPE system privilege can reference and execute methods of any type in the database.

Because system privileges are very powerful privileges that can affect the security of the entire database system, carefully consider what types of users require system privileges. For example:

- A database administrator is the only type of user that should have the powerful ALTER DATABASE system privilege, a privilege that allows someone to alter the physical structure and availability of the database system.

- Developers typically require several system privileges, including the CREATE TABLE, CREATE VIEW, and CREATE TYPE system privileges to build database schemas that support front-end applications.

- Every user in the system typically has the CREATE SESSION system privilege, the privilege that allows a user to connect to the database server.

At first, the overwhelming number of system privileges might appear intimidating. However, because each system privilege is a focused access right for a specific database operation, it's easy to provide each type of database user with just the right amount of privilege—no more or less power than what is necessary to accomplish their work.

Object Privileges

An *object privilege* is a privilege that gives a user the ability to perform a specific type of operation on a specific database object such as a table, view, or stored procedure. For example:

■ A user with the SELECT object privilege for the CUST view can query the view to retrieve information.

■ A user with the INSERT object privilege for the CUSTOMERS table can insert new rows into the table.

■ A user with the EXECUTE privilege for the PART_TYPE object type can use the type when building other database objects and execute the type's methods.

These examples are just a few of the object privileges that are available for tables, views, sequences, procedures, functions, packages, object types, and server file directories. Depending on how an application is designed, users might require object privileges for the underlying database objects that the application uses. For example, in a typical order-entry application, a user might need the SELECT, INSERT, UPDATE, and DELETE privileges for the CUSTOMERS, ORDERS, and ITEMS tables, as well as the SELECT and UPDATE privileges for the PARTS table. Because each object privilege is focused on the operation that it permits, you can manage database access with absolute control.

Granting and Revoking Privileges

You can give a user a system or object privilege by *granting* the privilege to the user with the SQL command GRANT. To withdraw a privilege from a user, you *revoke* the privilege from the user with the SQL command REVOKE. Oracle does not let just anyone grant and revoke privileges to and from users. Consider the following requirements when managing individual system and object privileges for database users:

■ You can grant a user a system privilege only if you have the system privilege with the administrative rights to grant the privilege to other users.

■ You can grant a user a database object privilege only if you own the associated database object or if you have the object privilege with the administrative rights to grant the privilege to other users.

NOTE
To grant a system or object privilege to every user in the database, grant the privilege to PUBLIC. PUBLIC is a special group in an Oracle database that you can use to make a privilege available quickly to every user in the system.

Privilege Management with Roles

The system and object privileges necessary to use a typical database application can be numerous. When a database application supports a large user population, privilege management can become a big job quickly if you manage each user's privileges with individual grants. To make security administration an easier task, you can use roles. A *role* is a collection of related system and object privileges that you can grant to users and other roles. For example, when you build a new database application, you can create a new role that has the database privileges necessary to run the program. After you grant the role to an application user, the user can start the application to connect to the database and accomplish work. If the privileges necessary to run the application change, all that's necessary is a quick modification of the role's set of privileges. All grantees of the role see the change in the role automatically and continue to have the privileges necessary to use the application.

Predefined Database Roles

Oracle has a number of predefined roles that you can use to grant privileges to database users:

CONNECT	A basic user role that lets the grantee connect to the database and then create tables, views, synonyms, sequences, database links, and data clusters in the associated schema.

RESOURCE	Intended for a typical application developer, this role lets the grantee create tables, sequences, data clusters, procedures, functions, packages, triggers, and object types in the associated schema.
DBA	Intended for administrators, this role lets the grantee perform any database function as it includes every system privilege. Furthermore, a grantee of the DBA role can grant any system privilege to any other database user or role.
SELECT_CATALOG_ROLE	Lets the grantee query administrator data dictionary views.
DELETE_CATALOG_ROLE	Lets the grantee delete records from the database audit trail (see the section "Database Auditing" later in this chapter for more information about auditing).
EXECUTE_CATALOG_ROLE	Lets the grantee execute the DBMS utility packages.
EXP_FULL_DATABASE, **IMP_FULL_DATABASE**	Lets the grantee export and import database information using the Export and Import utilities. See Chapter 10 for more information about these utilities.

Although Oracle provides predefined roles to help manage privileges for typical database users, an application that relies on these roles might not necessarily function correctly. That's because you can change a predefined role's privilege set or even drop the role altogether.

User-Defined Roles

You can create as many roles as you need for an Oracle database. After creating a role, you grant privileges and other roles to the role to build the role's set of privileges. Then you grant the role to users so that they have the privileges necessary to complete their jobs. For example, the following SQL command script creates a new role for a typical order-entry application and then grants the role to several database users:

```
CREATE ROLE order_entry;
GRANT SELECT, INSERT, UPDATE, DELETE ON sales.customers
 TO order_entry;
GRANT SELECT, INSERT, UPDATE, DELETE ON sales.orders
 TO order_entry;
GRANT SELECT, INSERT, UPDATE, DELETE ON sales.items
 TO order_entry;
GRANT SELECT, UPDATE ON sales.parts
 TO order_entry;
GRANT order_entry
 TO ssmith, tbrown, ptate;
```

Enabled and Disabled Roles

A grantee of a role does not necessarily have access to the privileges of the role at all times. Oracle allows applications to selectively enable and disable a role for each individual. After an application *enables* a role for a user, the privileges of the role are available to the user. As you might expect, after an application *disables* a role for a user, the user no longer has access to the privileges of the role. Oracle's ability to dynamically control the set of privileges available to a user allows an application to ensure that users always have the correct set of privileges when using the application. For example, when a user starts an order-entry application, the application can enable the user's ORDER_ENTRY role, using the SQL command SET ROLE so that the user can accomplish work. When the user finishes working, the application can disable the user's ORDER_ENTRY role so that the user cannot use the order-entry application privileges when working with a different application.

Default Roles

Each user has a list of default roles. A *default role* is a role that Oracle enables automatically when the user establishes a new database session. Default roles make it convenient to enable roles that users always require when working with Oracle, no matter which application they use.

Role Authentication

To prevent unauthorized use of a role, you can protect a role with authentication. Oracle can authenticate the use of a role using the same three authentication techniques as with database users: password authentication, operating system authentication, and global role authentication. See the previous section "User Authentication" for more information about these different authentication techniques. Oracle authenticates role usage when a user or application attempts to enable the role.

Resource Limitation

In a multi-user database system, it's prudent to limit each user's access to system resources. Otherwise, one user might consume an inordinate amount of database resource at the expense of other users. For example, when Oracle automatically terminates all database sessions that remain idle for an extended period of time, the server can eliminate unnecessary overhead and provide more memory, CPU cycles, and other system resources to sessions that are performing real work. The following sections explain the features of Oracle that you can use to limit access to several different system resources.

Tablespace Quotas

A user cannot create objects in a tablespace unless the user has a *quota* for the tablespace. A tablespace quota limits how much space a user's database objects can consume in the tablespace. A user can have a quota for zero, one, or all tablespaces in the database—it's entirely up to you. When you give a user a tablespace quota, you set the quota as a specific number of bytes in the tablespace or as an unlimited amount of space in the tablespace.

NOTE ←

When a user must have a unlimited quota for every tablespace in the database, you can grant the user the UNLIMITED TABLESPACE system privilege rather than giving the user an unlimited quota for each tablespace in the system.

Resource Limit Profiles

To control the consumption of several other types of system resources, you can use resource limit profiles. A *resource limit profile* is a set of specific resource limit settings that you assign to one or more database users. Using a resource limit profile, you can limit consumption of the following system resources:

- CPU time (in hundredths of a second), per session or per statement
- Logical disk I/Os, per session or per statement
- Concurrent database sessions per user
- The maximum amount of connect time and idle time (in minutes) per session
- The maximum amount of server memory available to a multithreaded server session

User Account Management

You can use resource limit profiles to enforce several other security policies for database users. Using a resource limit profile, you can control the following settings for each user account that is assigned the profile:

- The number of consecutive failed connection attempts to allow before Oracle locks the account
- The lifetime of the account's password, in days, after which the password expires
- The number of days that a user can use an expired password before locking the account
- The number of days that must pass or the number of times that an account's password must be changed before the account can reuse an old password
- Whether or not to check an account's password for sufficient complexity to prevent an account from using an obvious password

The Default Profile

Every Oracle database has a *default resource limit profile*. When you create
a new database user and do not indicate a specific profile for the user,
Oracle automatically assigns the user the default profile. By default, all
resource limit settings of the database's default profile are set to unlimited;
account management settings vary.

When you create a resource limit profile, you can set specific resource
limit settings or defer to the corresponding setting of the database's default
profile. At any time, you can alter the settings of a database's default profile
just like user-defined profiles.

Database Auditing

In some circumstances, it is necessary to *audit* or record information about
the activity in a database system. For example, you might want to audit the
activity in an Oracle database to gather statistics about what users are
doing. You can also use auditing to monitor the database for potential
security breaches.

Selective Auditing

Auditing is a feature of Oracle that you can enable or disable. When you
decide to enable the auditing of database activity, the system is subject to
the overhead necessary to generate audit records. To focus auditing and
minimize the extra work that Oracle must perform for database auditing,
you can choose exactly what you want to audit:

- You can audit particular SQL statements without regard to specific
  objects. For example, you can ask Oracle to generate an audit
  record each time that a user issues a DROP TABLE statement, no
  matter which table the statement targets.

- You can audit the use of powerful system privileges. For example,
  you can ask Oracle to generate an audit record each time a user
  makes use of the SELECT ANY TABLE system privilege to query a
  table in the database.

■ You can audit particular SQL statements for targeted database objects. For example, you can ask Oracle to generate an audit record each time a user deletes a record from the SALES.CUSTOMERS table.

■ For each auditing option that you enable, you can ask Oracle to generate an audit record for successful, unsuccessful, or all statement executions. Furthermore, you can focus each enabled auditing option to all or specific database users.

■ For each auditing option that you enable, you can ask Oracle to generate an audit record once per database session, no matter how many times the session executes the audited statement. Alternatively, you can ask Oracle to generate an audit record each time that a session executes the audited statement.

Audit Records and the Audit Trail

Oracle generates audit records only after you enable auditing and set particular auditing options. For example, you might decide to set auditing options for specific statements, objects, and users. Each audit record includes information about the audited statement, such as the operation that was audited, the user that performed the operation, and the date and time of the operation.

Oracle stores generated audit records in an *audit trail*. An audit trail is a storage area for auditing information. Oracle lets you store the audit records that it generates in either the database audit trail or the audit trail of the operating system that executes Oracle Server. If you decide to use the database audit trail, you can use SQL queries and predefined data dictionary views of the audit trail to view and find audit records easily. If you decide to use the operating system audit trail, you can centralize database auditing information with other auditing information that the operating system tracks.

Setting Audit Options

After an administrator enables auditing at the system level, you can set specific audit options using the SQL command AUDIT. For example, the following SQL command script turns on several audit options:

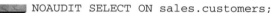

```
-- The following audit statement audits all unsuccessful
-- attempts to use the SELECT ANY TABLE system privilege
-- by the users SROGERS and JGIBBS. Oracle generates only
-- one audit record per session, no matter how many times
-- that the auditing criteria is met.
AUDIT SELECT ANY TABLE
 BY srogers, jgibbs
 BY SESSION
 WHENEVER NOT SUCCESSFUL;
-- The following statement audits all successful and unsuccessful
-- DELETE statements that target the SALES.CUSTOMERS table. Oracle
-- generates an audit record each time that the auditing criteria
-- is met.
AUDIT SELECT ON sales.customers
 BY ACCESS;
```

If you decide later that you no longer need to audit a particular operation, you can turn off auditing of the operation using the SQL command NOAUDIT.

```
NOAUDIT SELECT ON sales.customers;
```

What Is Trusted Oracle?

Many installations of Oracle require additional security features that are not present in the basic version of Oracle8. For example, government institutions commonly restrict access to data based on the classification of specific records—only the highest ranking officials should have access to "top secret" data. If you require such special security features, you can purchase a special release of Oracle8 called *Trusted Oracle*. This specialized feature of Oracle8 is not discussed in this book because it appeals to a select audience.

Summary

This chapter explained the security features of Oracle8 that you can use to limit and monitor access to a database.

■ Only a registered database user can access a database once Oracle authenticates a connection request.

- Once connected to a database, a user can perform only those operations that the user is privileged to execute. You can grant users individual system and object privileges or use roles to group related sets of privileges and more easily manage user privileges.

- Resource limit profiles let you limit a user's access to system resources such as CPU time, disk I/Os, and sessions.

- You can monitor user activity in a database using Oracle's auditing features.

CHAPTER
7

Database Storage

atabases store information in an organized manner. To store data, an Oracle database uses *storage structures*. An Oracle database has both logical and physical data storage structures that relate to one another.

- A *logical storage structure* is a conceptual organization of data such as a database or a table.

- A *physical storage structure* is a tangible unit of data storage such as a file or a data block.

In this chapter, you'll learn about the logical and physical storage structures in an Oracle database, including:

- Tablespaces

- Data files

- Control files

- Data, index, temporary, and rollback segments

- Extents

- Data blocks

- Data partitioning for tables and indexes

Tablespaces

A *tablespace* is a logical organization of data within an Oracle database that corresponds to one or more physical *data files* on disk. Figure 7-1 illustrates the relationship between a tablespace and its data files.

When you create a new database object such as a table or an index, Oracle stores the database object within the tablespace of your choice; when you do not indicate a specific tablespace for a new database object, Oracle stores the object in your account's default tablespace.

The physical storage of database objects within a tablespace maps directly to the underlying data files of the tablespace. Figure 7-2 demonstrates how Oracle might store various tables in different tablespaces.

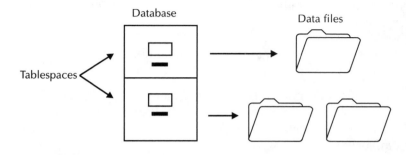

FIGURE 7-1. *Each tablespace in an Oracle database physically stores its data in one or more associated data files.*

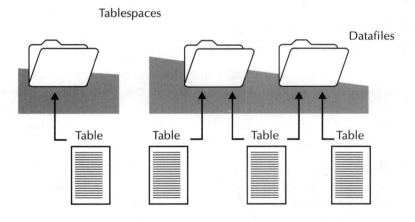

FIGURE 7-2. *Oracle stores objects in a tablespace in one or more data files that comprise the tablespace.*

Figure 7-2 shows how Oracle can store data for database objects within tablespaces that have only one data file compared to tablespaces that have multiple data files.

- When a tablespace has only one data file, the tablespace stores the data of all associated objects within the one file.

- When a tablespace has multiple data files, Oracle can store the data for an object within any file of the tablespace. In fact, Oracle might distribute the data of a single object across multiple data files of a tablespace.

The SYSTEM Tablespace

Every Oracle database has at least one tablespace, the *SYSTEM tablespace*. When you create a new Oracle database, you must indicate the names, sizes, and other characteristics of the data files that make up the physical storage for the SYSTEM tablespace.

Oracle uses the SYSTEM tablespace for several purposes:

- Oracle stores a database's data dictionary in the SYSTEM tablespace. As Chapter 2 states, a database's data dictionary is a set of internal system tables that stores information about the database itself. A database's data dictionary also includes other objects that Oracle uses for internal system processing.

- The SYSTEM tablespace of a database stores the source and compiled code for all PL/SQL programs such as stored procedures and functions, packages, database triggers, and object type methods. Databases that use PL/SQL extensively should have a sufficiently large SYSTEM tablespace.

- Database objects such as views, object type specifications, synonyms, and sequences are simple definitions that do not store any data. Oracle stores such object definitions in the data dictionary, which is in the SYSTEM tablespace.

Other Tablespaces

Although not required, an Oracle database typically has multiple tablespaces that logically and physically organize the storage of data within the database. Most Oracle databases have different tablespaces to separate the storage of the following:

- Application data from the internal data dictionary information in the SYSTEM tablespace

- An application's table data and index data

- The system's transaction rollback data

- Temporary data used during internal system processing

For example, suppose you are planning to build an Oracle database to support an accounting and a manufacturing application, and each application uses a different set of database tables. One way to organize the database is to create multiple tablespaces that separate the storage of each application's tables and indexes. Figure 7-3 demonstrates this configuration as well as distinct tablespaces for the system's temporary and rollback data.

By using multiple tablespaces for different sets of application data, you can manage the data for each application independently. For example, you can back up an active application's data frequently and a less active application's data less frequently.

NOTE
Later in this chapter you'll learn how you can partition (divide) an individual table or index among multiple tablespaces.

Online and Offline Tablespaces

Oracle lets you control the availability of data in a database on a tablespace-by-tablespace basis. That is, a tablespace can either be online or offline.

- The data in an *online tablespace* is available to applications and databases. Typically, a tablespace remains online so that users can access the information within it.

- The data in an *offline tablespace* is not available to database users, even when the database is available. An administrator might take a tablespace offline to prevent access to an application's data, because the tablespace is experiencing a problem, or because the tablespace contains historical data that is typically not required by anyone.

Database

```
+-----------------------------------+
|  SYSTEM Tablespace                |
+-----------------------------------+
|  TEMP Tablespace                  |
+-----------------------------------+
|  ROLLBACK Tablespace              |
+-----------------------------------+
|  ACCOUNTING Tablespace            |
+-----------------------------------+
|  ACCOUNTING_INDEX Tablespace      |
+-----------------------------------+
|  MANUFACTURING Tablespace         |
+-----------------------------------+
|  MANUFACTURING_INDEX Tablespace   |
+-----------------------------------+
```

FIGURE 7-3. *Using multiple tablespaces to logically and physically separate the storage of different sets of database information*

NOTE
A database's SYSTEM tablespace must always remain online because information in the data dictionary must be available during normal operation. If you try to take the SYSTEM tablespace offline, Oracle returns an error.

Permanent and Temporary Tablespaces

Most tablespaces in an Oracle database are permanent tablespaces. A *permanent tablespace* stores information that must persist across individual

SQL requests and transactions. For example, a permanent tablespace is necessary to store table, index, or transaction rollback information.

Oracle also lets you create temporary tablespaces in a database. A _temporary tablespace_ is a large temporary work space that transactions can use to process complicated SQL operations such as sorted queries, join queries, and index builds. Rather then inefficiently creating and dropping many small temporary segments in a permanent tablespace, Oracle can quickly provide temporary work areas for SQL statements by managing entries in a temporary tablespace's sort segment table.

NOTE
To learn more about temporary segments, see the section "Temporary Segments" later in this chapter.

When you create a new tablespace, you can create it as either permanent or temporary. You can always change a current tablespace's type to permanent or temporary, if necessary. If you decide to use a temporary tablespace, Oracle will not use the tablespace until you target the tablespace for temporary operations in one or more users' account settings.

Read-Only and Read-Write Tablespaces

When you create a new tablespace, it is always a _read-write tablespace._ That is, you can create, alter, and drop database objects within the tablespace, and applications can query, add, modify, and delete information from the database objects within the tablespace. When applications must actively change data in a tablespace, the tablespace must operate as a read-write tablespace.

In some cases, a tablespace stores historical data that never changes. When a tablespace's data never changes, you can make the tablespace a _read-only tablespace_. Making a static tablespace read-only can protect it from inappropriate data modifications. Making a tablespace read-only can also save time when performing database backups. That's because it's not necessary to back up a read-only tablespace when you back up the other tablespaces of the database.

After you create a new tablespace and add data to it, you can alter the tablespace and make it a read-only tablespace. If necessary, you can always switch a tablespace back to read-write mode so that applications can update the objects within the tablespace.

More About Data Files

A data file is a physical storage file on disk for a tablespace in an Oracle database. A tablespace can store all of its data in just a single data file, or a tablespace can have multiple data files to collectively store its data. The following sections explain more about the characteristics of the data files that make up the tablespaces in an Oracle database.

A Tablespace's Number of Data Files

When you create a tablespace, you can create one or more data files for the new tablespace. In general, you create a tablespace with multiple data files on different disks to distribute the disk I/O associated with accessing a tablespace's data. This technique is particularly useful when you explicitly partition database data. For more information about data partitioning, see the "Data Partitioning" section later in this chapter.

NOTE

An Oracle database has an upper limit to the number of data files that it can have. This limit is set during database creation. When planning a database and its tablespaces, make sure that you do not use too many data files to meet the storage requirements for the system or else you might reach the upper limit for the number of data files.

After you create a tablespace, you can always add more data files to the tablespace to increase its storage capacity. For example, when a tablespace uses data files that do not grow in size, you can allocate additional storage space for the tablespace by creating one or more data files for the tablespace. See the following sections for more information about data file space usage and sizing options.

Use of Data File Space

When you create a new data file for a tablespace, <u>Oracle preallocates the amount of disk space that you specify for the data file</u>. After you create a new data file, it is like an empty data bucket—the file contains no data, but it is a receptacle that is ready to store database information.

Any time you create a new data storage object such as a table or index in a tablespace, <u>Oracle designates a certain amount of space from the tablespace's data files to the new object</u>. Allocating data file space to a new database object reduces the remaining amount of available free space in the data file. As applications insert and update data in a data storage object, the preallocated space for the object can eventually become full.

If data consumes all of a data storage object's available storage space, Oracle can automatically allocate additional space from the tablespace's data files for the object. Allocating more space to a data storage object to extend the storage capacity of the object further reduces the amount of available free space in the tablespace's data files.

Coalescing Free Space in a Tablespace's Data Files

As you create data storage objects in a tablespace and these objects extend their storage capacity, <u>the free space areas in the tablespace's data files can become fragmented and small</u>. Oracle might not be able to complete subsequent free space allocations for new or existing objects if the free space areas on disk are not large enough. To fix this problem, Oracle can coalesce many small adjacent free space areas into fewer large free space areas. Figure 7-4 illustrates the concept of free space coalescing.

<u>Oracle periodically coalesces a tablespace's free space automatically as an internal system operation</u>. However, Oracle also lets you coalesce a tablespace manually when you know that this operation is necessary. For example, the following statement coalesces the RBSEG tablespace's free space:

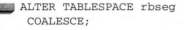

```
ALTER TABLESPACE rbseg
  COALESCE;
```

Data File Sizes

In general, the size of a data file remains constant. As objects in a tablespace allocate space from the corresponding data files, the tablespace

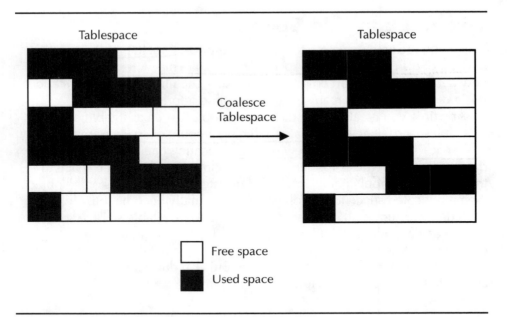

FIGURE 7-4. *Free space coalescing*

can become full if all of the data files in the tablespace become full. When applications attempt to insert or update data within a tablespace that's full, Oracle returns errors until more storage space becomes available for the tablespace. To increase the storage capacity of a full tablespace, you have a few different options:

- You can add one or more new data files to the tablespace

- You can manually resize one or more of the existing data files in the tablespace

- You can configure one or more of the data files in the tablespace to automatically extend when the tablespace becomes full and requires more space

NOTE
Certain operating systems allow Oracle to use devices as data files. For example, a raw partition on a UNIX disk can be a data file for a tablespace. In such cases, extending the size of a data file does not make any sense.

Each option has certain advantages and disadvantages. For example, the first two options are fine if you are a watchful administrator who frequently monitors the storage capacity of your database's data files. When you notice that a tablespace is running low on free space, you can add more files to the tablespace or increase the size of one of the tablespace's data files. In contrast, the third option allows a tablespace's storage capacity to grow automatically, without manual assistance. If you choose to manually or automatically extend the storage allocation for a data file, do so conservatively—fragmented allocations of disk space across a disk drive can decrease database performance.

Data File Corruption

Unfortunately, operating system files are always vulnerable to disk and I/O problems. Such problems can corrupt the integrity of a file. At the expense of system performance, you can configure an Oracle Server to detect and log block-level data file corruptions.

Online and Offline Data Files

Oracle controls the availability of individual data files of a tablespace. A data file can either be *online* (available) or *offline* (not available). Under normal circumstances, a data file is online. When Oracle attempts to read or write a data file and cannot do so because some type of problem prevents this from happening, Oracle automatically takes the data file offline. The encompassing tablespace remains online because other data files of the tablespace might still be available. You can take a data file offline manually when a known problem exists. Once the problem is fixed (for example, after a data file recovery), you can bring an offline data file back online manually.

NOTE
The data files of a database's SYSTEM tablespace must always remain online because the data dictionary must always be available during system operation. If Oracle experiences a problem reading or writing a data file in the database's SYSTEM tablespace, the system will not operate correctly until you fix the problem.

Control Files

Every Oracle database has a *control file*. A database's control file contains information about the physical structure of the database. For example, a database's control file includes the name of the database as well as the names and locations of all files associated with the database. A database's control file also keeps track of internal system information to log the current physical state of the system, including information about tablespaces, data files, and system backups.

NOTE
Starting with Oracle8, a database's control file logs information about database backups. Therefore, the control files for Oracle8 databases are much larger than control files for databases managed by previous versions of Oracle.

When you create a new database, Oracle creates the database's control file. Subsequently, Oracle updates the database's control file automatically with internal information that it needs to record. Additionally, every time that you change a physical attribute of a database, Oracle updates the information in the database's control file. For example, when you create a new tablespace with one or more data files, or add a data file to an existing tablespace, Oracle updates the database's control file to log information about the new data files.

Mirrored Control Files

An Oracle database cannot function properly without its control file. To ensure database availability in the event of an isolated disk failure, Oracle lets you *mirror* a database's control file to multiple locations. When you mirror a database's control file to multiple locations, Oracle updates every copy of the control file at the same time. If one copy of the control file should become inaccessible due to a disk failure, other copies of the control file remain available and permit database processing to continue without interruption.

Segments, Extents, and Data Blocks

Just as Oracle preallocates data files to serve as the physical storage for tablespaces in a database, Oracle preallocates segments of data blocks as the physical storage for database objects such as tables, indexes, data clusters, and other data storage objects. Oracle allocates groups of contiguous *data blocks* for a database object as *extents*. A *segment* is the collection of all the extents dedicated to a database object. Figure 7-5 demonstrates the relationship among a table, its data segment, extents, and data blocks.

When you create a new data storage object such as a table or an index, you can indicate the tablespace in which to create the corresponding segment. Oracle then allocates data blocks from one or more of the data files in use by the target tablespace.

Now that you have a general understanding of segments, extents, and data blocks, the following sections explain more about each topic.

Data and Index Segments

Oracle creates different types of segments for different types of database objects. For example, when you create a table, Oracle creates a corresponding *data segment* to store the table's data. Oracle also creates a data segment when you create a data cluster; a data cluster's data segment

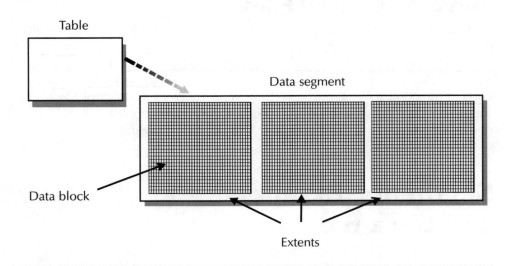

Table

Data segment

Data block

Extents

FIGURE 7-5. *Dedicating physical data storage for a table as extents (groups of contiguous data blocks) in a table's data segment*

stores the data for all of the tables that you put in the cluster. Similarly, when you create an index, Oracle creates a corresponding *index segment* to store the index's data.

Temporary Segments

SQL statements often require temporary work areas. For example, when you create an index for a large table, Oracle typically must allocate some temporary system space so that it can sort all of the index entries before building the index's segment. When processing a SQL statement that requires temporary work space, Oracle allocates small *temporary segments* from a tablespace in the database. When the statement completes, Oracle releases the segments back to the tablespace so that other objects can use the space. Thus the term "temporary segment."

Temporary Tablespaces

To optimize temporary segment allocation, Oracle also lets you create temporary tablespaces in a database. You can think of a temporary

tablespace as one large temporary segment that all transactions can use for temporary work space. A temporary tablespace can more efficiently   ←
provide temporary work space to transactions because Oracle inserts and deletes simple table entries in the temporary tablespace's segment table rather than physically allocating and deallocating segments on demand.

Rollback Segments

Transactions can complete either with a commit or a rollback. Typically, a transaction ends with a commit, which permanently records the transaction's changes to the database. A rollback undoes all effects of the transaction as though the transaction never occurred. To provide for transaction rollback, Oracle must keep track of the data that a transaction changes until the transaction commits or rolls back.

Oracle uses a special type of segment called a *rollback segment* (sometimes called an *undo segment*) to record rollback data for a transaction. Should you choose to roll back a transaction, Oracle reads the necessary data from a rollback segment to rebuild the data as it existed before the transaction changed it. Figure 7-6 illustrates how Oracle uses rollback segments to "undo" the effects of a transaction that is rolled back.

How Oracle Writes to a Rollback Segment

Oracle writes information to rollback segments differently than it does with other types of segments. Figure 7-7 shows how Oracle writes information to the multiple extents in a rollback segment.

As Figure 7-7 shows, a rollback segment is a circle of extents. As transactions write to the *current extent* of a rollback segment and eventually fill it with rollback information, the transactions then *wrap* to the next extent of the segment to continue recording rollback information. If a transaction is so long that it wraps across all extents of a rollback segment and the current extent becomes full, Oracle must allocate an additional extent so that the system does not overwrite earlier rollback information that would be necessary to roll back the long transaction. Oracle can shrink back rollback segments to an optimal number of extents after they grow larger than their original size. Later in this chapter you'll learn more about specific storage parameters that you can set to control extent allocation and deallocation for rollback segments.

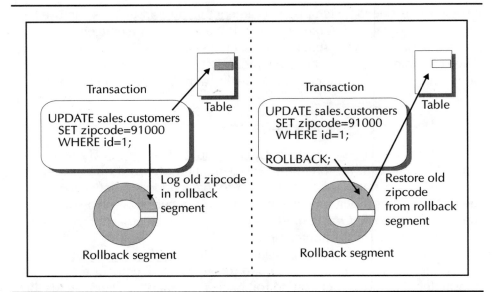

FIGURE 7-6. *Rollback segments keep track of the data that transactions change and facilitate transaction rollback.*

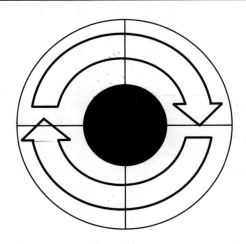

FIGURE 7-7. *Oracle writes rollback information circularly to the extents that comprise a rollback segment.*

The SYSTEM Rollback Segment

Every Oracle database has at least one rollback segment, the SYSTEM rollback segment. When Oracle creates a new database, it automatically creates the SYSTEM rollback segment in the database's SYSTEM tablespace.

A database's SYSTEM rollback segment alone cannot adequately support a production database system. After you create a new database, you should create additional rollback segments to support the planned transaction loads of the database.

Multiple Rollback Segments

Typically, an Oracle database has multiple rollback segments that reside in a tablespace specifically set aside for rollback segment data. You can create any number of rollback segments for a database. Each rollback segment can be a different size and have different storage attributes. You'll learn more about segment storage, including rollback segment storage, later in this chapter.

When you start a new transaction, Oracle automatically assigns it to an available rollback segment in the database. Oracle assigns transactions to rollback segments on a round-robin basis to distribute the load across all available rollback segments.

Once Oracle assigns a transaction to a rollback segment, the segment records the changed data for all of the transaction. Multiple transactions can share a single rollback segment, but a transaction never uses more than one rollback segment.

Targeting Specific Rollback Segments

An application can explicitly target a rollback segment at the very beginning of a new transaction. For example, before starting a large batch operation, you can target a sufficiently large rollback segment in the database. By doing so, you can avoid both assigning the large transaction to a small rollback segment, and forcing Oracle to allocate additional space for the segment; the end result is that you reduce the overhead necessary to record rollback data for the transaction and improve the performance of the operation.

Online and Offline Rollback Segments

Just like tablespaces and data files, a rollback segment is available if it is *online* and unavailable if it is *offline*. Typically, a rollback segment is online so that transactions can use it to record rollback information. However, some administrative operations require that you first take rollback segments offline. For example, to take a tablespace offline that contains rollback segments, you must first take all rollback segments in the tablespace offline. After you bring the tablespace back online, you can then bring the rollback segments back online as well.

Public and Private Rollback Segments

A rollback segment in a database can be either public or private. A *public rollback segment* is a rollback segment that Oracle automatically acquires access to and brings online for normal database operations. On the other hand, an Oracle Server acquires a *private rollback segment* only if its server parameter file explicitly lists the name of the private rollback segment. Private rollback segments are useful when you are using Oracle's Parallel Server option and want the various servers for the same database to acquire a mutually exclusive set of the database's rollback segments. Unless you use Oracle with the Parallel Server option, it's much easier to create and use public rollback segments.

Deferred Rollback Segments

When a disk problem forces Oracle to take one or more data files offline, it's typical to take associated tablespaces offline so that users do not notice file access errors when using applications. However, when you take a tablespace offline and Oracle cannot access all of the tablespace's data files, Oracle might create a deferred rollback segment in the SYSTEM tablespace. A *deferred rollback segment* contains transaction rollback information that Oracle could not apply to the damaged offline tablespace. Oracle keeps track of this information so that when you recover the damaged tablespace and bring it back online, Oracle can roll back the transactions that affected the tablespace and make its data consistent with the other data in the database.

Other Functions of Rollback Segments

Oracle also uses rollback segments to provide read-consistent sets of data for concurrent transactions in a multi-user database system and to help during database recovery. To learn more about the function of rollback segments in read consistency and database recovery, see Chapters 9 and 10, respectively.

Data Blocks

A *data block* is the unit of disk access for an Oracle database. When you work with a database, Oracle stores and retrieves data on disk using data blocks. For example, when you query a table, Oracle reads all of the data blocks into the server's memory that contain rows in the query's result set.

When you create a database, you can specify the block size that the database will use. A database's block size must be equal to or a multiple of the server's operating system block size. For example, if the server's operating system block size is 512K, a database on such a server could be 512K, 1024K, 2048K, and so on.

Data Block Allocation

When you create a new data storage object such as a table, index, or rollback segment, Oracle allocates one or more extents for the object's segment. An extent is a set of contiguous data blocks in a data file of the tablespace that stores the object's segment. If all data blocks in a segment's existing extents are full, Oracle allocates a new extent for the segment the next time a transaction requests the storage of some new data.

Data Block Availability and Free Lists

Every data and index segment in an Oracle database has one or more data block free lists. A *free list* is a catalog of data blocks that are available to hold new data for the corresponding table, cluster, or index. Figure 7-8 shows how data blocks can go on and off an object's free lists as transactions insert, update, and delete information from a table.

In Figure 7-8, you can see how a data block might go on and off a table's free list. When a transaction wants to insert a new row into the table, all data blocks on the free list are candidates to hold the data for the

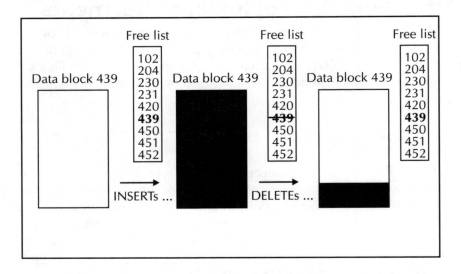

FIGURE 7-8. *A data block going on an off and object's free list, depending on how full it is*

new row. As transactions insert more and more rows into the table, data blocks eventually become full (or nearly full) such that Oracle removes them from the table's free list. A block can return to the table's free list after a transaction deletes rows from the table.

NOTE
See the section "Block Thresholds" later in this chapter, which explains how to control when Oracle puts data blocks on a segment's free lists.

Row Chaining and Data Block Size

When you insert a new row into a table, Oracle puts the new row into a data block that's on the table's free list. Optimally, Oracle puts all of a row's data into one data block, assuming that the row can fit within the space of one data block. This way, when you request a row in a table,

Oracle has to read only one data block from disk into memory to retrieve all of a row's data.

If a row's length is greater than the data block size, Oracle *chains* the row among two or more data blocks. Figure 7-9 illustrates row chaining.

Row chaining, while unavoidable in this situation, is not desirable. That's because Oracle must read multiple data blocks from disk into memory to access a row's data. More disk I/Os always slows system performance. Therefore, row chaining should be avoided if at all possible.

Typically, the default block size for an installation of Oracle Server is the optimal setting for most databases. However, databases with certain characteristics can benefit from block sizes that are larger than the default. For example, when many tables in a database will have rows that exceed the default block size, you can reduce the amount of row chaining in the database by creating the database with a larger block size.

Oracle can also create a row chain when you update a row in a table or an index. This type of row chaining happens when

■ you update the row so that it is longer than the original row, and

■ the data block that holds the row does not have enough empty space to accommodate the update.

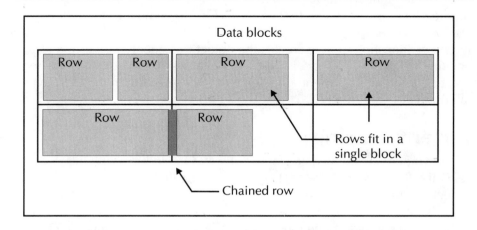

FIGURE 7-9. *Storing pieces of a row in a chain that spans multiple data blocks*

When you expect that updates to the rows in a segment will increase row sizes, you can prevent row chaining by reserving extra data block space for updates. See the section, "Block Thresholds" later in this chapter, which explains how to control space usage within data blocks.

Object Storage Settings

With great detail, Oracle lets you control the storage characteristics for segments in a database. The following sections explain several storage settings that you can set for different data storage objects.

Tablespace Placement

When you create a new data storage object, including a table, data cluster, index, snapshot (see Chapter 11 for information about snapshots), or rollback segment, you can explicitly indicate in which tablespace to create the object's segment. For example, the following CREATE ROLLBACK SEGMENT statement creates a new public rollback segment in the RBSEG tablespace:

```
CREATE PUBLIC ROLLBACK SEGMENT rbseg_10
  TABLESPACE rbseg;
```

Provided that you have the necessary quota in the tablespace and the privileges necessary to create the object, Oracle completes the request. If you omit a tablespace specification when creating a new table, data cluster, index, or snapshot, Oracle creates the object's segment in your user account's default tablespace; if you omit a tablespace specification when creating a rollback segment, Oracle creates the segment in the SYSTEM tablespace.

Extent Settings

When you create a new data storage object, Oracle lets you control several different storage settings related to allocation of extents for the object's segment:

- You can determine the number of extents to allocate when creating the segment. Oracle must allocate at least one extent when creating a new segment.

- You can limit the maximum number of extents that Oracle can ever allocate for the segment.

- You can control the size of the segment's extents. You can set the size of the segment's initial extent as well as the size of subsequent extents, including a growth factor to apply before allocating new extents for the segment.

➤ For example, the following CREATE TABLE statement controls how Oracle allocates extents for the new CUSTOMERS table's data segment:

```
CREATE TABLE sales.customers
  ( ... column specifications ... )
  STORAGE (
   INITIAL 500K
   NEXT 500K
   MINEXTENTS 1
   MAXEXTENTS 10
   PCTINCREASE 50  );
```

When Oracle creates the data segment for the CUSTOMERS table, the server allocates one initial extent, 500K in size, for the segment. When this initial extent fills, <u>Oracle allocates the next extent, 500K in size</u>, <u>and</u> updates the segment's <u>next extent size to 750K</u> (that is, 500K increased by   ←PCT INCREASE 50 percent). When a new extent is needed, Oracle allocates the next extent, 750K in size, and updates the segment's next extent size to 1,125K (that is, 750K increased by 50 percent). Extent allocation for the data segment continues in this manner until Oracle allocates the tenth extent, which is the limit for the number of extents for the segment. Of course, you can alter an object's storage settings, for example, to increase maximum number of extents for the object.

NOTE
You can also set a segment's MAXEXTENTS setting to UNLIMITED so that the segment can allocate an unlimited number of extents.

Unique Storage Settings for Rollback Segments

As explained earlier in this chapter, Oracle writes information to the extents of a rollback segment in a circular fashion. Additionally, Oracle can grow and shrink a rollback segment as different sized transactions log their rollback information in the segment. Accordingly, you can set some special storage parameters for each rollback segment.

■. At all times, a rollback segment can have no fewer than two extents.

■. You can set an *optimal size* for a rollback segment. If a rollback segment grows larger than its optimal size, Oracle eventually deallocates one or more extents from the segment to shrink it back to its optimal size.

For example, the following CREATE ROLLBACK SEGMENT statement creates a rollback segment and specifies its storage settings:

```
CREATE PUBLIC ROLLBACK SEGMENT rbseg_11
  TABLESPACE rbseg
  STORAGE (
    INITIAL 100K
    NEXT 100K
    MINEXTENTS 3
    MAXEXTENTS 100
    OPTIMAL 310K );
```

Data Block Settings

For each type of segment, Oracle lets you control how to use the space within the data blocks of the segment. The following sections explain the various storage settings that relate to data blocks.

Free List Settings

When you create a table, cluster, index, or snapshot, you can indicate the number of free list groups to create for the corresponding segment. A *free list group* is a group of one or more data block free lists for a data storage object's segment. By default, Oracle creates one free list group with one free list per data or index segment. If you are using Oracle with the Parallel Server option, it's possible to reduce contention among servers for free list lookups and improve system performance by creating multiple free list groups with multiple free lists. For example, the following statement creates an index with multiple free list groups and free lists per group:

```
CREATE INDEX sales.customer_name
  ON sales.customers (lastname, firstname)
  STORAGE (
  ... other storage options ...
   FREELIST GROUPS 2
   FREELISTS 2  );
```

Block Thresholds

Earlier in this chapter, you learned how data blocks can go on and off a segment's free lists as they become full or emptied. For tables, clusters, indexes, and snapshots, Oracle has two settings, PCTFREE and PCTUSED, that let you specifically control when data blocks go on and off a data storage object's segment free lists:

■ You can set a maximum threshold, PCTFREE, that controls how much data block space to reserve for future updates to rows. When a data block becomes PCTFREE full, Oracle removes the block from the corresponding segment's free lists.

■ You can set a minimum threshold, PCTUSED, that controls when to put a data block back on the corresponding segment's free list. For example, the default PCTUSED for all segments is set to 40 percent. Therefore, when transactions delete rows from a data block so that it becomes only 39 percent full, Oracle puts the block back on the corresponding segment's free lists.

Figure 7-10 demonstrates how the settings for PCTFREE and PCTUSED control when data blocks go on and off a segment's free lists.

For example, the ORDERS table contains small rows that transactions frequently update to increase their row length. The following statement creates the ORDERS table to set aside extra space for updates and put its data blocks back on the free list when it becomes partially empty:

```
CREATE TABLE sales.orders
  ( ... column specifications ... )
  PCTFREE 20
  PCTUSED 60 ;
```

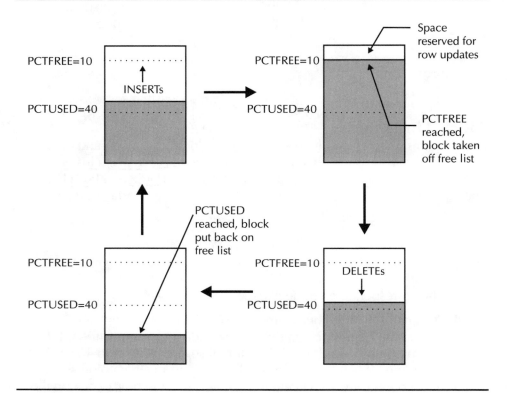

FIGURE 7-10. *Oracle removes a data block from a free list when it becomes PCTFREE full. Oracle returns the block to a free list when it becomes PCTUSED full.*

Transaction Entries

When a transaction updates a data block of an object, Oracle allocates a transaction entry in the data block. A *transaction entry* is a small amount of space in the header of a data block that Oracle uses to hold internal processing information until the transaction commits or rolls back. Oracle lets you set two storage parameters, INITRANS and MAXTRANS, that you can use to tune how the system allocates transaction entries within the data blocks of a table, data cluster, index, or snapshot:

■ INITRANS determines how much data block header space to preallocate for transaction entries. When you expect many concurrent transactions to touch a data block, you can preallocate more space for associated transaction entries and avoid the overhead of dynamically allocating this space when necessary.

■ MAXTRANS limits the number of transactions that can concurrently use a data block.

Setting Defaults for Object Storage

In most cases, storage settings for objects are optional specifications that you can use to control how Oracle stores data for each object. Oracle always has defaults for storage settings. The following sections explain how you can determine default object storage settings for data storage objects in an Oracle database.

User Defaults

As Chapter 6 explains, Oracle lets you set each user's default and temporary tablespaces. When the user creates a new database object and does not explicitly indicate a tablespace for the object, Oracle stores the new object in the user's default tablespace. A user's temporary tablespace is where Oracle allocates temporary work space for the user's SQL statements, whenever necessary.

Tablespace Defaults

When you create a new table, data cluster, index, or snapshot in a tablespace, and choose not to specify extent settings for the new object, the object's segment assumes the default extent storage settings of the tablespace. For each tablespace you can specify the defaults for the following:

■ Size for a segment's initial and subsequent extents

■ Minimum and maximum number of extents for a segment

■ Growth factor for a segment's subsequent extents

For example, the following statement alters a tablespace's default extent storage settings:

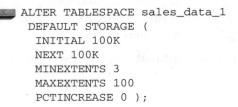

```
ALTER TABLESPACE sales_data_1
  DEFAULT STORAGE (
    INITIAL 100K
    NEXT 100K
    MINEXTENTS 3
    MAXEXTENTS 100
    PCTINCREASE 0 );
```

Unique Data Storage for Multimedia Data

When a table in a database includes a column that uses a LOB datatype (for example, CLOB, BLOB, or NCLOB) or a BFILE datatype, Oracle stores only a small locator inline with each row in the table. A *locator* is a pointer to the location of the actual LOB or BFILE data for the row. For CLOB, BLOB, and NCLOB columns, a LOB locator points to a storage location inside the database; for a BFILE column, a BFILE locator points to an external file managed by the server's operating system. Figure 7-11 illustrates the concept of locators for LOB and BFILE columns.

Notice in Figure 7-11 that a LOB column can have storage characteristics independent from those of the encompassing table. This makes it easy to address the large disk requirements typically associated with LOBs. In this example, the table stores all non-LOB and non-BFILE data for each row together in one tablespace, a LOB column's data in another tablespace, and a BFILE column's data in the server's file system. By doing so, you can distribute the storage of primary table data and related multimedia data to different physical locations (for example, disk drives) to reduce disk contention and improve overall system performance.

More About LOB Locators

To provide for efficient access to LOB data, Oracle stores a CLOB or BLOB column's pointers within a corresponding B-tree index. By doing so, Oracle can quickly access specifically requested *chunks* (pieces) of individual LOBs in a column.

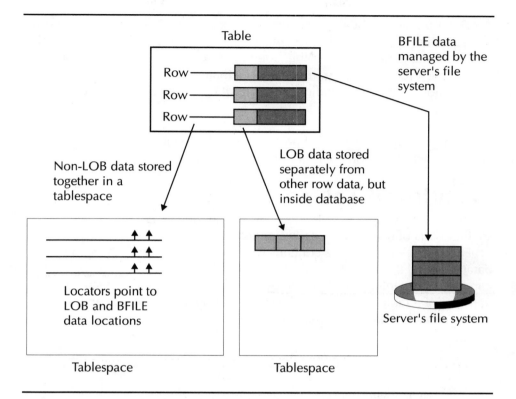

FIGURE 7-11. *Distributing the storage of primary table data and related multimedia data to different physical locations to reduce disk contention*

Data Partitioning

Large tables (and indexes) can create or magnify several problems in production database systems because of their size and storage characteristics. For example, consider the following scenarios:

■ A table becomes so large that associated management operations take longer to complete than the time window which is available.

■ A query requires Oracle to complete a full table scan of a very large table. Application and system performance suffers while Oracle reads the numerous data blocks for the corresponding table.

■ A mission-critical application depends primarily on a single large table. The table becomes unavailable when just a single data block in the table is inaccessible due to a disk failure. An administrator must recover the entire tablespace that contains the table before the table and corresponding mission-critical application can be brought back online.

To help reduce the types of problems that large tables and indexes can create, Oracle8 supports *partitioned tables* and *indexes*.

Partitioned Tables

As Figure 7-12 shows, Oracle8 lets you divide the storage of tables into smaller units of disk storage called *partitions*.

Each partition of a table contains the same columns with the same datatypes and the same integrity constraints. However, each table partition can have different physical attributes. For example, Oracle can store each partition of a table in separate tablespaces, and each partition can have different extent and data block storage settings.

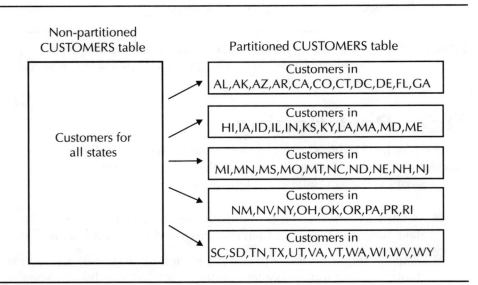

FIGURE 7-12.   *Oracle8 supports the partitioning of table rows by range.*

Oracle8 supports *range partitioned tables.* A row's partition key value determines in which partition Oracle stores a row. A table's partition key is a column or ordered set of columns (up to 16) that characterize the physical partitioning of table rows. To prevent the overhead associated with migrating rows among table partitions, applications should never update data in a table's partition key.

You can determine the data range for individual table partitions by specifying the non-inclusive upper bound for each partition. Each partition, except for the first, has an implicit low value, which is the upper bound of the previous partition. Therefore, it's important to declare table partitions ← with ranges that ascend in value. For example, consider the following CREATE TABLE statement. It demonstrates how you might create a large, partitioned USA_CUSTOMERS table in an Oracle8 database. Oracle places table rows into different partitions according to each customer's state.

```
CREATE TABLE sales.usa_customers
( id NUMBER(5) PRIMARY KEY,
  lastname VARCHAR2(50) NOT NULL,
  firstname VARCHAR2(50) NOT NULL,
  address VARCHAR2(100),
  city VARCHAR2(50),
  state CHAR(2),
  zipcode VARCHAR2(15),
  phone VARCHAR2(15),
  fax VARCHAR2(15),
  email VARCHAR2(100) )
  PARTITION BY RANGE ( state )
  ( PARTITION p1  VALUES LESS THAN ('H')      -- AL,AK,AZ,AR,CA,CO,CT,DC,DE,FL,GA
      TABLESPACE data01,
    PARTITION p2  VALUES LESS THAN ('MI')     -- HI,IA,ID,IL,IN,KS,KY,LA,MA,MD,ME
      TABLESPACE data02,
    PARTITION p3  VALUES LESS THAN ('NM')     -- MI,MN,MS,MO,MT,NC,ND,NE,NH,NJ
      TABLESPACE data03,
    PARTITION p4  VALUES LESS THAN ('S')      -- NM,NV,NY,OH,OK,OR,PA,PR,RI
      TABLESPACE data04,
    PARTITION p5  VALUES LESS THAN (MAXVALUE) -- SC,SD,TN,TX,UT,VA,VT,WA,WI,WV,WY
      TABLESPACE data05 );
```

Placing Rows into Data Partitions

To illustrate how Oracle places rows into a range partitioned table, think about what happens when an application inserts a customer from the state of Arkansas. Oracle performs a comparison with the first character in the state code AR with the value that defines the first table partition, P1. Since "A" is less than "H," Oracle places the new row into partition P1, which is physically stored in a data file of tablespace DATA01. Similarly, when you insert a new customer from New Jersey, Oracle places the new customer record into partition P3 (NJ is less than NM), which is physically stored in a data file of tablespace DATA03, and so on.

Using MAXVALUE

In the previous example, notice the declaration of partition P5. This partition stores all rows with a value greater than the upper bound of the previous partition, P4. For example, when you insert a new customer from Wyoming, Oracle places the new row into partition P5, which is physically stored in a data file of tablespace DATA05. If the USA_CUSTOMERS table did not include a partition with an upper bound MAXVALUE, Oracle would not allow applications to insert customers from SC, SD, TN, TX, UT, VA, VT, WA, WV, WI, and WY.

NOTE *MUST DEFINE THE "MAXVALUE"*

When a table's partition key accepts nulls, Oracle sorts rows with null partition keys greater than all other values except MAXVALUE.

Partitioned Indexes

Oracle8 also supports range partitioned indexes for non-clustered tables. Just as with tables, each partition of an index has the same logical attributes (index columns), but can have different physical characteristics (tablespace placement and storage settings). An index's partition key determines in which partition Oracle stores index entries. An index's partition key must include one or more of the columns that define the index. The declaration of index partition ranges is identical to declaring table partitions, as the following example shows:

```
CREATE INDEX usa_customers_state
  ON usa_customers ( state )
  PARTITION BY RANGE ( state )
    ( PARTITION p1  VALUES LESS THAN ('H')       -- AL,AK,AZ,AR,CA,CO,CT,DC,DE,FL,GA
        TABLESPACE data01,
      PARTITION p2  VALUES LESS THAN ('MI')      -- HI,IA,ID,IL,IN,KS,KY,LA,MA,MD,ME
        TABLESPACE data02,
      PARTITION p3  VALUES LESS THAN ('NM')      -- MI,MN,MS,MO,MT,NC,ND,NE,NH,NJ
        TABLESPACE data03,
      PARTITION p4  VALUES LESS THAN ('S')       -- NM,NV,NY,OH,OK,OR,PA,PR,RI
        TABLESPACE data04,
      PARTITION p5  VALUES LESS THAN (MAXVALUE) -- SC,SD,TN,TX,UT,VA,VT,WA,WI,WV,WY
        TABLESPACE data05 );
```

Partitioned Index Options

Should you always create partitioned indexes for partitioned tables? What columns should a partitioned index incorporate? How should you structure the partitions in an index? These are good questions to answer before deciding how to index partitioned tables in your database.

First things first. It makes sense to partition an index of a partitioned table only when the index itself is large enough to justify partitioning. Choosing the key columns for a partitioned index is no different than choosing the key columns for a non-partitioned index—index table columns that SQL statements use within a WHERE clause's search criteria.

Once you decide to create a partitioned index for a table, you must then decide how to structure the index's partitions. In general, you should consider two options: to create the index with partitions that match, or with partitions that are different than the corresponding table's partitions. The following sections explain each option.

Equi-Partitioned Objects

Two or more database objects are *equi-partitioned* if they have identical logical partitioning attributes. The USA_CUSTOMERS table and the USA_CUSTOMERS_STATE index of the previous code examples are equi-partitioned because they have the same number of partitions, the same data ranges for each partition, and the same columns that define their respective partition keys.

Equi-partitioned objects can yield benefits in several situations. Consider the following three examples:

- You can equi-partition a master table and a corresponding detail table. Consequently, Oracle can complete joins of the two tables very fast because all corresponding master-detail rows are within the same data partition. The reduction in disk access described here is similar to that when using data clusters to "pre-join" master and detail tables.

- You can equi-partition a table and its primary key index. When an administrative operation for a specific table partition makes the partition unavailable, only the corresponding index partition becomes unavailable as well. If the table and its index were not equi-partitioned, two or more index partitions would likely become unavailable due to the table partition maintenance operation.

- You can equi-partition a table and an index when you know that operations on a specific table partition tend to affect the corresponding index partition only. For example, if you perform a bulk data load into the table and the load updates data in just one table partition, you only have to rebuild the corresponding index partition.

When you equi-partition an index with its table, all keys in a particular index partition refer only to the rows in the corresponding table partition—thus, a partitioned index that is equi-partitioned with its table is a *local partitioned index*. Oracle can use the local index partitions to generate excellent query plans. Additionally, an administrator affects only one index partition when performing a maintenance operation on a table partition.

NOTE   ←

When you define a partitioned index that is equi-partitioned with its table, the index is easier to create than the previous example demonstrates. For example, the following creates a local, equi-partitioned index for the USA_CUSTOMERS table:

```
CREATE INDEX usa_customers_state
  ON usa_customers ( state )
```

```
LOCAL
  ( PARTITION p1 TABLESPACE data01,
    PARTITION p2 TABLESPACE data02,
    PARTITION p3 TABLESPACE data03,
    PARTITION p4 TABLESPACE data04,
    PARTITION p5 TABLESPACE data05 );
```

Notice in this example that range specifications and a maximum index value are not necessary. Local partitioned indexes automatically inherit these characteristics from their equi-partitioned table. However, you can always set the storage characteristics for each index partition independent of corresponding table partitions.

Global Partitioned Indexes

In some cases, it might be beneficial to create a global partitioned index that is not equi-partitioned with its table. A *global partitioned index* can contain the keys from all partitions of the corresponding table. Global indexes can provide better performance than local indexes in OLTP environments because they minimize the number of index probes. However, if you modify an underlying table partition, you might also affect many or all partitions of a corresponding global index for the duration of the table operation. When deciding what type of partitioned index to create, use application characteristics as your primary determining factor.

Partition-Extended Table Names

Oracle8 offers unique command syntax, a partition-extended table name, that application developers can use to declare SQL statements that are optimal for partitioned tables. A *partition-extended table name* is a simple but powerful declarative syntax that lets applications view individual partitions of a table as tables themselves. For example, the following query retrieves all the customers in California specifically from the corresponding table partition:

```
SELECT * FROM usa_customers PARTITION (p1);
```

While partition-extended table names can help to improve the performance of certain SQL statements, developers should think carefully about using such syntax in an application's SQL statements. That's because partition-extended table names reveal the underlying physical storage characteristics of a table's data. In general, it is not wise to code application SQL statements that create dependencies on the physical storage of a table—such dependencies can break an application if the physical storage of the table changes in the future.

If you decide to develop applications using partition-extended table names, understand also that partition-extended table names are an Oracle-specific extension to ANSI SQL. If you want to use partition-extended table names and preserve application portability, try creating views with the extended table names and using standard SQL statements against the views. For example:

```
CREATE VIEW v1 AS SELECT * FROM t1 PARTITION (p1)
    SELECT * FROM v1;
```

Partition Management

Oracle8 offers complete support for the management of partitioned tables and indexes. For example:

- You can convert a non-partitioned table to a partitioned table, and vice-versa.

- You can add partitions after the existing partitions of a table.

- You can split or merge partitions in the middle of a table.

- You can drop partitions of a table that do not contain any rows.

- You can truncate individual partitions in a table rather than the entire table.

What About Corresponding Indexes?

When you modify the partitions in a table, Oracle automatically completes an equivalent operation to synchronize any corresponding equi-partitioned indexes of the table. Alternatively, when you modify the partitions of a table that has a global partitioned index, you can rebuild the index to synchronize it with the modified table.

Summary

This chapter has explained the logical and physical database storage structures, including databases, tablespaces, data files, control files, segments, extents, and data blocks.

- A database's control file keeps track of internal system information about the physical structure of the database.

- Tablespaces are logical storage divisions within an Oracle database.

- Each tablespaces has one or more data files to physically store its data.

- A segment is the collection of data blocks for a data storage object such as a table, data cluster, index, or snapshot.

- An extent is a set of contiguous data blocks allocated to an object's segment.

- A data block is the unit of physical disk access for an Oracle database.

Additionally, you learned how to partition the data of large tables and indexes to improve the performance and manageability associated with these objects.

PART
IV

Oracle8 Software Architecture

CHAPTER
8

Oracle Software
Structures

racle8 Server is a sophisticated DBMS that manages access to almost any size database that you can imagine. Hundreds or even thousands and tens of thousands of concurrent users can connect to a single database server, locally or across a computer network. To accomplish these extraordinary tasks efficiently and reliably, Oracle creates and uses numerous software structures. This chapter explains the many software structures that Oracle8 uses to function, including:

- Database servers and instances

- Oracle server processes

- Oracle memory structures

- Net8, Oracle's networking software for distributed processing environments

Database Servers and Database Instances

An Oracle *database server*, commonly referred to as a *database instance*, is the collection of server-side processes and memory areas that Oracle uses to manage access to a database. Figure 8-1 is a basic illustration that shows you the shape of an Oracle database instance's processes and memory areas.

Server Startup and Shutdown

Before anyone can work with an Oracle database, someone must perform a *startup* on a database server. This process includes starting a database instance, *mounting* (associating) the database to the instance, and *opening* the database. After a server startup, the database is generally available for use with applications.

Conversely, you can make a database unavailable by performing a database server *shutdown*. A server shutdown is the reverse of a server startup: first, you *close* the database, *dismount* it from the instance, and then shut down the instance. After a server shutdown, users cannot access the database until after you restart the server.

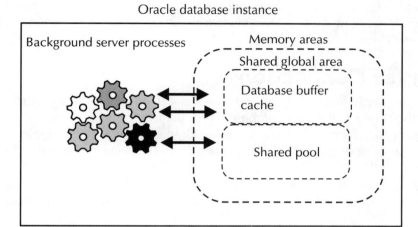

FIGURE 8-1.   *An Oracle database instance*

Server Crashes

A *server crash* is an abnormal server shutdown. For example, an unfortunate operating system operation or problem could unexpectedly kill one or more of a server's background processes. Consequently, the database server might crash. Oracle has built-in features that protect the work of all committed transactions, and automatically performs the necessary recovery from an instance that crashes. See Chapter 10 for more information about Oracle8's database protection mechanisms.

Oracle's Parallel Server Option and High Availability

Many sites use Oracle to support mission-critical applications. A mission-critical application, by definition, has stringent high-availability requirements. Such sites can tolerate little or no downtime due to a server crash. In such circumstances, *Oracle's Parallel Server option* can help. In a parallel server configuration, multiple database instances, running on different nodes of a loosely-coupled computer, mount and open the same Oracle database in parallel. Users can work with the database through any instance that is mounted to the database. If an isolated system failure causes one of the instances to crash, other servers remain available so that users can continue work uninterrupted. See Chapter 12 for more information about configuring Oracle for parallel processing computers and Oracle's Parallel Server option.

Server Connections

After an Oracle instance is up and running, you can establish a connection with the server to perform database work. Behind the scenes, the mechanisms of the database instance work to complete your requests and the requests of others. At the same time, the database instance automatically protects the work of all transactions while preserving the integrity of the shared database. The following sections explain more about the processes and memory structures that comprise an Oracle database server.

Oracle8 Processes

During server startup, Oracle creates a set of operating system processes on the *host* (server computer). As users connect to the instance, Oracle creates additional processes to manage their connections and perform database work on their behalf. The following sections explain the various operating system processes that run as part of an Oracle database instance.

Server-Side Background Processes

Every Oracle database instance contains a set of server background processes. A *background process* is a server process that performs a specialized system function. Figure 8-2 and the following sections explain more about the most common server background processes that you'll find in an Oracle database instance.

The Database Writer Process (DBWR)

When you modify some database data (for example, insert, update, or delete a row in a database table), Oracle does not simply modify the data in a data file. This type of processing would be extremely inefficient in a large multi-user system because the system would constantly be reading data from and writing data back to the database's data files. Instead, a

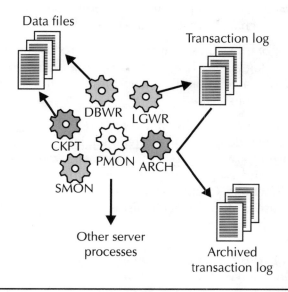

Data files

Transaction log

DBWR   LGWR

CKPT

PMON   ARCH

SMON

Other server
processes

Archived
transaction log

FIGURE 8-2.   *The background processes of an Oracle database instance*

server process working on behalf of your session reads one or more data blocks from a data file into the server's memory. Oracle then makes the change that you request in the server's memory. Eventually, the *database writer process (DBWR)* writes modified data blocks in memory back to the database's data files. To consolidate disk accesses, reduce unnecessary overhead, and make Oracle8 perform optimally, an instance's DBWR writes modified data blocks from memory to disk only in certain situations: if DBWR sits idle for several seconds, if a process wants to read a new data block into memory but no free space is available, or when the system performs a checkpoint. The section "The Checkpoint Process" explains checkpoints.

The Log Writer Process (LGWR)

The *log writer process (LGWR)* records information about the changes made by all transactions that commit. Oracle performs transaction logging as follows:

1. As you carry out a transaction, Oracle creates small records called *redo entries* that contain just enough information necessary to regenerate the changes made by the transaction.

2. Oracle temporarily stores your transaction's redo entries in the server's redo log buffer. The server's *redo log buffer* is a small memory area that temporarily caches transaction redo entries for all system transactions.

3. When you ask Oracle to commit your transaction, LGWR reads the corresponding redo entries in the redo log buffer and writes them to the database's transaction log. The database's *transaction log* is a set of files dedicated to logging the redo entries created by all system transactions. Chapter 10 discusses the transaction log and other database protection mechanisms.

NOTE

Oracle does not consider a transaction as "committed" until LGWR successfully writes your transaction's redo entries and a commit record to the transaction log.

The Archiver Process (ARCH)

The *archiver process (ARCH)* automatically backs up the transaction log files after LGWR fills them with redo entries. The sequential set of archived transaction log files that ARCH creates is collectively called the database's *archived transaction log*. If a database experiences a serious failure (for example, a disk failure), Oracle uses the database backups and the archived transaction log to recover the database and all committed transactions. Chapter 10 explains more about Oracle's protective mechanisms, including database backups and the archived transaction log.

NOTE

Automatic transaction log archiving is an optional feature of Oracle. Therefore, the ARCH process is present only when you use this feature.

The Checkpoint Process (CKPT)

Periodically, DBWR performs a checkpoint. During a *checkpoint,* DBWR writes all modified data blocks in memory back to the database's data files. The purpose of a checkpoint is to establish mileposts of transaction consistency on disk. After performing a checkpoint, the changes made by all committed transactions have been written to the database's data files. Therefore, a checkpoint indicates how much of the transaction log's redo entries Oracle must apply if a server crash occurs and database recovery is necessary.

During a checkpoint, Oracle must also update the headers in all of the database's data files to indicate the checkpoint; normally, LGWR performs this operation. However, when your database has a large number of data files, many data file updates due to checkpoints can detract from LGWR's ability to log transactions as they commit. To relieve some of the burden on LGWR, an Oracle database instance can start a special *checkpoint process (CKPT)* dedicated to updating data file headers during checkpoints.

The System Monitor Process (SMON)

During database processing, an Oracle instance's *system monitor process (SMON)* performs many internal operations, some of which you might never even realize. For example, SMON periodically coalesces the free extents in a tablespace's data files to create larger free extents. SMON does its work quietly in the background during times of low activity or when certain operations are required.

The Process Monitor Process (PMON)

Occasionally, user connections do not end gracefully. For example, a network error might unexpectedly disconnect your database session before you can disconnect from Oracle. An instance's *process monitor process (PMON)* notices when user connections have been broken. PMON cleans up after orphaned connections by rolling back a dead session's transaction and releasing any of the session's resources that might otherwise block other users from performing database work.

Distinct versus Multithreaded Background Processes

On some operating systems, Oracle implements each background process as a distinct operating system process. However, with other operating systems, such as Microsoft Windows NT, each Oracle background process executes as a lightweight thread inside a single background server process.

Process Options to Support User Connections

An Oracle instance creates and uses a separate set of processes to support database user sessions that connect to the server. Oracle can support user connections to an Oracle instance in any type of computing environment. For example, Oracle can support users that connect to an Oracle database server across a network using a PC or network computer. Oracle can also support users that start a host session and connect to an Oracle instance on the same computer. The following sections explain the different process architectures that Oracle uses to support user connections in different types of computing environments.

Client/Server Process Architectures

A *client/server* application is another name for a *distributed processing* application system. In a distributed processing application, the tasks performed by the application are "distributed" across two or more distinct processing components. In a client/server application, there are three components—the client, the server, and a network that connects clients and the server. Figure 8-3 illustrates a typical client/server configuration.

The following sections explain each component of a client/server system.

The Client

The *client* is the front-end of the application that you use to perform work. The client is typically in charge of the following types of operations:

- Presenting a user interface with which you can interact, such as a form for data entry

- Validating data entry, such as checking that you enter a valid date in a date field

- Requesting information from a database server, such as customer records or sales orders

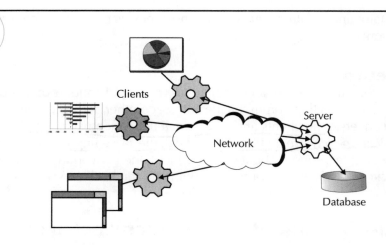

FIGURE 8-3. *A typical client/server configuration*

- Processing information returned from a database server, such as filling a form with data, calculating field totals on a report, or creating graphs and charts

The Server

The *server* is the back-end of the application. Behind the scenes, a database server works to manage a database among all the users and applications that use it to store and retrieve data. The server is responsible for the following operations:

- Opening a database and making it accessible to applications

- Preventing unauthorized database access with tight security controls

- Preventing destructive interference among concurrent transactions accessing the same data sets

- Protecting a database with bulletproof database backup and recovery features

■ Maintaining data integrity and consistency as many users perform work

The Network

Typically, the client and server components of an application execute on different computers that communicate with each other across a *network*. In order to converse, the clients and servers in a network must all employ *communication software* that lets them speak the same lingo. Later in this chapter, you'll learn more about Oracle's Net8, the networking software that lets clients and servers communicate in an Oracle client/server network.

Oracle-Specific Process Architectures

Now that you have a general understanding of client/server architecture, let's take a look at the specific process architectures that an Oracle server uses to support client connections.

Dedicated Servers

The simplest process architecture that Oracle can use to support client connections is the *dedicated server architecture*. Figure 8-4 shows a dedicated server architecture.

In a dedicated server configuration, Oracle starts a dedicated *foreground server process* for each client that connects to the instance. A client's foreground server process performs database work for its client only. For example, when you send an UPDATE statement to Oracle, your foreground server process checks server memory for the necessary data blocks; if they are not already in memory, your server process reads the blocks from disk into server memory; finally, your server process updates the data blocks in server memory.

The dedicated server process configuration is not particularly efficient for large user populations. That's because each dedicated server process performs work for only one user session. If a dedicated server process sits idle a large percentage of the time (for example, as a salesperson talks to a customer and fills out a form), the inactive server process unnecessarily consumes server resources. Multiply this by hundreds or thousands of users and the processes necessary to support user connections quickly exhaust all of a server's resources. Dedicated server connections are typically used

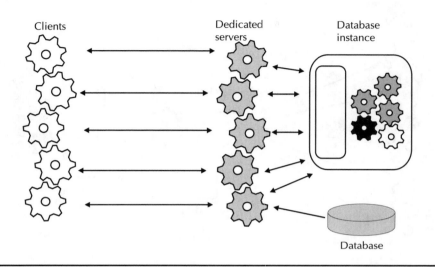

FIGURE 8-4.   *A dedicated server architecture*

only for intensive batch operations that keep the server process busy a large percentage of the time. Dedicated server connections are also required to execute certain administrative tasks (for example, server startup, shutdown, and database recovery). Instead, most client/server configurations use a multithreaded server process configuration.

Multithreaded Servers

The typical process architecture that Oracle uses to support client connections is the *multithreaded server architecture*. Figure 8-5 illustrates a multithreaded server configuration.

A multithreaded server configuration is a small collection of server-side processes that, together, can efficiently support large user populations. The components in a multithreaded server configuration include dispatchers, shared servers, and queues.

■   A *dispatcher process* receives client requests and places them in the server's *request queue*. A dispatcher process also returns the results for requests back to the appropriate client. An Oracle database

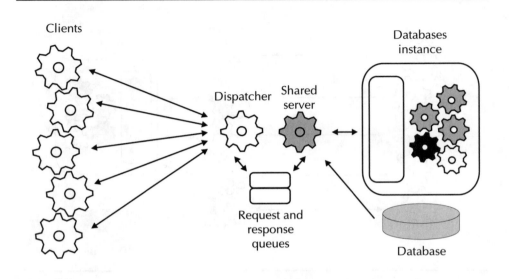

FIGURE 8-5. *A multithreaded server architecture*

instance must start at least one dispatcher process for every network protocol that it plans to support (for example, TCP/IP, IPX/SPX, DecNet).

■ A *shared server process* executes the requests that it finds in the server's request queue and returns corresponding results to the server's *response queue*. An Oracle instance can start one or more shared server processes. After instance startup, Oracle automatically adjusts the number of shared servers as the transaction load on the system fluctuates; when there are many requests waiting for execution in the request queue, Oracle starts additional shared servers to handle the load; conversely, when the requests in the queue are cleared, Oracle can stop unnecessary shared servers to reduce the process overhead on the host computer.

A multithreaded server configuration is very efficient for typical application environments because a small number of shared server processes perform the work for many connected clients. Consequently, very little process overhead is necessary to support large user populations and the host computer running Oracle can perform better.

Single-Task Server Process Architecture

In a host-based environment, you use a dumb terminal or terminal emulator to establish an operating system session on the host computer. Using this operating system session, you can run the client application of your choice and connect to the database instance on the same computer—a network does not sit between the front and back ends of the application.

To support host-based environments, Oracle has a *single-task server process architecture*. Figure 8-6 shows Oracle's single-task process architecture.

A single-task process is very efficient for host-based environments because just one process executes both the client and foreground server portions of the application. However, not all host operating systems can support Oracle's single-task configuration—only operating systems that can adequately protect the boundary between client and server code can use a

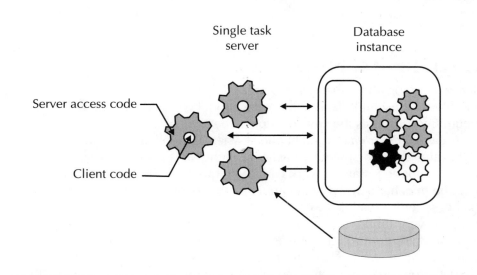

FIGURE 8-6. *A host-based system uses a single-task server process architecture.*

single-task configuration. For example, Digital's VAX VMS operating system can support single-task configurations for host-based connections, but most UNIX servers cannot; instead, most UNIX servers must employ a multithreaded or dedicated server configuration to support both client/server and host-based connections to an Oracle instance.

Memory Areas and Data Caching

Disk access is a necessary evil in all computer systems. Why? To permanently store data, the computer must write the data to a disk. To subsequently read the data, the computer must retrieve the information from the disk. But relatively speaking, disk I/O is typically one of the slowest operations that a computer can perform. Therefore, the less disk access that is necessary, the faster that a computer and applications using the computer will appear to perform.

To minimize disk access and speed up the performance of computer systems, applications typically create *random access memory (RAM)* areas that temporarily *cache* (store) data stored on disk. An application can manipulate data in a memory cache almost instantly and consolidate relatively costly disk access only when necessary or when it is most efficient. By using memory caches, the application and the entire system perform much faster.

Cache Hits, Misses, and Reloads

Before learning about the memory areas that an Oracle instance creates and uses, it's useful to learn a bit more about how data caching works. Figure 8-7 illustrates the key concepts of data caching.

A *cache hit* (or *cache get*) happens when an application requests data that is already in the memory cache. A cache hit is good because disk access is not necessary to work with the requested data. On the other hand, a *cache miss* happens when an application requests data that is not in the cache, so a disk read is necessary to put the data into the cache. A cache reload is very similar to a cache miss. A *cache reload* happens when an application requests data that was in the cache, but has since been *aged* from the cache (written back to disk)—therefore, the application must read the data from disk back into memory. As you might imagine, the fewer the number of cache misses and reloads, the less disk access and the better the system will perform.

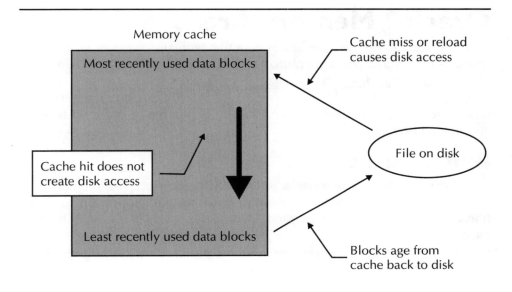

FIGURE 8-7.   *To cache data intelligently, an application uses a caching algorithm that maximizes cache hits and minimizes cache misses and cache reloads.*

A memory cache is typically a fixed chunk of memory that does not grow or shrink in size. Consequently, there is a limit as to how much data the cache can hold. If the memory cache is full of data and some new data must be read into the cache, the application must decide what blocks to age from the cache to make room for the new data. To keep the most frequently used data blocks in memory and minimize the number of cache misses and reloads, the application implements an intelligent *caching algorithm* that decides when to age blocks from the cache. A common caching algorithm is the *most-recently-used/least-recently-used (MRU/LRU) caching algorithm*. Basically, this algorithm keeps the most-recently-used data blocks in the cache and writes the least-recently-used blocks back to disk when more space is necessary.

Oracle8 Memory Areas

Oracle is a database management system that typically manages large amounts of data. To perform optimally, Oracle creates and uses many different memory caches to minimize disk I/O and maximize server performance, including the buffer cache, the shared pool, and program global areas. The following sections explain each of the memory areas of an Oracle instance.

Buffer Cache

An Oracle instance's *buffer cache* is typically the largest server memory area. The buffer cache stores database information that application transactions have recently requested. Figure 8-8 shows an instance's buffer cache.

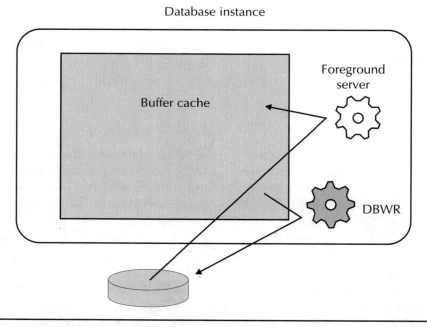

FIGURE 8-8. *Foreground server processes read data into an Oracle instance's buffer cache to perform database work. Eventually, the DBWR background process writes dirty data blocks from the buffer cache back to the database's data files.*

When you update a row in a table, a foreground server process reads the data block that contains the row from a data file on disk into the buffer cache. Then, the server process can modify the data block in server memory. Should another user's transaction request to update the same row or another row in the same data block, the buffer cache already contains the block and can avoid disk access. Eventually, the DBWR writes *dirty* (modified) data blocks back to the data files. See the section, "The Database Writer Process" earlier in this chapter for more information about how DBWR works.

Buffer Cache Size

One of the easiest ways to tune the performance of an Oracle server is to correctly size the instance's buffer cache. The objective is to make the buffer cache large enough so that it can hold the set of database information most frequently used by applications, but not excessively large such that it hoards all of the host computer's memory. Before server startup, you can set a server parameter that determines the size of the instance's buffer cache and then start up the server. After running the server for a representative amount of time, you can analyze the ratio of buffer cache hits to cache misses and reloads to determine how well the buffer cache is helping your system minimize block I/O. To resize the buffer cache, you must shut down the server, alter the setting of the buffer cache parameter, and then restart the database server—you cannot dynamically resize the buffer cache size while the database server is running.

The Shared Pool

An instance's *shared pool* memory area is another primary server memory area. An instance's shared pool has two components: the library cache and the dictionary cache. Figure 8-9 and the following sections describe an instance's shared pool.

The Library Cache and Shared SQL

The *library cache* stores and shares parsed representations of the most recently executed SQL statements and PL/SQL programs. For example, when you issue a SQL statement, Oracle parses the statement and determines the most efficient execution plan for the statement. Then, Oracle caches the statement in the shared pool. If another user issues the

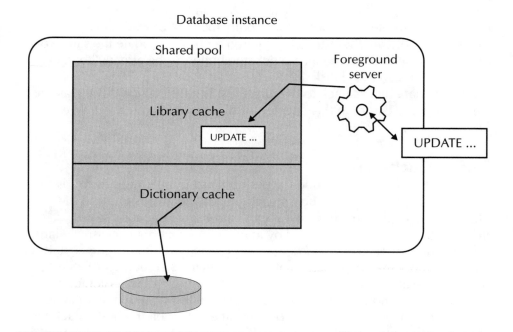

FIGURE 8-9.   *An instance's shared pool contains two memory areas: the library cache and the dictionary cache.*

same statement, Oracle can share the statement already in memory rather than perform identical steps necessary to execute the statement again. By caching statements in memory, Oracle's *shared SQL* reduces the server overhead necessary to execute a set of application statements.

The Dictionary Cache
During system processing, Oracle continually requests and updates information in the database's data dictionary. To maximize the performance of the system's internal operations, an Oracle instance's *dictionary cache* stores the most recently used data dictionary information.

Shared Pool Size

Like the buffer cache, you can adjust the size of the shared pool by setting a configuration parameter before server startup. After performance analysis, you can adjust the size of an instance's shared pool by shutting down the server, modifying the shared pool's configuration parameter, and restarting the database server.

The System Global Area (SGA)

The *system* or *shared global area (SGA)* encompasses the buffer cache and the shared pool. Therefore, the SGA is a general term that you can use to refer to all of the shared memory used by an Oracle instance.

Program Global Areas (PGA)

For each connected client, Oracle creates a private memory area called a *program* or *private global area (PGA)*. A PGA is a relatively small amount of server memory that holds session-specific information. For example, a client's server process uses its PGA to hold the state of the session's program variables and packages.

Sort Areas

The previous chapter explains how Oracle uses temporary segments (or a temporary tablespace) as work space to sort a large amount of information for ordered queries, index builds, and other demanding server operations. Oracle uses temporary segments only when it cannot complete the entire operation in a sort area. A *sort area* is a small amount of server memory that a session can use as a temporary work space.

All sessions connected to an Oracle instance can create and use a temporary sort area in server memory. You can adjust the size of the sort areas that Oracle creates for user sessions with a server parameter before server startup.

Oracle8 Networking and Net8

Computer applications typically operate using a client/server system that incorporates a network of computers. To transmit data between the clients and servers in your Oracle environment, you must use Oracle's network communication software. *Net8,* known as *SQL*Net* in previous versions of Oracle, is networking software that makes it possible for Oracle clients and servers to communicate across a network. Executing on both the clients and servers of the system, Net8 makes the presence of the network in a client/server system transparent—an application developer does not have to code low-level application logic (for example, network protocol calls) to access Oracle data across a network. Instead, a client application uses standard SQL statements to request data from a remote Oracle server as if the database were on the same machine as the client. Figure 8-10 and the following sections explain the many components of Oracle Net8 networking software.

Transparent Network Substrate (TNS) and Other Net8 Layers

The Net8 software running on both clients and servers in an Oracle network includes three different layers: the Net layer, the TNS layer, and a protocol adapter.

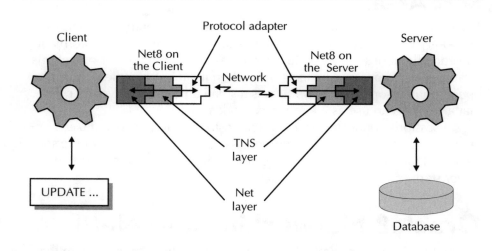

FIGURE 8-10. *Net8 makes the network between the clients and servers of an application transparent.*

■ The *Net layer* on the client permits an application to transparently access a remote database using SQL as if the database were on the same computer. The Net layer on the server permits the server to receive and send data in response to client SQL requests as though the client were running on the same machine as the server.

■ The *Transparent Network Substrate (TNS) layer* is software that provides Oracle clients and servers a common application programming interface to all industry-standard network protocols. By plugging network protocol adapters into TNS, clients and servers can communicate using any network protocol.

■ An Oracle *protocol adapter* is necessary to translate generic TNS functionality to and from a specific network communication protocol. Net8 has protocol adapters for all common network protocols, including TCP/IP, IPX/SPX, DecNet, LU6.2, and more.

When a client application executes a SQL statement, the statement passes through each layer of Net8 running on the client and is finally packaged and sent across the network. At the server end, Net8 opens the network package and passes the request through the various Net8 layers in reverse order and finally feeds the SQL statement to the database server as though it were issued by a local application. After statement processing, the server returns the results in the reverse order through Net8 and the network back to the client.

TNS Connections, Initiators, and Destinations

A *TNS connection* is a communication pathway between two nodes in the network. A TNS connection is a persistent pathway that transmits data between two TNS components. In every TNS connection, one node is the *initiator* and the other is the *destination*. Typically, the initiator of a TNS connection is a client and the destination is an Oracle database server. However, servers can also communicate with one another in an Oracle distributed database system using TNS connections. See Chapter 12 for more information about distributed database systems.

Connection Pooling

Typical database connections support applications that sit idle a large percentage of the time. For example, when using a typical order-entry application, the salesperson does not actually send or receive any database information across the TNS connection while filling out a screen form with order information.

To limit the number of physical network connections and make more efficient use of network resources, Net8 can *pool* a preset number of TNS connections. Figure 8-11 illustrates the basics of connection pooling.

With connection pooling, a database session that sits idle can temporarily allow another session to use its physical TNS connection to the database server, and later reclaim its connection when the session needs to communicate with the server. Consequently, connection pooling allows many sessions to communicate with a database server by sharing a

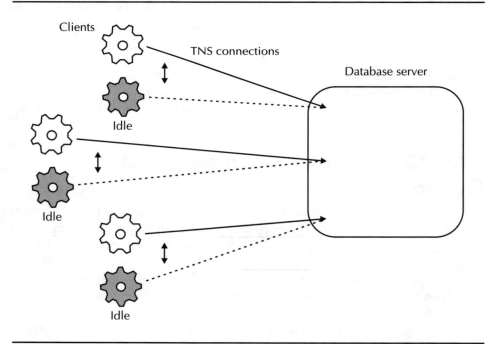

FIGURE 8-11. *Connection pooling allows database sessions to use a set number of physical TNS connections and reduce network overhead.*

predetermined number of available TNS connections. Fewer network resources are necessary to support typical applications, and less server overhead typically translates to better server performance.

The server does not begin pooling TNS connections until after the preset number of physical network connections are open. To open a subsequent TNS connection, the database server must first locate an idle session and then logically reassign the idle session's connection to the new connection. The preset limit of physical network connections is a limit that you can set as a configuration parameter before server startup.

Multiplexing

To further reduce the overhead of systems that must support many network connections, Net8 can *multiplex* many network connections into a single physical network transport. Figure 8-12 illustrates Net8 multiplexing.

The objective of multiplexing is to reduce the operating system overhead on the host computer that's necessary to support many network connections. By concentrating many network connections into a single

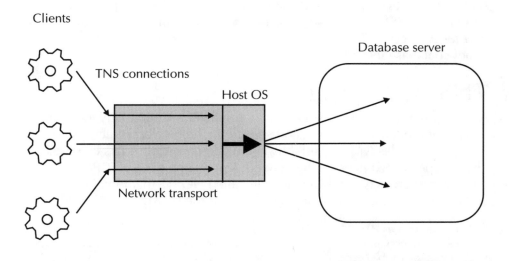

FIGURE 8-12. *Multiplexing many network connections into a single physical network transport to reduce the operating system overhead*

network transport, you reduce number of processes and open network sockets on the server computer necessary to support large user populations.

The TNS Listener

A *TNS listener* is necessary to establish TNS network connections. A TNS listener is a process that receives the connection request of an initiator, resolves the given address to the network address of the destination, and establishes a TNS connection to the destination. For example, when you start an application and request a connection to the SALES database, your connection request is forwarded to the network's TNS listener, which then resolves the address of SALES to the computer that is running an instance for the SALES database. The TNS listener then requests the instance to establish a TNS connection between your client application and the instance's multithreaded server configuration (or a new dedicated server).

Web Listeners

More and more companies are using the Internet and private intranets to provide access to the information in Oracle databases. Using a standard web browser, you can establish a connection to an Oracle database and perform work. To support web-based connections to an Oracle database server, the host computer must run a special type of listener process called an *Oracle Web listener*. A web listener is a process that facilitates *hypertext transfer protocol (HTTP)* communication between web applications and an Oracle database instance.

TNS Addressing

All computer networks use an addressing scheme that uniquely identifies the location of each computer and service on the network. Network configuration files typically establish network names that users can use to identify specific services on the network. For example, on a TCP/IP computer, there is typically a small file called HOSTS that identifies the IP addresses of computers that are accessible on the network.

```
# This is a sample HOSTS file.
# This file contains the mappings of IP addresses to host names. Each
# entry should be kept on an individual line. The IP address should
```

```
# be placed in the first column followed by the corresponding host name.
# The IP address and the host name should be separated by at least one
# space.
# IP Address      Host Name                        Alias
127.0.0.1         localhost
128.126.50.100    alitest1.animatedlearning.com    alitest1
128.126.50.101    client1.animatedlearning.com     client1
128.126.50.100    alitest1.animatedlearning.com    oranamesrvr0
```

Similarly, Oracle TNS networks also require address mappings that describe where TNS services can be found on the network, such as TNS listeners and Oracle database servers. One way to accomplish TNS addressing is to create and distribute *TNS configuration files* to each client and server in the network. Then, when a client initiates a TNS connection, it can use the local copy of the appropriate configuration file to resolve the TNS service address.

When your network uses configuration files to set up a TNS network, the most common TNS configuration files include the following: ·

File Name	Description
TNSNAMES.ORA	The TNSNAMES.ORA configuration file resides on both clients and servers in an Oracle network. TNSNAMES.ORA contains address information that TNS running on a client or server uses to establish connections to other Oracle services in a network.
SQLNET.ORA	The SQLNET.ORA configuration file resides on both clients and servers in an Oracle network. SQLNET.ORA contains special configuration parameters that configure a SQL*Net connection from a client or server to another Oracle service in a network.
LISTENER.ORA	The LISTENER.ORA configuration file resides only on servers that run a TNS listener process. LISTENER.ORA configures one or more TNS listener processes. The file describes the names, addresses, and databases that correspond to one or more listener processes.

Oracle Names

Configuring and maintaining large Oracle networks can be a challenging administrative task. When you use TNS configuration files for network addressing, each client and server must have the most recent copy of the configuration files or else applications might not work properly. Distributing files to the nodes in the system can be particularly difficult when the network contains hundreds or thousands of clients that need access to network services. And putting configuration files in a shared, central network location does not work well because the files become hot spots that create bottlenecks.

To solve many network management problems in an Oracle network, you can employ an optional TNS service component called Oracle Names. *Oracle Names* is name server software that an Oracle client/server system can use to centrally manage network names and corresponding addresses. Rather than use configuration files, a client contacts an Oracle Names server to resolve the address to other network services in the Oracle network. You can start redundant names servers in the same network to distribute loads and prevent single points of failure from making the network unavailable. And if the network changes in some way, all that's necessary is a quick change to the names servers in the system and all clients automatically see new address information automatically.

Multiple Network and MultiProtocol Interchanges

The previous sections explain the basic components of a simple TNS network that operates within just one network community. A TNS *community* is a logical area of a network in which all nodes communicate using the same network protocol. Large organizations are likely to have several different network communities. When a mix of network communities must support a single Oracle client/server application, a *MultiProtocol Interchange* is necessary in the TNS network configuration. An interchange provides a way for an Oracle client/server system to join different network communities and hide the complexities of inter-network connectivity from the client and server portions of a database application. Figure 8-13 illustrates a more complex TNS network that includes multiple communities and an interchange.

A MultiProtocol Interchange is Oracle networking software that executes on a computer that is a member of two or more network communities. A TNS connection that utilizes interchanges to span multiple network communities has a path. A *TNS connection path* is the series of

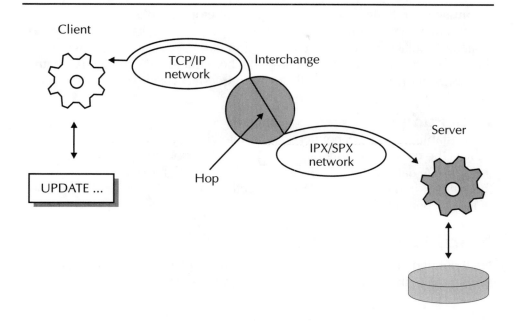

FIGURE 8-13.   *MultiProtocol Interchanges can join different network communities to create one large TNS network that supports client/server applications.*

hops across communities and available interchanges that are necessary to make a TNS connection.

The Navigator

Multiple paths can join nodes of different communities when a TNS network contains several communities and interchanges. The *Navigator* component of an interchange makes sure to establish optimal TNS connections between nodes. During connect time, the Navigator makes navigation decisions based on current network availability and the cost of using certain networks.

The Connection Manager

The *Connection Manager* of an interchange manages its TNS connections. An interchange's Connection Manager has a listener process to catch incoming interchange connection requests. Before establishing an interchange connection, the Connection Manager consults the Navigator to evaluate available paths for the connection. If the Navigator indicates that the interchange is necessary to complete the optimal TNS connection path, the Connection Manager establishes the requested TNS connection.

Data Pumps

After establishing a TNS connection, an interchange's Connection Manager assigns the connection to a *data pump*. A TNS connection uses its assigned interchange data pump as a bi-directional avenue to move data between the initiator and destination. The Connection Manager manages the number of pumps per interchange and the number of connections per pump.

Net8 Configuration

Net8 configuration is accomplished using the *Net8 Configuration Wizard*, a simple utility that makes it easy to create and maintain Oracle networks.

Summary

This chapter has explained the many software components that you will configure and work with when you use Oracle8.

■ An Oracle instance is a set of operating system processes and memory structures that, after started, provide for application access to a database.

■ Oracle uses a number of background processes (for example, DBWR, LGWR, ARCH, CKPT, SMON, and PMON) to perform specialized internal functions.

■ Oracle can use either dedicated or multithreaded server configurations to support user connections to a database instance.

■ Oracle uses single-task processes to support host-based connections to a database instance.

■ Oracle creates several different memory caches to reduce disk access and improve server performance. The primary memory structures in an Oracle database instance include the buffer cache, the shared pool (library and dictionary caches), program global areas, and sort areas.

■ When an Oracle database server must support a client/server application, clients and servers in the system must run Net8, Oracle's networking software.

■ Net8 can support all types of networks, including simple, single-protocol networks and complex, multiprotocol networks.

CHAPTER
9

Shared Database
Access Mechanisms

anaging access to a shared database among hundreds or thousands of users can be a very challenging task. This chapter explains Oracle8's features that allow for safe, concurrent user access to a database. Topics in this chapter include:

- The concepts of data concurrency and consistency
- Oracle's automatic and manual database locking mechanisms
- Oracle's multiversioning mechanism

The Three Cs—Contention, Concurrency, and Consistency

All multi-user computer systems must manage the problems of contention, concurrency, and consistency related to the resources that users share. For example, in a computer network, a file server must prevent multiple users from updating the same file at the same time—otherwise, users might interfere with each other and cause lost work. Print servers typically use a queuing mechanism to prevent two users from using a network printer at exactly the same time.

Contention, concurrency, and consistency are closely related terms but have important differences:

- *Contention* happens when two users try to access simultaneously the same resource such as a file or a printer.

- *Concurrency* happens when multiple users can access the same resource as though each user has access to the resource in *isolation*. Concurrency is high when a user notices no apparent wait to access the shared resource. Conversely, concurrency is low when a user must wait a noticeable period of time to access the shared resource.

- *Consistency* happens when a user accesses a shared resource and the resource exhibits the same characteristics among operations.

The following section introduces Oracle's concurrency and consistency mechanisms.

Oracle's Concurrency and Consistency Mechanisms

Oracle is a database management system that typically manages multi-user access to a single database. Consequently, Oracle has concurrency and consistency mechanisms that address contention for the same database resources, allowing for safe, simultaneous user access to the database. At the same time, Oracle's concurrency and consistency mechanisms do not complicate database access or unnecessarily detract from system performance. For example, if you and another user want to update the same row in a table at nearly the same time, Oracle uses automatic locking mechanisms to *serialize* the transactions as if they were occurring in *isolation*. When you want to query a table that another transaction is currently modifying, Oracle's *multiversioning mechanism* automatically allows your query to proceed immediately by reading data as it existed before the open transaction modified the data.

Locking and multiversioning are two of the mechanisms that Oracle uses to safely manage multi-user access to an Oracle database. Later in this chapter, you'll learn more about these mechanisms. But first, let's learn about the basic types of concurrency problems that all multi-user database systems must address.

Transactions and Interference

Transactions in a multi-user database system have the potential to interfere with each other in several different ways, including lost updates, dirty reads, non-repeatable reads, and phantoms.

Lost Updates

A *lost update* happens when the system lets two transactions update the same data at the same time. For example, consider what might happen if your and another user's transactions can update the PARTS table at the same time to change a specific part's inventory quantity. One update will overwrite the other such that one of the updates is lost. To prevent lost updates and other forms of destructive interference, almost all database systems use some type of data locking mechanism to serialize access to specific sets of data.

Dirty Reads

A *dirty read* happens when one transaction reads the uncommitted changes made by another open transaction. For example, assume that another user starts a transaction and modifies the CUSTOMERS table to change the address of a customer. Before the user commits the transaction, you start a new transaction and query the CUSTOMERS table. If your query retrieves the modified address of the customer, the database system has allowed you to perform a dirty read.

In some cases, dirty reads can create problems for database applications. For example, suppose that you query the CUSTOMERS table before making a change to a customer's address. After reviewing the customer's current address, you find that another transaction has already made the necessary update. Therefore, you skip the update yourself. However, what you did not know was that the transaction that modified the customer's address was still in progress, and that later the transaction rolled back instead of committing. Consequently, the customer's address remains out of date. In this scenario you have made an incorrect decision based on the data provided by a dirty read.

Repeatable and Non-Repeatable Reads

A *repeatable read* happens when a query, executed multiple times in the same transaction, consistently returns the same set of data and ignores the changes made by other uncommitted and committed transactions. Only after the current transaction ends and a new one begins do queries see the effects of other committed transactions.

In contrast, a *non-repeatable read* happens when a query, executed multiple times in the same transaction, produces inconsistent sets of data due to the changes made by other committed transactions.

PHANTOMS   A phantom is a specific type of non-repeatable read. A *phantom* is a row that is inserted and noticed by a query executed multiple times in the same transactions. For example, assume that you issue a query to display all of the orders placed today. Later, in the same transaction, you rerun the query only to find that new orders have been placed since the original execution of your query. Phantoms can cause problems with applications that first identify a set of rows to update and then subsequently perform further analysis before updating individual rows, one by one, in the same transaction.

Isolation Levels

→To deliver predictable behavior for different types of applications that operate in a multi-user database system, the ANSI/ISO standard for SQL defines several different isolation levels of database operation. A transaction's *isolation level* determines whether statements in the transaction can see the results of other uncommitted and/or committed transactions that occur during the course of the transaction. For example, if you execute the same query twice in a transaction, the transaction's isolation level determines whether each execution of the query will return the same set of results and ignore the effects of other uncommitted and/or committed transactions. Figure 9-1 illustrates how the effects of one transaction can interfere with consistency of query results seen by another transaction in a multi-user environment.

In Figure 9-1, Transaction 1 sees the effects of Transaction 2, even though Transaction 2 has not yet committed. More specifically, the second execution of the query in Transaction 1 sees a phantom inserted by Transaction 2.

Each isolation level permits more or less interference among concurrent transactions. There is a direct tradeoff between concurrency and

Transaction I	Transaction 2
SELECT * FROM sales.orders; ID CUST_ID ORDER_DATE SHIP_DATE PAID_DATE S ------- ----------- ------------------ -------------- -------------- --- 1 1 21-OCT-97 F	
	INSERT INTO sales.orders VALUES (2,8,SYSDATE,NULL,NULL, 'F');

SELECT * FROM sales.orders;
 	
ID   CUST_ID ORDER_DATE SHIP_DATE PAID_DATE S
------- ----------- ------------------ -------------- -------------- ----
  1   1 21-OCT-97   F
  2 **8 21-OCT-97** **F**	

...	...

FIGURE 9-1. *Isolation levels determine exactly how concurrent transactions can interfere with one another in a multi-user environment.*

performance as you use different isolation levels. For example, when an isolation level permits more interference, simultaneous transactions experience a higher degree of concurrency and very good performance. Alternatively, when an isolation level permits less interference, simultaneous transactions experience a lower degree of concurrency and are more likely to wait for each other's work to complete. Table 9-1 lists the different types of interference that each isolation level permits.

By default, Oracle transactions operate using the read committed isolation level. When necessary, an application can issue a SET TRANSACTION statement to explicitly start and run a transaction using the serializable isolation level.

```
-- starts a transaction in serializable isolation level
SET TRANSACTION
 ISOLATION LEVEL SERIALIZABLE;
... other transaction statements ...
COMMIT;
-- starts a transaction in read committed isolation level
SET TRANSACTION
 ISOLATION LEVEL READ COMMITTED;
... other transaction statements ...
COMMIT;
```

Additionally, Oracle's multiversioning mechanism—discussed later in this chapter—offers some unique isolation options that are not part of the SQL standard.

Isolation Level	Dirty Reads	Non-Repeatable Reads	Phantoms
Read Uncommitted	✓	✓	✓
Read Committed	✗	✓	✓
Repeatable Read	✗	✗	✓
Serializable	✗	✗	✗

TABLE 9-1. *The read uncommitted, read committed, repeatable read, and serializable ANSI/ISO isolation levels describe acceptable levels of interference among concurrent transactions in a multi-user database system.*

Oracle's Locking Mechanisms

To prevent destructive interference among concurrent transactions, Oracle locks various database resources during normal system processing. Just as a lock on your house's front door prevents someone from entering your house while you are away, a lock on a database resource prevents someone else from using the resource in a way that would interfere with your work. The following sections explain how Oracle locks database resources to prevent destructive interference in a database system.

Automatic and Explicit Locking

By default, a transaction automatically acquires all necessary locks for database resources when you perform a database operation. For example, suppose that you start a new transaction and update a customer's address. Before updating the requested row, Oracle checks to make sure that no other open transaction has a lock on the row. If another transaction holds the lock on the target row, your transaction waits until the other transaction ends and releases its lock on the row. If the row is not locked, Oracle automatically acquires a lock on the row for your transaction. Your transaction maintains the lock on the row until you commit (or roll back) the transaction so that other transactions cannot modify the row and cause a lost update.

Oracle's default locking mechanisms are adequate for most applications. However, there are situations in which a transaction can perform or operate better if it explicitly locks data in anticipation of performing a database operation. For example, suppose that you design a transaction that will update most of the rows in a table. If the table is large, it can be much more efficient to lock the entire table before performing the update rather than allow Oracle's default locking mechanisms to acquire row locks as it updates each row in the table. Additionally, acquiring a table lock first ensures that the complete operation can proceed. For example, during the execution of an UPDATE statement that targets all rows in a table, Oracle might update almost all of the table rows and then hit a locked row, which might require the application to roll back all of the updates to the previous rows. The following sections explain more about the different locking levels that Oracle uses to lock data, such as row- and table-level locks.

Lock Levels

In general, Oracle can lock database resources in one of two lock modes: shared or exclusive. Figure 9-2 and the following sections explain more about shared and exclusive locks.

Shared Locks

A *shared lock* on a database resource gives a transaction shared access to the resource—other transactions can also acquire shared locks on the same resource. For example, both transactions in Figure 9-2 have a shared lock on the same table. This lets each transaction update different rows in the same table at the same time.

Shared locks allow for high degrees of transaction concurrency. However, transactions cannot always acquire shared locks for all types of resources and operations. For example, although each transaction in Figure 9-2 can acquire a shared lock on the same table at the same time, each transaction also acquires exclusive locks for the rows that it updates so that other transactions cannot concurrently update the same rows and cause lost updates.

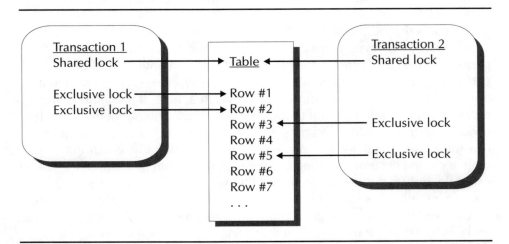

FIGURE 9-2.   *Shared and exclusive locks allow for more and less concurrency among database operations.*

Exclusive Locks

In contrast to a shared lock, an *exclusive lock* on a resource gives a transaction sole access to the resource. For example, in Figure 9-2, after Transaction 1 acquires an exclusive lock on rows 1 and 2, the other transaction cannot acquire a shared or exclusive lock on the same rows until after transaction 1 commits (or rolls back).

Obviously, exclusive locks are more restrictive and establish a lower degree of concurrency than do shared locks. Consequently, Oracle's automatic locking algorithms do not acquire an exclusive lock on a database resource unless an exclusive lock is absolutely necessary to prevent destructive interference with other concurrent transactions.

DML Locks

Oracle automatically acquires locks on the tables and indexes in a database when transactions perform DML operations (INSERTs, UPDATEs, and DELETEs). To provide for high degrees of concurrency and prevent destructive interference, Oracle can acquire both row-level and table-level locks as DML operations proceed. The following sections explain more about row and table locks and when Oracle uses them during transaction processing.

Row Locks

A transaction acquires an exclusive lock on a specific row in a table when the transaction inserts, updates, or deletes the row. By locking data at the row level, multiple concurrent transactions can update the same table and not interfere with each other unless they happen to request access to the same row.

For example, when your transaction contains the following statement, it acquires an exclusive lock on the target row in the CUSTOMERS table:

```
UPDATE sales.customers
  SET ...
  WHERE last_name = 'Ellison' AND first_name = 'Lawrence';
```

If another transaction comes along and attempts to update Larry Ellison's record in the CUSTOMERS table before you commit or roll back your transaction, Oracle notices that you have an exclusive row lock for the row and forces the other transaction to wait.

In anticipation of updates, a transaction can exclusively lock specific rows in a table using a SELECT ... FOR UPDATE statement. For example, the transaction that contains the following statement acquires exclusive row locks for all customer records that have a zip code equal to 95000:

```
SELECT * FROM sales.customers
  WHERE zipcode = 95000
  FOR UPDATE
  NOWAIT;
```

When you issue a SELECT ... FOR UPDATE statement and include the NOWAIT keyword, Oracle returns control to you if it cannot acquire row locks on all target rows immediately. Without the NOWAIT keyword, a SELECT ... FOR UPDATE statement waits until your transaction can acquire row locks on all target rows.

Table Locks

When a transaction acquires a lock on a row, the transaction automatically acquires a lock on the table that contains the row. When a transaction updates one or more rows in a table, a companion lock at the table level is necessary to prevent a conflicting DDL operation that might destructively interfere with the updates to the table rows.

For example, when you update a row in the CUSTOMERS table, your transaction acquires an exclusive lock on the row that you update. Your transaction also acquires a lock on the CUSTOMERS table so that another transaction cannot alter or drop the CUSTOMERS table before you commit your transaction.

Transactions can acquire shared or exclusive locks on tables during transaction processing. In general, a transaction always acquires a shared lock on a table when it performs a basic DML operation such as an INSERT, UPDATE, or DELETE statement. A transaction acquires an exclusive lock on a table only when the transaction contains a LOCK TABLE statement that explicitly requests an exclusive lock. For example, a transaction that contains the following LOCK TABLE statement acquires an exclusive lock on the CUSTOMERS table:

```
LOCK TABLE customers
  IN EXCLUSIVE MODE
  NOWAIT;
```

Again, the NOWAIT keyword returns control to you if Oracle cannot immediately acquire the requested table lock; without the NOWAIT keyword, your transaction waits until the exclusive table lock is available for the CUSTOMERS table.

NOTE
Oracle actually has several different levels of table locks not mentioned here, including row share, row exclusive, share, share row exclusive, and exclusive; each successive type of table lock is more restrictive than the previous. However, to keep the explanations in this chapter relatively simple, we focus on the simple distinction between shared and exclusive locks, and row- and table-level locks.

Deadlocks

A *deadlock is* an interesting situation that occurs when two transactions cannot proceed because each transaction requests a conflicting set of locks. Figure 9-3 illustrates two transactions in a deadlock.

In Figure 9-3, Transaction 1 has an exclusive lock on Row #1 in the table and is waiting for Transaction 2 to release the exclusive lock for Row #2. Meanwhile, Transaction 2 currently has the exclusive lock on Row #2 and is waiting for Transaction 1 to release its lock on Row #1. Consequently, neither transaction can proceed and both transactions wait for each other in a deadlock situation.

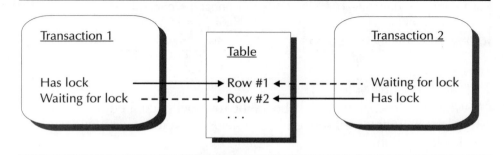

FIGURE 9-3.   *Two transactions in a deadlock*

Deadlocks typically happen because of poor transaction design. For example, consider the following two transactions that are poorly designed. Each transaction contains multiple updates to the PARTS table and ends up in a deadlock because they each lock rows that the other transaction needs.

Transaction 1	Transaction 2
UPDATE sales.parts SET onhand = onhand - 10 WHERE id = 1;	UPDATE sales.parts SET onhand = onhand - 10 WHERE id = 2;
UPDATE sales.parts SET onhand = onhand - 10 WHERE id = 2;	UPDATE sales.parts SET onhand = onhand - 10 WHERE id = 1;
waiting for Transaction 2 to release lock on Part 2	waiting for Transaction 1 to release lock on Part 1

The design problem with the transactions above is that each transaction contains multiple, unrelated updates to the PARTS table. A better transaction design that would avoid deadlocks is to make each update to the PARTS table in a separate transaction, as follows:

Transaction 1	Transaction 2
UPDATE sales.parts SET onhand = onhand - 10 WHERE id = 1;	UPDATE sales.parts SET onhand = onhand - 10 WHERE id = 2;
COMMIT; -- row locks released	COMMIT; -- row locks released
UPDATE sales.parts SET onhand = onhand - 10 WHERE id = 2;	UPDATE sales.parts SET onhand = onhand - 10 WHERE id = 1;
COMMIT; -- row locks released	COMMIT; -- row locks released

With the transaction design above, the row locks acquired by each update are released sooner, which helps to avoid the previous deadlock situation.

DEADLOCK RESOLUTION   When a transaction issues a statement that causes a deadlock, Oracle automatically detects the deadlock and rolls back the statement causing the deadlock.

Lock Escalation

Lock escalation is a technique that many database servers use to reduce the amount of system overhead associated with data locking. For example, consider a database server that locks table data at the row level. However, after a transaction acquires a certain number of row locks on the same table, the database server might convert its many row-level locks into a single table-level lock to conserve the system resources necessary to lock the table's data.

At first glance, lock escalation might seem like an acceptable operation to make more efficient use of server resources. However, lock escalation can be a villain that causes deadlocks. Oracle does not escalate locks and typically experiences a deadlock only because of poor transaction designs.

Queries and Locking

The previous sections in this chapter do not mention the types of locks that Oracle acquires when a transaction issues a query on a table. That's because Oracle does not lock rows or tables when querying data. However, to provide read consistency for queries without locking, Oracle uses a unique multiversioning mechanism to generate repeatable reads and consistent results for transactions. See the section "Multiversioning" later in this chapter for more information about Oracle's multiversioning mechanism.

DDL Locks

The previous sections explain the locks that Oracle automatically uses to protect DML operations such as INSERT, UPDATE, and DELETE statements. Oracle also automatically locks data when you perform various DDL operations using CREATE, ALTER, and DROP statements. The following sections explain when Oracle acquires shared and exclusive DDL locks for database objects.

NOTE
Each DDL operation completes within its own transaction. Therefore, a transaction acquires and holds necessary DDL locks for only as long as it takes to complete the DDL operation itself.

Exclusive DDL Locks

DDL statements that create, alter, or drop a database object require an *exclusive DDL lock* on the target object. For example, when you execute an ALTER TABLE statement to add a new integrity constraint to a table, your transaction acquires an exclusive DDL lock for the table. This way, other users cannot modify or drop the table until after your ALTER statement completes.

Shared DDL Locks

Some DDL statements can acquire *shared DDL locks* on database objects. DDL statements that establish dependencies among database objects typically require shared DDL locks. For example, assume that you create a new package and the package's procedures and functions refer to many different database tables. When you create the package, your transaction acquires an exclusive DDL lock on the package and also acquires shared DDL locks on the referenced tables. The shared DDL locks prevent another transaction from acquiring an exclusive lock on a referenced table to alter or drop the referenced table before Oracle finishes compiling your package. However, the shared locks do not prevent other transactions from also acquiring shared DDL locks on the referenced tables, for example, to create stored procedures that use the tables.

Parse Locks

Oracle uses the shared pool to cache parsed and optimized SQL statements and PL/SQL programs so that users running the same application can experience better throughput. A cached object in the shared pool acquires parse locks on the database objects that it references. A *parse lock* is a unique type of DDL lock that Oracle uses to keep track of dependencies between a shared pool object and the database objects that it references. If a transaction alters or drops a database object while a shared pool object holds a parse lock on the database object, Oracle invalidates the shared pool object. Then, the next time the application issues the SQL statement or PL/SQL program, Oracle knows to reparse and reoptimize the statement to take into account the new version of the referenced database object that has changed.

Internal Latches

The locks that Oracle uses to serialize access to internal system structures are called _latches_. For example, before a transaction can write information to a database instance's redo log buffer, it must acquire the latch to this memory cache. Oracle optimizes database performance by making sure that database operations hold latches for a very short duration, which maintains a high level of database concurrency, even in demanding application environments.

Multiversioning

Earlier in this chapter, you learned about the ANSI/ISO isolation levels that characterize different levels of interference among concurrent transactions. A transaction's isolation level determines whether statements in the transaction can see the results of other uncommitted and committed transactions that occur during the course of the transaction. For example, if you execute the same query twice in a transaction running in repeatable read-isolation level, each query returns the same set of results and ignores the effects of other uncommitted and committed transactions.

No matter which isolation level you choose for a transaction, it is typically desirable that the set of data returned for an individual statement be consistent within itself. In other words, Oracle returns database information that is consistent with the point in time at which you issue a new statement. No matter if the statement is quick or takes a long time to complete, Oracle hides the changes that uncommitted and committed transactions perform after the exact point in time at which you execute the statement.

Oracle can do this, without locking any data, using its unique _multiversioning_ mechanism. Using the system's rollback segments, Oracle can actually generate multiple versions of the database's information to satisfy the requests of concurrent SQL statements, including a mix of queries and DML statements. The following explains how Oracle performs its magic.

System Change Number

Every transaction that commits increments the database's *system change number (SCN)*. For the purposes of this discussion, you can think of an SCN as a unique identifier for a committed transaction. The header of a data block records the SCN of the most recently committed transaction that touched the block. When a query starts, Oracle performs the following operations to produce a read-consistent set of data for the query's return set:

1. At the start of the query, Oracle observes the system's current SCN. To make the rest of this discussion simpler, let's call this the *query SCN*.

2. As Oracle executes the query, it must read data blocks to build the return set of the query. For each data block that it reads, Oracle compares the query SCN to the SCN in the header of the data block, and

   ■ If the SCN in the data block is equal to or older than the query SCN, Oracle can use the data in the block to build the result set of the query, or

   ■ If the SCN in the data block is greater than the query SCN, Oracle reads information from the system's rollback segments to regenerate a version of the data block's information as it existed at the query SCN.

Figure 9-4 illustrates how Oracle uses multiversioning to return a set of information that is consistent with the SCN at the start of the query.

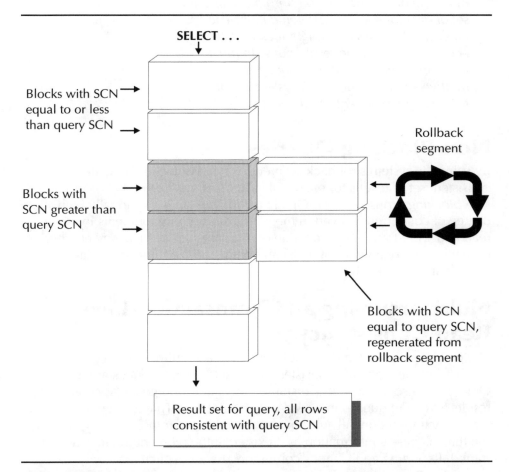

SELECT . . .

Blocks with SCN equal to or less than query SCN

Blocks with SCN greater than query SCN

Rollback segment

Blocks with SCN equal to query SCN, regenerated from rollback segment

Result set for query, all rows consistent with query SCN

FIGURE 9-4.   *Oracle can use information in rollback segments to create a consistent set of data for any SQL statement.*

NOTE
Few database systems other than Oracle use a multiversioning strategy to return a consistent set of data for each SQL statement. Instead, other database systems might lock data to accomplish the same result, but with much less concurrency. Without locking or multiversioning, a database system might return an inconsistent set of results.

Non-Blocking Queries

By using the system's rollback segments instead of locking to generate a consistent set of results for each SQL statement, queries in the system are *non-blocking.* Consequently, Oracle can deliver an exceptionally high degree of concurrency, even in mixed transaction environments in which read and write transactions operate on the same set of data. Any number of readers and one writer of data can operate on the same set of data records simultaneously.

Multiversioning and Transaction-Level Read Consistency

The previous discussion describes how Oracle's multiversioning mechanism can generate consistent result sets for individual statements. Oracle can also use its multiversioning mechanism to generate consistent results across all queries in a read-only transaction. That is, after you start a read-only transaction, all subsequent queries in the transaction consistently see the database's information as it existed at the moment the transaction started. Reporting applications commonly use an explicit read-only transaction to encompass several queries and produce a report with consistent data.

Again, Oracle uses the system's rollback segments to regenerate older versions of data blocks, as necessary. If a read-only transaction is long running in a database that experiences frequent data updates, Oracle must use more and more information in the system's rollback segments to generate the necessary version of the database for the transaction.

To begin a read-only transaction and establish read consistency for all subsequent transaction queries, the first statement in the transaction must be a SET TRANSACTION statement:

```
SET TRANSACTION READ ONLY;
```

Snapshot Too Old Errors

In specific situations, Oracle's multiversioning mechanism might not be able to generate a read-consistent set of data for a statement or transaction. This happens if Oracle writes over information in a rollback segment that a long-running query or read-only transaction subsequently requests to build a set of results. In such cases, your transaction will return an Oracle error called "snapshot too old."

To avoid such errors, the first thing to do is examine the design of your transactions and queries. If read-only transactions are unnecessarily long, simply reduce their size to solve your problem. If you receive "snapshot too old" errors for individual queries, you can create more or larger rollback segments in the system to reduce the likelihood that Oracle will overwrite rollback segment information too early.

Remember, It's All Automatic

If you are new to database systems and Oracle, data locking and multiversioning might seem convoluted and too complicated to understand. However, remember that all of Oracle's concurrency mechanisms have default behaviors that, in most cases, deliver acceptable transaction concurrency and application performance automatically. You have to understand Oracle's concurrency mechanisms only when you want to fine-tune an application or develop an application that delivers specific concurrency characteristics. Otherwise, go ahead and start using Oracle and let it automatically manage transactions that concurrently access your database.

Summary

This chapter has explained the many concurrency mechanisms in Oracle8:

- Multi-user database systems must use concurrency mechanisms to prevent undesirable transaction interference such as lost updates, dirty reads, non-repeatable reads, and phantoms.

- Oracle uses shared and exclusive locks to prevent destructive interference among multiple, concurrent transactions. Oracle's DML locks control access to table and index data when transactions insert, update, and delete rows. Oracle's DDL locks control access to database objects when you create, alter, and drop database objects.

- Oracle's patented multiversioning mechanism uses the system's rollback segments to create consistent result sets for SQL statements and transactions. Because queries use multiversioning and not locks, they are non-blocking and allow for exceptionally high levels of database concurrency.

CHAPTER 10

Database Protection

hen you bet your business on some software, it better have the capability to protect your valuable data from any type of problem—from simple system crashes that are the result of unexpected power outages, to more serious problems such as hard-disk failures. This chapter explains the sophisticated database backup and recovery mechanisms of Oracle that you can use to protect and repair your databases. Topics in this chapter include:

- Possible failures to prepare for
- Oracle's Recovery Manager utility
- The transaction log
- Database backups
- Database recovery

Different Types of Problems

Before you begin learning about Oracle's database protection mechanisms, you should have a general idea of the types of problems that can adversely affect your database system. Knowing what types of problems are possible will help you to better protect your Oracle databases from an unfortunate catastrophe.

System and Server Crashes

Perhaps the most common type of problem that affects the availability of computer systems are crashes. A *crash* is the sudden failure of the system in question. Unexpected power failures, software bugs, and operating system process failures are inevitable problems that commonly cause crashes. For example, a bug in your computer's operating system might cause an Oracle background process to suddenly fail, which, in turn, causes an Oracle database server to crash (this is commonly called a database *instance crash*).

In general, Oracle instance crashes do not damage physical database structures permanently. The primary problem with an instance crash is that all of the work and data in the instance's memory at the time of the crash is lost unless the data was written to disk. For example, when an Oracle database instance crashes, all of the data in the instance's buffer cache that was not yet written back to the data files is lost forever. However, this isn't a cause for alarm—later in this chapter you'll see how the database's transaction log contains data on disk that can recover all committed work lost during a simple instance crash.

File Loss from User Error, Corruption, or Disk Failure

The loss of an important database file due to operator error, file corruption, or a disk failure is a serious problem that you must be prepared for, even though it might never occur. For example, let's say you're working overtime, you're tired, and you accidentally delete a data file. You won't be able to recover from this user error unless you are ready.

■ To restore the lost data file, you must have a database backup that contains the deleted data file.

■ To recover all work committed since the backup was taken, you must have the necessary transaction log groups.

→ Oracle's database backup and recovery mechanisms include all that you need to completely protect and recover your database from any type of file loss.

Site Disaster

A company that uses Oracle to run its entire business might have particularly strict requirements for the protection of its data. Such requirements often include contingency plans to prepare for total site disasters that result from earthquakes, fires, and other natural or unnatural catastrophes. Later in this chapter you'll see how Oracle's standby database feature can provide the necessary protection.

Overview of Database Protection Mechanisms

Before explaining the many database protection features of Oracle that you'll learn about in this chapter, let's get a brief look at them and understand how they function together to protect an Oracle database.

Figure 10-1 introduces the primary database protection features: database backups and the transaction log.

- Regular and frequent *database backups* make it possible to restore files that are lost due to user error, file corruption, or disk failures.

- The database's *transaction log* is a group of operating system files that record the database changes made by committed transactions. During the commit of a transaction, Oracle writes enough information in the transaction log to redo its work should the database require recovery.

An Example Backup and Recovery Scenario

With a database backup and the transaction log, Oracle can recover the database from all types of problems, even serious problems such as a disk crash. To better understand the function of database backups and the

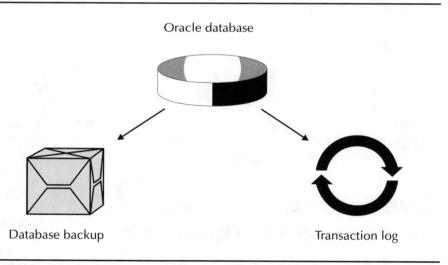

Oracle database

Database backup

Transaction log

FIGURE 10-1. *Database backups and the transaction log are the primary features of Oracle that enable you to recover a database from problems.*

transaction log, let's study a brief example of how you can protect and recover an Oracle database from a disk failure:

■ Every night, you back up your Oracle database. Among other files, each database backup includes a backup of all the database's data files.

■ One day, a disk crashes that contains one of the database's data files. Consequently, a part of the database is unavailable and needs recovery. Although it is not necessary, you shut down the database so that you can perform the recovery.

■ First, you address the disk with the problem. Unfortunately, you have a serious disk failure and must replace the broken drive with a new drive.

■ Next, you use the most recent database backup to restore the lost data file to the replacement disk drive. The restored version of the data file is missing the work of transactions that committed after the backup was taken.

■ Finally, you perform database recovery. During database recovery, Oracle reads the transaction log to "redo" (apply) the work of past committed transactions to the restored data file, which makes the data file current.

■ After completing database recovery, you open the database and make it available to applications.

This simplified example gives you a general understanding of how you will use the database's transaction log (and, in the case of a disk failure, also use database backups) to perform database recovery. With this perspective in mind, read the following sections of this chapter to learn more about the protective mechanisms of Oracle.

Introduction to Recovery Manager

With Oracle8, you perform most database backup and recovery tasks using a new administration utility, Recovery Manager. *Recovery Manager* is a client-side utility that lets you configure the backup and recovery of multiple Oracle databases. Figure 10-2 illustrates Recovery Manager.

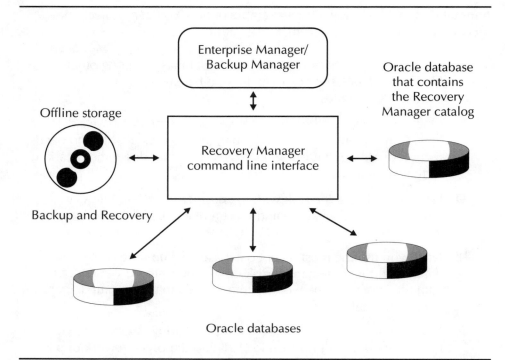

FIGURE 10-2.   *Recovery Manager is a client-side utility that you can use to back up and recover multiple Oracle databases.*

Recovery Manager has many features to make your database protection strategy comprehensive, automated, and relatively easy to perform. In general, you can use Recovery Manager to back up an Oracle database. If the database subsequently requires a recovery operation, you use Recovery Manager to restore all damaged database files and then perform the necessary database recovery operation.

The Recovery Catalog
The backup and recovery mechanisms used by previous versions of Oracle are still available with Oracle8. However, Recovery Manager greatly simplifies and automates the process of database backup and recovery by

automatically keeping track of backup information in a recovery catalog. A *recovery catalog* is a set of database tables and views that Recovery Manager uses to record specific information about each database backup that you perform. When a database requires recovery, Recovery Manager uses information in its catalog to recover the damaged database with available backups and an appropriate recovery action.

The catalog that keeps track of a database's backup information must always be available to Recovery Manager. This way, if the database is damaged, Recovery Manager can read the catalog to direct recovery of the damaged database. To ensure the availability of recovery information for a database, you do not create the Recovery Manager catalog in the same database that you are trying to protect. Instead, you create a recovery catalog in an Oracle database and then use Recovery Manager and this catalog to manage the protection of one or more remote Oracle databases that are not at the same physical location as the catalog (see Figure 10-2). When a database becomes damaged, the recovery catalog that contains backup information about the database is still intact and available to Recovery Manager.

When you operate a single Oracle database and cannot maintain a recovery catalog separate from the database that you are trying to protect, you can use Recovery Manager in a special operational mode. In this mode, Recovery Manager logs all of the recovery information about a database in the database's control file. However, not all of the functionality of Recovery Manager is available when you use this special operational mode. For example, you cannot perform point-in-time recovery or store scripts of Recovery Manager commands when you use the database's control file rather than a complete recovery catalog.

The Recovery Manager Command Line Interface

The underlying interface of the Recovery Manager utility is available on every operating system as a command language interpreter (CLI) that accepts simple commands. For example, the following sequence of Recovery Manager commands connects to the target SALES database for a backup operation, specifies the location of the recovery catalog in the HQ database, registers the SALES database in the recovery catalog at the HQ database, and then backs up the entire SALES database using two different tapes.

```
TARGET "system/manager@sales" RCVCAT "rman/rman@hq";

REGISTER DATABASE;

CREATE JOB bkup_full_01 {
 ALLOCATE CHANNEL t1 NAME "tape1";
 ALLOCATE CHANNEL t2 NAME "tape2";
 BACKUP FULL;
}

EXECUTE JOB bkup_full_01;
```

You can automate the execution of repetitive Recovery Manager commands by assembling and running stored scripts. In the context of Recovery Manager, a *script* is a series of Recovery Manager commands. Rather than store scripts in a computer's file system as a file, Recovery Manager stores scripts in the recovery catalog so that they are available to any administrator working with Recovery Manager. For example, you might create and save a script of Recovery Manager commands that you always use to back up your database. You can manually run the script when you want to perform a database backup operation, or automate the execution of the script with a job so that Recovery Manager runs the script for you.

Backup Manager—A Graphical User Interface to Recovery Manager

On most operating systems, you might never see the Recovery Manager command line interface or have to enter a single Recovery Manager command. Instead, you can use a graphical user interface to Recovery Manager such as the Enterprise Manager-Backup Manager. Third-party utilities might also use Recovery Manager to perform database backup and recovery mechanisms.

Now that you have a general understanding of Recovery Manager, you can begin learning about the specific features of Oracle that you use to protect a database from loss of data. The next section explains the database's transaction log.

The Transaction Log or Redo Log

An Oracle database's *transaction log*, also called the *redo log*, is an important component of the database that protects the work of all committed transactions. The job of the transaction log is to record immediately the changes made by committed transactions. Should the database need recovery from an instance crash, disk failure, or some other type of problem, Oracle reads the transaction log during an appropriate recovery operation to "redo" the work of all committed transactions that are missing from the database.

Transaction Log Structure

The transaction log of a database is a group of operating system files on the host computer. As Figure 10-3 illustrates, a database's transaction log is made up of two or more log groups. Together, this set of log groups is called the *online transaction log*.

Each *log group* is a set of one or more identical operating system files that records the log entries of committed transactions. During server startup, LGWR chooses one of the groups in the transaction log and then

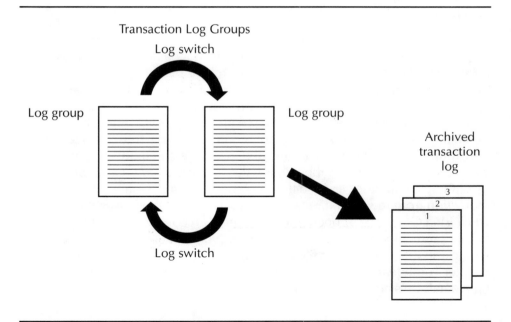

FIGURE 10-3. *An Oracle database's transaction log contains two or more log groups.*

uses the group to begin recording log entries. The log group being written to by LGWR at any given time is the *current log group.* A log group has a static size and eventually fills with information. Once LGWR fills the current log group, Oracle performs a *log switch.* During a log switch, Oracle closes the current log group, opens the next log group, and begins writing log entries to the new current log group.

NOTE

To optimize the logging of transaction redo entries, Oracle sometimes allows LGWR to write an open transaction's redo entries in anticipation of a commit. Therefore, at any given time, the transaction log might contain a small number of changes to the database made by uncommitted transactions. However, Oracle notes these redo entries appropriately so that if database recovery is necessary, the server automatically clears the uncommitted changes from the database.

To enable Oracle to recover from damage to a database's data files, you must configure the server to permanently archive log groups after they fill. Operating in this mode after a log switch, the archiver (ARCH) background server process archives the previous current group as a file on a disk. Oracle names each archived log group with a unique *log sequence number,* which serves as a permanent record of the log entries written to the group. The sequence of log groups that Oracle continuously generates by archiving log groups as they fill is called the *archived transaction log.* Most Oracle databases archive transaction log groups to offer full protection from media failures—you can refer to this mode as either *ARCHIVELOG mode* or operating with "*media recovery enabled.*" To further protect the archived transaction log, you can use Recovery Manager to back up the archived log files to offline storage such as tape. Later in this chapter you'll learn more about Recovery Manager and how you can back up a database's archived transaction log.

NOTE
When you choose not to archive log groups, you can boost server performance a small degree. However, the consequences can be significant because Oracle can protect your database from simple system crashes only and not from more serious problems such as disk failures.

After Oracle fills the final log group in the transaction log, LGWR performs a log switch back to the first log group, and then recycles through the log groups in the same order as before. When Oracle reuses a log group to record log entries, LGWR overwrites the previous entries in the group. If you have configured your server to archive log groups after they fill, the log entries are preserved as part of the database's archived transaction log. By cyclically using and reusing the log groups in the database's transaction log, an Oracle database server can continuously record transaction log entries in a relatively small, predefined amount of disk space.

Log Members and Fault-Tolerance
The transaction log is a critical component in Oracle's database protection scheme. To prevent an isolated disk failure from damaging the log groups in the transaction log, you can *mirror* (or multiplex) the transaction log by creating log groups with multiple members (files) that reside on different disks. Figure 10-4 shows a mirrored transaction log with log groups that contain multiple members.

As Figure 10-4 shows, all members of a log group are replicas—as LGWR writes to a log group that has multiple members, the server process writes to all members concurrently. Should one of the members in the current log group become damaged due to a disk failure or user error, LGWR can continue to write to the log group as long as one or more of the members are available.

When you operate your database server to archive filled log groups, ARCH reads one or more of the members in a mirrored log group to create an archived copy of the group. To protect the archived transaction log from single points of failure, you can also mirror the archived transaction log. That is, you can configure ARCH to write two or more replicas of each filled log group to distinct offline archive areas.

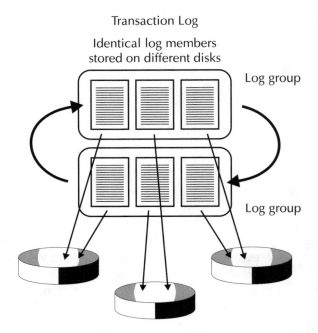

Transaction Log

FIGURE 10-4. *To protect a transaction log from an isolated disk failure, you can create log groups with multiple members on different disks.*

Checkpoints

Periodically, Oracle performs a checkpoint. During a *checkpoint*, DBWR writes all modified data blocks in the instance's buffer cache back to the data files that contain those blocks. The purpose of a checkpoint is to establish mileposts of transaction consistency on disk. After performing a checkpoint, Oracle knows that the changes made by all committed transactions have been written to the database's data files. Therefore, a checkpoint indicates how much of the transaction log's redo entries Oracle must apply if a simple server crash occurs and database recovery is necessary.

Oracle performs checkpoints at different times and at different levels. For example, Oracle performs a *database checkpoint* during each log switch. During a database checkpoint, DBWR writes all modified data blocks in the buffer cache back to all of the database's data files. In contrast, when you take a tablespace offline, Oracle performs a *tablespace checkpoint*. During a tablespace checkpoint, DBWR writes the modified data blocks in the buffer cache that correspond to data files of the tablespace only.

Protect the Database Control File

The information in a database's control file describes the physical structure of the database. Oracle also uses information in the database's control file about checkpoints and transaction logging information to manage various types of database recovery operations. New in Oracle8, the server can also use a database's control file to record information about database backups. Considering these important functions, it's no wonder that a database cannot function properly without its control file.

To protect a database's control file and database availability from disk failures, you should always mirror the database's control file to multiple locations just like you do with the log groups in a database's online transaction log. When you mirror a database's control file to multiple locations, Oracle updates every copy of the control file at the same time. If one copy of the control file becomes inaccessible due to a disk I/O problem or failure, other copies of the control file remain available and permit database processing to continue without interruption.

Database Backups

Database backups are an important part of a comprehensive database protection strategy. A *database backup* is a collection of all of the files that comprise the database. If you damage or lose a file that is part of a database, you can extract a copy of the lost file from a database backup to restore the file in the database.

To back up an Oracle8 database, you can use Recovery Manager or a GUI to Recovery Manager such as Enterprise Manager-Backup Manager. Recovery Manager has many different options that you can use to back up an Oracle database. Table 10-1 and the next few sections introduce each type of database backup.

Type of Backup	Description
Database Backup (Whole Database Backup)	Includes all data files of all tablespaces, as well as the database's control file. *This is the most common type of backup that you perform to protect a database.*
Open Database Backup (Hot Database Backup) (Inconsistent Database Backup)	Database backup taken while the database is open and operational. Because the data in the backup does not correspond to any single transaction-consistent time point, the backup is said to be *inconsistent.*
Closed Database Backup (Cold Database Backup) (Consistent Database Backup)	Database backup taken after you shut down the database cleanly (that is, after a planned shutdown that completes normally). Because the data in the backup corresponds to a transaction-consistent time point, the backup is said to be *consistent.*
Tablespace Backup	Includes all data files of a tablespace.
Online Tablespace Backup (Hot Tablespace Backup) (Inconsistent Tablespace Backup)	Tablespace backup taken while the database is open and the tablespace is online. Online tablespace backups are also called *hot backups* or *inconsistent tablespace backups.*
Offline Tablespace Backup (Consistent Tablespace Backup)	Tablespace backup taken while the database is open but the tablespace is offline. If you take a tablespace offline cleanly, a subsequent offline backup of the tablespace is considered *consistent.*
Data File Backup (Data File Copy)	Backup of a single data file.
Backup Set (Recovery Manager)	Made with Recovery Manager, a backup set contains multiple database files of the same type—either data files or archived log groups, but not both in the same set. A backup set can also contain a backup of the database's control file.

TABLE 10-1.   *Summary of Oracle Backup Terminology*

Type of Backup	Description
Full Backup Set (Recovery Manager)	Made with Recovery Manager, a full data file backup set includes all blocks of all data files in the backup set.
Incremental Backup Set (Recovery Manager)	Made with Recovery Manager, an incremental data file backup set includes just the blocks of data files that have been modified since the previous backup of the set.
Logical Backup (Export/Import)	Made with the Export utility, a logical backup can include all schema objects in the database, all the schema objects in a particular schema, or a single table.

TABLE 10-1. *Summary of Oracle Backup Terminology* (continued)

Whole Database Backups

A *database backup*, or *whole database backup*, includes a copy of all database data files and the database's control file. A database backup is common type of backup that you perform to protect an Oracle database. With Oracle, you can make two different types of database backups: an open database backup and a closed database backup.

Open Database Backups

An *open database backup*, also called a *hot database backup*, is a database backup that you perform while the database is open and operational. Open database backups are useful for environments in which high availability is required by one or more applications. You cannot perform an open database backup unless you always operate your database with media recovery enabled (that is, in ARCHIVELOG mode).

Because the data in the data files of an open database backup are being modified by transactions throughout the course of the backup, the backup is said to be *inconsistent* or *fuzzy*. That is, there is not a single transaction-consistent time point to which all data blocks correspond. Don't worry, though. After restoring a data file from an inconsistent database backup, Oracle's recovery mechanism regenerates missing transactions so that all data blocks in the file are in a transaction-consistent state that corresponds with all other data blocks in the database.

Closed Database Backups

A *closed database backup* is a database backup that you perform after a planned database shutdown. A closed database backup is an option for systems where high availability is not critical. A closed database backup is also the **only** option for databases that operate without media recovery enabled (that is, in NOARCHIVELOG mode).

To perform a closed database backup, the preceding shutdown of the database must complete normally—you cannot perform a closed database backup after a system crash or an abnormal shutdown. During a normal database shutdown, Oracle rolls back any open transactions, performs a database checkpoint, and then closes the database's data files and control file. All files that comprise the database are in a transaction-consistent state with one another. Therefore, a closed database backup is often called a *consistent* database backup.

Tablespace Backups

Oracle also lets you back up individual tablespaces in a database. A *tablespace backup* is a backup of all the data files that comprise the tablespace. Tablespace backups are useful when you want to back up particular divisions of a database that applications modify more frequently than others.

When you operate with media recovery enabled, you can perform two different types of tablespace backups: online tablespace backups and offline tablespace backups.

Online Tablespace Backups

An *online tablespace backup*, also called a *hot tablespace backup*, is a tablespace backup that you perform while the database is open and the tablespace is online. Because the data in the tablespace can be modified as the backup progresses, the backup is said to be inconsistent.

Just as with open database backups, an online tablespace backup is useful when high availability is a must. Rather than shutting down the database or taking a tablespace offline for a backup, you simply back up the tablespace while applications are using it.

Offline Tablespace Backups

An *offline tablespace backup* is a tablespace backup that you perform while the database is open but the tablespace is offline. If you take a tablespace offline normally (that is, Oracle can successfully perform a tablespace checkpoint and close all associated data files), the backup data generated from an offline tablespace backup is consistent.

Recovery Manager Backup Concepts

Recovery Manager is the utility that you use to perform most of the work to protect an Oracle database. When using Recovery Manager or one of the graphical user interfaces to the Recovery Manager CLI, you can perform open and closed database backups, online and offline tablespace backups, and more. The following sections explain some additional concepts and terms to understand before working with Recovery Manager.

Backup Sets

A *backup set* is a set of backup files that are all of the same type. For example, a *data file backup set* contains one or more of the data files that comprise a database. Recovery Manager also lets you make an *archive log backup set*, which contains a number of the database's archived log groups. A data file or archived log backup set can also contain a backup of the database's control file. Regardless of the file type, you can refer to an individual file in a backup set as a *backup piece*.

When Recovery Manager creates a backup set, the data blocks of all the files in the set are interspersed together to create one large storage unit that is the backup set. Additionally, to reduce the total size of a data file backup set, Recovery Manager does not write data blocks in the set that have never contained data in the database (for example, new blocks in a new data file)—in a sense, this compresses the size of the data file backup set. Considering these attributes of a backup set, when a database recovery operation is necessary and a file has been damaged, you must first use Recovery Manager to extract and restore a copy of the lost file from the proper backup set.

Recovery Manager can write a backup set as a file in the server's file system on disk. After performing a backup, you can manually copy or move the backup set to tape for permanent, offline storage. Alternatively, if your hardware vendor offers a media management library or subsystem to

interface with Oracle and Recovery Manager, you can have Recovery
Manager write backup sets directly to other types of storage devices
such as a tapes.

One advantage of organizing and using backup sets is that they enable
you to complete your database backups as quickly as possible. When you
request Recovery Manager to create a backup set, Recovery Manager can
uses Oracle's parallel processing mechanisms to complete the backup
process as quickly as possible. By carefully planning the size of each
backup set, you can continuously stream the data of the backup set to back
up storage for maximum throughput. And if you are performing a backup
while the database is open, correctly configured backup sets produce
minimal impact on your system performance during the backup.

Full and Incremental Data File Backup Sets

When you back up the data files of a database or tablespace with Recovery
Manager, you can perform either a full backup or an incremental backup. A
full backup of a data file backup set includes all data blocks of all data files
in the backup set. A full backup is also called a *level 0 backup*. In contrast,
an *incremental backup* of a data file backup set includes just the blocks of
data files in the backup set that have been modified since the previous
backup of the set. The advantage of incremental backups is that it typically
takes less time to back up a subset of a backup set's data rather than the
entire backup set.

When you use incremental backups, you can set the *level* of the
incremental backup. In general, a level *n* backup includes the blocks of the
backup set that have been modified since the most recent level *n* backup or
less. For example, suppose you back up a data file backup set on Sunday
with a level 0 backup (a full backup).

- On Monday, you perform a level 2 backup of the data file backup
  set. The backup set includes only the blocks that have changed
  since the level 0 backup on Sunday.

- On Tuesday, you perform another level 2 backup of the data file
  backup set. The backup set includes only the blocks that changed
  since the level 2 backup on Monday.

- On Wednesday, you perform a level 1 backup of the data file backup set. The backup set includes only the blocks that have changed since the level 0 backup on Sunday.

- On Thursday, you perform a level 2 backup of the data file backup set. The backup set includes only the blocks that have changed since the level 1 backup on Wednesday.

- On Friday, you perform another level 2 backup of the data file backup set. The backup set includes only the blocks that changes since the level 2 backup on Thursday.

- On Saturday, you perform a level 1 backup of the data file backup set. The backup set includes only the blocks that have changed since the level 1 backup on Wednesday.

- On Sunday, you perform a level 0 backup of the data file backup set, and so on.

As this simple example demonstrates, most database backup strategies include a mix of both full and incremental data file backup sets. Oracle allows you to make incremental backups of a data file backup set up to eight levels deep.

Image Copies
You can also back up parts of a database by using Recovery Manager to create image copies. An *image copy* is a direct copy of a single data file, archived log group, or the database's control file. Image copies differ from backup sets in several ways:

- You can make an image copy of a file on a disk only—for example, you cannot make an image copy on a tape directly.

- An image copy of a file is an exact block-by-block copy of the file. For example, Recovery Manager does not compress an image copy of a data file by eliminating unused data blocks in the file.

■ Because an image copy is a file that directly corresponds with a database file, you do not need to extract or restore image copies from backup sets before performing database recovery. Using Recovery Manager, you can simply "switch" the location of the damaged file to the location of a corresponding image copy and then perform database recovery to make the file current. Because a restore operation is not necessary with an image copy, recovery is quicker—this is useful for applications that require high-availability.

Channels

When Recovery Manager performs a database backup, image copy, restore, or recovery operation, it allocates at least one channel for the task. A Recovery Manager *channel* is two things: a connection to the database that is the target of the operation, and a specification of the name and type of I/O device to use for the operation. For example, the following Recovery Manager command allocates two channels for a full database backup:

```
CREATE JOB bkup_full_01 {
    ALLOCATE CHANNEL t1 NAME "tape1";
    ALLOCATE CHANNEL t2 NAME "tape2";
 BACKUP FULL;
}
```

When you specify more than one channel for a Recovery Manager operation such as a backup, image copy, file restore, or recovery, Recovery Manager automatically parallelizes the operation to complete the job quickly.

Backup Tags

When you create a backup set or an image copy, you can assign it a *tag*, which is a logical name. Recovery Manager automatically associates the backup set or image copy with its tag in the recovery catalog. You can use a tag when you need to perform a recovery or want to overwrite the previous version of a backup set or image copy with a new one.

Corrupt Data File Blocks

When Recovery Manager performs the backup of a data file, it automatically searches the file for corrupt data file blocks. By default,

Recovery Manager does not tolerate any corrupt data file blocks in a backup. However, by altering some parameters for a backup, Recovery Manager can back up a file with corrupt blocks and log the address and the type of corruption in the control file. Using a data dictionary view, you can review backups for corrupt blocks. After finding corrupt blocks in a data file backup, you can verify the data file itself and then perform the backup again.

Logical Database Backups

To supplement the physical, block-by-block backups of a database's data files, archived log groups, and the control file that you make with Recovery Manager, you can make logical backups of an Oracle database's data. A *logical backup* is a backup of database information that corresponds to the specific schemas and schema objects in the database (for example, tables). To make and use logical database backups, you use the Oracle utilities Export and Import.

The Export Utility

Using Oracle's *Export* utility, you can logically back up all or a subset of data in an Oracle database. For example, Export lets you selectively export:

- All objects in the database
- The objects in a specific schema
- A single table

You can export database information while the database is open and in use. Export ensures that the export data for an individual table is consistent with itself. However, when you export a schema or the entire database while the database is open and being modified, the export data that you generate is not necessarily consistent—if all export data must be consistent, you must take additional measures to ensure that an Export file is a transaction-consistent snapshot of the data that you are exporting. This means that applications and their transactions cannot make any changes to the database data that you are exporting until after the export operation completes. This requirement alone can severely impact database concurrence.

The Import Utility

To recover lost data from an Export file, you use the companion Oracle utility, *Import*. With Import, you can read an Export file to restore specific database tables, schemas, or an entire database.

The Proper Use of Export and Import

Oracle's Export and Import utilities should never be your first or complete choice to protect an Oracle database. That's because an export of a database, schema, or table can never guarantee complete recovery from a database failure. It is very important to understand that after you import data from an Export file, there is no recovery process to complete—the work of all committed transactions that completed after you performed the export is lost forever. For these reasons, use database exports only as a supplement to true database backups and transaction logging.

Other Uses for Export/Import

Besides using Export and Import for supplemental database protection, you can use the utilities to move data from one database to another. For example, when you configure different databases in an Oracle distributed database system to replicate large amounts of data using Oracle's data replication features, you can use the Export and Import utilities to initially transfer data between sites during configuration. See Chapter 11 for more information about Oracle's distributed database and data replication features.

Database Recovery

Hopefully, your database will never have a problem and you will never have to use the transaction log and database backups to recover lost work. However, if you do, rest assured that Oracle has the necessary mechanisms to complete the job. The following sections explain Oracle's database recovery mechanisms and options that you have to repair a damaged database.

Roll-Forward and Roll-Back Recovery Stages

All types of database recovery include two stages: roll-forward and roll-back. Figure 10-5 illustrates what happens during the roll-forward and roll-back recovery stages.

During the *roll-forward recovery*, Recovery Manager applies the necessary transaction log groups to "redo" all committed transactions not present in the current data files of the database. When you are recovering from a simple system crash, all necessary log entries are present in the current set of online transaction log groups. After more serious damage

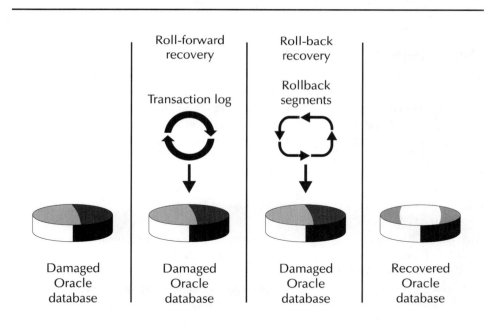

FIGURE 10-5. *A database recovery includes two stages: roll-forward and roll-back.*

such as a disk failure, you might need to use backup data files and archived log groups to complete roll-forward recovery.

After roll-forward recovery, Oracle must perform roll-back recovery. During *roll-back recovery*, Oracle uses information in the database's rollback segments to "undo" the database changes made by any transactions that were open (uncommitted) when the system crashed. After roll-back recovery completes, the database contains all work as of the last committed transaction before the problem that necessitated the recovery.

Now that you have a general understanding of how Oracle performs all database recovery operations, Table 10-2 and the following sections explain more specifically the different types of database recovery situations.

Type of Recovery	Description
Crash Recovery	The automatic recovery operation that Oracle performs to recover from a simple system crash.
Media Recovery (Disk Failure Recovery)	A recovery operation that is necessary after one or more of a database's data files are lost. Before performing a media recovery, you typically have to restore one or more lost data files from a backup set or switch to available image copies.
Complete Recovery (Database, Tablespace, or Data File Recovery)	A recovery operation that recovers the work of all committed transactions.
Incomplete Recovery (Point-In-Time, Cancel-Based, or Change-Based Recovery)	A recovery operation that recovers only some of the work of committed transactions.
Database Recovery (Closed Database Recovery)	A database recovery is a type of complete recovery that recovers lost work in all data files of the database. You perform a database recovery while the database is mounted but closed.

TABLE 10-2. *Summary of Oracle's Recovery Options*

Type of Recovery	Description
Tablespace Recovery (Open Database Recovery)	A tablespace recovery is a type of complete recovery that recovers lost work in all data files of a specific tablespace. You can perform a tablespace recovery while the database is open and the damaged tablespace is offline, or while the database is mounted but closed.
Data File Recovery (Open Database Recovery)	A data file recovery is a type of complete recovery that recovers lost work in a specific data file. You can perform a data file recovery while the database is open and the damaged tablespace is offline, or while the database is mounted but closed.
Time-Based Recovery (Point-in-Time Recovery)	A time-based recovery is a type of incomplete recovery that recovers the work of committed transactions in a database up to a specific point in time (for example, up to Monday at 8:05 AM, just before a user dropped an important table).
Change-Based Recovery	A change-based recovery is a type of incomplete recovery that recovers the work of committed transactions in a database up to a specific system change number (SCN).
Cancel-Based Recovery	A cancel-based recovery is a type of incomplete recovery that recovers the work of committed transactions in a database up to the application of a specific log group.

TABLE 10-2.   *Summary of Oracle's Recovery Options* (continued)

Crash Recovery

Unfortunately, power failures and software problems are common events that can cause an Oracle database server to crash unexpectedly. When a system crash happens, your Oracle database server does not shut down cleanly. More specifically, at the time of the crash, the server might be managing many open transactions that have modified database information. Additionally, during a system crash, Oracle does not have time to perform a database checkpoint to make sure that all modified data blocks in the server's buffer cache are written back to the database's data files safely. Considering these side effects of a system crash, it's likely that the data in the data files of the database are inconsistent and missing some changes made by committed transactions—the database's transaction log contains the only permanent records of some committed transactions. Database recovery is thus necessary.

After a system crash, Oracle automatically performs crash recovery as part of the subsequent server startup. To perform *crash recovery*, Oracle uses the redo entries in the online transaction log to perform roll-forward recovery on the existing, intact data files of the database (by definition, a system crash does not permanently damage any of the database's data files). After performing the roll-back recovery stage, crash recovery is complete and Oracle automatically opens the database for general use. Although it might take longer to start up Oracle after a system crash, crash recovery is completely transparent and happens without any work on your part.

Media Recovery— Recovery from File Damage

After a disk failure or a user error causes the loss of one or more of a database's data files, you must perform a *media recovery* operation. During a typical media recovery, you must perform the following steps:

1. Fix all hardware problems.

2. Restore lost data files.

3. Make available the transaction log groups necessary to perform recovery.

4. Perform an appropriate media recovery operation.

The following sections explain each step in more detail.

NOTE
Recovery from the loss of a data file is not possible unless you always operate the database with media recovery enabled (that is, in ARCHIVELOG mode). When you choose to operate the database with media recovery disabled (that is, you choose not to archive filled transaction log groups), database recovery is not possible from media failures. Your only option is to perform a restore operation using the most recent closed database backup. Understand that if this is the case, the work of all committed transactions performed since the backup is lost forever.

Fix Hardware Problems

After you lose one or more data files because of a hardware failure, you should fix the hardware problem if it might prevent the server from operating properly in the future. For example, if a disk drive crashes and you want to continue to use the drive for the database, you should either fix or replace the drive before performing recovery.

Restore Lost Data Files

Before you can recover a lost file, there must be an intact version of the file in place to recover. When a database's data files are lost because of a hardware failure or a user error, you must restore copies of all damaged data files. You can use Recovery Manager and backup set or image copies to restore lost data files.

■ Using Recovery Manager, you can extract and restore a copy of a lost data file from available data file backup sets. Recovery Manager automatically uses information in the recovery catalog to restore files from the most recent full backup, and then successively from subsequent incremental backups, if available.

■ When an image copy of a damaged data file is currently available on disk, you can use Recovery Manager to perform a file switch. When Recovery Manager performs a *switch*, it updates the database's control file so that the damaged data file's pointer is switched from the damaged data file to the intact image copy of the file.

Mount Necessary Archived Log Groups

After you restore a data file from a backup set or switch to an image copy, Oracle must recover the file by performing roll-forward and roll-back recovery. Depending on how long ago the backup of the data file was made and how much work has been done since the backup, roll-forward recovery of the restored data file might require a significant amount of redo entries from the database's transaction log. Therefore, you must ensure that all of the archived log groups necessary to compete recovery of the damaged data file are available to Recovery Manager. To meet this requirement, Recovery Manager can use information in the recovery catalog to restore archived log files from backup sets before starting recovery.

Perform Recovery with Recovery Manager

After you prepare for recovery from media failure by fixing hardware and restoring necessary data files and archived log groups, you can start an appropriate database recovery operation using Recovery Manager. Recovery Manager automatically uses the information in the recovery catalog (or control file) to carry out the stages of database recovery and fix your damaged database. The following sections explain several different type of media recovery operations.

Complete Recovery

A *complete recovery* operation is one that recovers the work of all committed transactions. Complete recovery operations, including database recovery, tablespace recovery, and data file recovery, are the most typical types of recovery that you perform when a problem damages a database.

Database Recovery

The simplest way to recover all lost work in a database using only one operation is to use Recovery Manager to perform a database recovery. A *database recovery* is a type of complete recovery that recovers lost work in all data files of the database. Recovery Manager identifies damaged data files and automatically recovers them using information in the recovery catalog, available data file backup sets, and the database's transaction log.

A database recovery is appropriate when many data files of the database require recovery and the database can be unavailable during the recovery operation. To perform a database recovery, the database is mounted but closed.

Tablespace Recovery

When selected portions of a database have been damaged and high availability is a requirement, consider using tablespace recovery. A *tablespace recovery* is a type of complete recovery that recovers lost work in all data files of a specific tablespace. You can use Recovery Manager to perform a tablespace recovery while the database is open and the damaged tablespace is offline, or while the database is mounted but closed.

NOTE
If a problem damages any data file of the SYSTEM tablespace, the database cannot operate properly. Therefore, you must shut down the database after such a failure; you cannot perform tablespace recovery of the SYSTEM tablespace while the database is open.

Data File Recovery

When a single data file has been damaged, consider using a data file recovery. A data file recovery is a type of complete recovery that recovers lost work in a specific data file. You can use Recovery Manager to perform a data file recovery while the database is open and the damaged tablespace is offline, or while the database is mounted but closed.

NOTE
You cannot recover a damaged data file of the SYSTEM tablespace while the database is open.

Incomplete Recovery

In most situations, Recovery Manager applies all available transaction log groups to perform a complete database recovery (for example, with database, tablespace, or data file recovery). In rare circumstances, you might consider performing an incomplete recovery operation. When you perform an incomplete recovery, Oracle recovers only some of the work of committed transactions by applying a limited amount of the redo entries in the database's transaction log.

For example, assume that on Monday at 8:06 AM, you accidentally drop an important database table—no other damage has been done to the database. If you have a recent Export file that contains the table, you can import the table to recover nicely from this problem; however, luck would have it that you do not use Export to perform supplemental database backups. Even so, you can still recover the lost table by performing an incomplete recovery operation. For example, you might restore the entire database from the most recent backup to a different computer and then perform a point-in-time recovery up to the time 8:05 AM. Then, you can export the table and import it back into the production database to recover from your mishap.

Oracle and Recovery Manager support three different types of incomplete recovery: time-based recovery, change-based recovery, and cancel-based recovery.

Time-Based Recovery

A *time-based recovery*, also called a *point-in-time recovery*, is a type of incomplete recovery that recovers the work of committed transactions in a database up to a specific point in time (for example, up to Monday at 8:05 AM, just before a user dropped an important table).

Change-Based Recovery

A *change-based recovery* is a type of incomplete recovery that recovers the work of committed transactions in a database up to a specific *system change number (SCN)*. Oracle assigns a unique SCN to every transaction that commits. If you know the SCN of the last transaction that you want to reflect in a database recovery, you can perform change-based recovery.

Cancel-Based Recovery

A *cancel-based recovery* is a type of incomplete recovery that recovers the work of committed transactions in a database up to the application of a specific log group. To perform cancel-based recovery, you must be able to indicate the last log sequence to apply as part of the recovery.

Recovery Optimizations

Down time costs money. Therefore, Recovery Manager automatically uses many different optimization features to complete all types of database recovery operations as fast as possible. Consequently, you can get a damaged database back up and running quickly. For example, Recovery Manager automatically makes use of Oracle's parallel processing capabilities to complete a database recovery as fast as possible.

What About Damage to Log Groups and the Control File?

If you read the previous section closely, you'll notice that there is no mention of the fact that serious failures might damage the database's transaction log groups and its control file. You might be asking yourself what type of database recovery is necessary after these types of files are damaged or lost. If you mirror the database's online and archived transaction log as well as the database's control file on different disks to protect them from isolated disk failures and user errors, you'll never have to worry about recovering from the loss of these critical database files. As long as one copy of a log group or control file is always accessible, the database can continue to function properly without interruption.

In contrast, when you lose a data file, database recovery is usually necessary because Oracle does not provide any facility to mirror data files. Oracle can always perform database recovery as long as you have a backup of the lost data file and at least one copy of all log groups and the database's control file.

After a disk failure, the database's transaction log or control file might become unprotected (that is, unmirrored). For example, if you mirror the database's control file to two different disks and one disk fails, the control file is now unprotected because there is no mirror. When such situations arise, the most urgent step that you can take is to reconfigure the database's log groups and control file and protect them with at least one mirror. Otherwise, the database is vulnerable to an isolated disk failure.

NOTE

Even when you mirror the database's transaction log groups and control file, the database theoretically still remains vulnerable to total site disasters (for example, fires, floods, and other catastrophes). If these types of situations worry you, consider using Oracle's standby database feature or data replication for ultimate database protection—the following section discusses these advanced database protection features of Oracle8.

High-Availability Options

Oracle's backup and recovery mechanisms can protect a database from almost any type of failure that occurs. However, if you plan to use Oracle to manage your entire business and support mission-critical applications, you might want to design a database protection strategy with some additional contingency plans. For example, will you be able to recover your business's lost data if an earthquake totally destroys your building? If so, how long will it take for you to actually recover any damaged databases, and is this time window satisfactory to your business's customers and workers? Fortunately, Oracle has a couple of features that can satisfy even the most extreme high-availability requirements. The next couple of sections discuss these features: standby databases and subset failover sites.

Standby Databases

A *standby database* is a database that mirrors a *primary database*. In a standby database configuration, the primary database is open and in use with applications, while the standby database is closed and perpetually in a special standby database recovery mode. If a failure of some type happens to make the primary database unavailable, you can activate the standby database immediately and applications can continue to work after switching connections. Figure 10-6 illustrates a standby database configuration.

In a standby database configuration, both the primary database and the standby database operate with media recovery enabled. As the primary database archives a transaction log group, you transfer the log to a standby database site as soon as possible. Once you have an archive log group at the standby database site, you can apply it to the standby database to make it a more recent version of the primary database.

The process of transferring logs from the primary database site to the standby database site and then applying them to the standby database is not automatic. To automate these tasks, you must use the facilities available to you through your operating system. For example, if you are using two UNIX computers to manage the primary and standby databases, you might start *cron* jobs at each site. The cron job at the primary database site can periodically check for new archived transaction logs and use FTP to transfer the files to the standby database site. At the standby database site, a cron

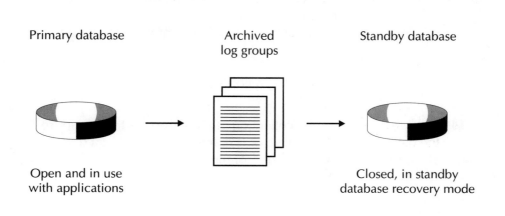

Primary database   Archived   Standby database
                          log groups

Open and in use   Closed, in standby
with applications   database recovery mode

FIGURE 10-6.   *A standby database configuration*

job can look for new archived log groups and apply them to the database when found.

To protect a database's availability from complete site disasters such as floods, fires, and earthquakes, you must operate the primary and standby databases on different computers at physically different locations. Additionally, you should prepare your system's network configuration so that clients can connect to the standby database should a site switchover be necessary.

Failover Sites and Data Replication

Oracle's standby database feature is a good solution when you need to protect the availability of an entire database from extreme situations such as site disasters. However, some environments might not need the full database protection that a standby database configuration supports, or require the standby database to always be available for database access by applications. In such circumstances, consider using Oracle's advanced data replication features to create a failover site instead. See Chapter 11 to learn more about Oracle's advanced data replication features.

Summary

Protecting an Oracle database from unforeseen problems is one of the most important jobs that you can perform as a database administrator. This chapter has explained the many features of Oracle that you can use to back up, restore, and recover databases when inevitable problems affect your system.

- A database's transaction log records the changes made by committed transactions.

- A database backup is a collection of all of the files that comprise the database. If you damage or lose a file that is part of a database, you can extract a copy of the lost file from a database backup to restore the file in the database.

■ A database recovery operation recovers the work lost due to some type of problem. Configured correctly, Oracle can recover a database from all types of problems, including simple system crashes, more serious disk failures, and even complete site disasters.

■ You use Recovery Manager to automate the process of backing up Oracle databases and recovering them when necessary.

PART
V

Specialized Oracle
Environments

CHAPTER
11

Distributing and Replicating Data

ith the proliferation of networks and affordable small computer systems, almost all companies other than small businesses no longer centralize the storage of all business information in a single database. Important information that all corporate users require access to is likely to be scattered among many databases at many different physical locations. To pull many databases together and make their information accessible to all users in the system, you can use Oracle8's distributed database and data replication features. This chapter explains the architecture of an Oracle distributed database system and how you can use data replication to coordinate and maintain local data replicas in multiple Oracle databases. This chapter's topics include the following:

- An introduction to Oracle's distributed database architecture

- SQL operations and transactions in a distributed database

- Location transparency

- Unique security issues for distributed databases

- The concepts of data replication

- Oracle's basic and advanced data replication features

Distributed Database Architecture

A *distributed database* is a set of databases that appears to users and applications as a single database. In most cases, the databases that comprise a distributed database reside on separate computers that communicate using a network. After you configure an Oracle distributed database system, all of the data in the system is available to applications as though it resides in one logical database. For example, a transaction like the one in Figure 11-1 can include DML statements that modify the data in several databases.

Cooperation and Autonomy

Each database server in a distributed database system manages access to its local database—there is no one location that is in charge of managing the entire system. However, all servers in the system must cooperate with one

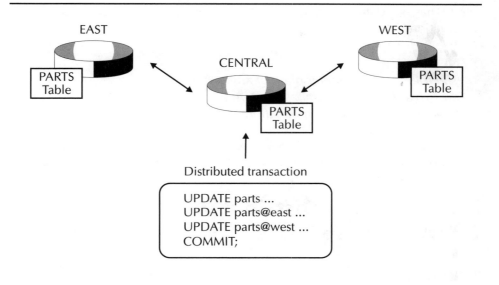

FIGURE 11-1. *In a distributed database, a single transaction can access the data in one or more Oracle databases.*

another to ensure that the data throughout the distributed database system is consistent and accurate.

An Extension of Client/Server

In Chapter 8, you learned about distributed processing and client/server application systems. Oracle distributed database systems are simply an extension of the basic client/server model because a database server in a distributed database system can act as both a client and a server, depending on its current operation in carrying out a transaction's work. For example, take a close look at Figure 11-1. When the computer that manages the CENTRAL database executes the first statement in the transaction, it acts as a database server because the statement is accessing the PARTS table in the local database. However, when the transaction issues the second and third statements, the same computer now acts as a client because it forwards the SQL statements to the remote EAST and WEST database servers to update remote PARTS tables. Recall that a *database server* is the Oracle software that manages a database, and that a *client* is an application requesting information from a database server.

NOTE
The role that a computer plays at any given time in a distributed database system is typically transparent to applications. However, it is useful to understand this concept so that you can better understand how Oracle's distributed database architecture functions.

Networks and Distributed Database Systems

Most distributed database systems incorporate a number of databases managed by different servers at different physical locations. When this is the configuration, a network is necessary to enable server-to-server communication. Furthermore, all servers (and clients) in an Oracle distributed database system must use Oracle's networking software, Net8, so that they can communicate with one another across the network.

Database Services and Naming in a Distributed Database

All services (print queues, mail servers, etc.) available on a network must have unique names so that users and applications know where to access them. In a distributed database system, a database server or instance is simply a *database service* that is available on the network. As you might expect, a database service in a distributed database system must have a unique name so that applications and other database servers know where to access the information that the server manages. In an Oracle distributed database system, each database service's unique name is its *global database name*. A global database name consists of two parts:

■ The first part is the database's basic name that you give to it during creation. A database's name is no longer than eight characters.

■ The second part is the database's network domain. A database's network domain indicates the logical location of the database in the network.

For example, Figure 11-2 shows a network of databases at the hypothetical company COMPWORLD.

For example, the COMPWORLD network includes three databases: EAST, CENTRAL, and WEST. The corresponding global database names (service names) are EAST.COMPWORLD, CENTRAL.COMPWORLD, and WEST.COMPWORLD.

To reference specific schema objects in a distributed database that are not local to your database, you can extend the name of the object using its global database name. For example, notice that in Figure 11-2, there is a PARTS table in each of the EAST, CENTRAL, and WEST databases. If you are running an application, say SQL*Plus, and connected to the CENTRAL database, you can query the PARTS table in the EAST

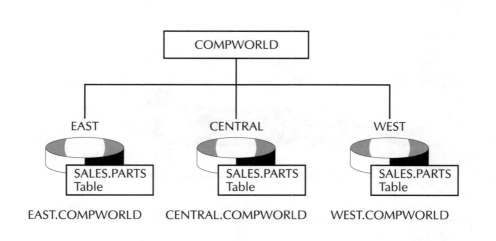

FIGURE 11-2. *An Oracle database's global database name is the database's network domain prefixed by the database's basic name.*

database by identifying the object with its fully qualified name in the distributed database:

```
SELECT * FROM sales.parts@east.compworld;
```

To complete the request, the local CENTRAL database server implicitly uses a database link that connects to the remote EAST database. The next section introduces database links.

Database Links

To permit access to remote databases in a distributed database, you must define database links in your local database. A *database link* specifies a unidirectional communication path from one Oracle database to another. Figure 11-3 illustrates a database link from one database to another in an Oracle distributed database system.

In typical configurations, the name of a database link must match the global name of the database to which the link points. Due to this requirement, database links effectively establish a global object naming scheme in a distributed database system. For example, the following SQL

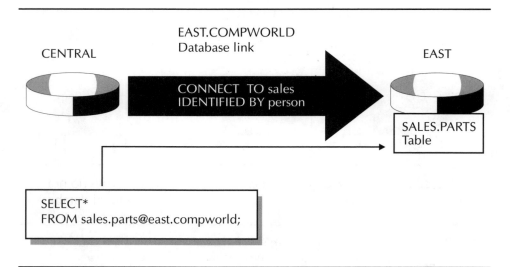

FIGURE 11-3. *A database link is a communication path from one Oracle database to another.*

statement creates a database link in the local CENTRAL database that describes a path to the remote EAST.COMPWORLD database:

```
CREATE DATABASE LINK east.compworld ... ;
```

After creating a database link, applications connected to the local CENTRAL database can access data in the remote EAST.COMPWORLD database. For example, the following UPDATE statement updates a row in the PARTS table of the remote EAST database:

```
UPDATE sales.parts@east.compworld
  SET unit_price = 100.50
  WHERE id = 1;
```

Fixed User, Connected User, and Current User Database Links

When you create a database link, you can indicate specific connection information that your local database server uses to establish a session in the remote database. The type of database link that you choose to create has specific security implications. First, let's learn about fixed user database links. A *fixed user database link* is one that includes a specific username and password in its definition. For example, the following CREATE DATABASE LINK statement creates a fixed user database link to the remote EAST.COMPWORLD database:

```
CREATE DATABASE LINK east.compworld
  CONNECT sales IDENTIFIED BY person;
```

The local database server uses the embedded credentials to establish sessions in the remote database. A fixed user database link passes connection information to the remote server as plaintext when establishing a session. Therefore, it is wise to encrypt server login packets when using fixed user database links.

Alternatively, *connected user* and *current user database links* do not embed a username/password in the definition. Instead, the local database server uses the credentials of the connected user or the current user to establish a session with and request data from the remote server. To understand the subtle difference between connected user and current user database links and the security implications, you first must understand the difference in the terms "connected user" and "current user."

■ A *connected user* is the user connected to the local database running an application. For example, when I run an application at my local database, I connect as SBOBROWS. The connected user in this context is SBOBROWS.

■ A *current user* is the user context in which an operation is being performed. For example, if I connect to a database as SBOBROWS and run an application that calls the TOTAL_ORDER method of the SALES.ORDER_TYPE object type, the current user running the method is SALES, not SBOBROWS.

Connected user database links can be used in any distributed database configuration. Connected user database links provide accountability for remote server operations because you can track which remote users do what operations in the distribute database system.

Current user database links let you exactly duplicate the security contexts when running operations locally or remotely. However, you can only use current user database links when you use global authentication of database users. See the section "Global Users and Roles" later in this chapter that discusses global user and role authentication in an Oracle distributed database system.

Public, Private, and Global Database Links

Oracle lets you create database links within three different domains of the distributed database system: private, public, and global database links.

■ A *private database link* is a database link that you create in a specific schema of a database. Only the owner of a private database link or PL/SQL subprograms (packages, procedures, functions, triggers, and object type methods) in the schema can use a private database link to access data and database objects in the remote database. This attribute of private database links makes them secure relative to public and global database links.

■ A *public database link* is a database link that you create in the PUBLIC domain of a database. All users, packages, methods, and so on in a database can use a public database link to access data and schema objects in the remote database. Public database links simplify the management of database links when all users of a local database require access to a remote Oracle database.

■ A *global database link* is a database link managed by an Oracle Names server. When you create a names server for a Net8 network, the names server automatically creates and manages global database links for every Oracle database in the network. All users and programs in any database can use a global database link to access data and schema objects in the remote database. By using Oracle Names to manage database links for all databases in a large distributed system, link management is centralized and simple.

Shared Database Links

Efficient use of computer resources always produces better performance for applications, especially in demanding environments. To reduce the number of network connections from one database server to another, consider using shared database links. A *shared database link* can enable multiple sessions originating from the local database to share a single connection to the remote database. Consequently, you can reduce the overhead necessary to support inter-database communication.

NOTE
Shared database links are useful only when the local server uses a multithreaded server configuration, and when multiple local users simultaneously access the same remote database. Otherwise, shared database links can actually increase the overhead necessary to establish remote server connections.

Heterogeneous Distributed Databases

In a heterogeneous distributed database system, at least one of the databases is a non-Oracle system. A supplemental product set, the *Oracle Open Gateways*, enables your distributed database to mix Oracle and non-Oracle systems together to form a distributed database system. When you use a gateway, applications can connect to your local Oracle database server and access the data in the non-Oracle system.

Applications and Distributed Databases

When developing applications to work in a distributed database system, you must understand several unique issues. The following sections explain how you can develop applications to access remote data in a distributed database with SQL statements and PL/SQL programs.

Remote Queries

A *remote query* is a SELECT statement that retrieves information from one or more remote tables that all exist at the same remote node. For example, the following remote query retrieves information from the remote ORDERS and CUSTOMERS tables at the WEST database:

```
SELECT o.id, c.company_name
  FROM sales.orders@west.compworld o, sales.customers@west.compworld c
  WHERE o.cust_id = c.id;
```

Distributed Queries

In contrast, a *distributed query* retrieves information from two or more different databases. For example, the following distributed query joins information from the local ORDERS table and the remote CUSTOMERS table:

```
SELECT o.id, c.company_name
  FROM sales.orders o, sales.customers@west.compworld c
  WHERE o.cust_id = c.id;
```

Remote Updates

A *remote update* is an update that modifies data in a remote table. For example, the following remote update modifies a row in the PARTS table of the EAST database:

```
UPDATE sales.parts@east.compworld
  SET unit_price = 100.50
  WHERE id = 1;
```

Distributed Updates

In contrast, a *distributed update* modifies data on two or more servers, all in one operation. The only way that you can perform a distributed update in an Oracle distributed database system is to create a stored procedure, object method, etc. that includes two or more remote updates, each of which updates data in different databases. For example, you can consider the following anonymous PL/SQL block as a distributed update:

```
BEGIN
UPDATE sales.parts@east.compworld
  SET ... ;
UPDATE sales.items
  SET ... ;
END;
```

Remote Procedure Calls (RPCs)

PL/SQL lets developers store application logic in a database server as stored procedures (packages, object type methods, etc.). Oracle's distributed database architecture is not limiting with respect to procedure calls—applications can call both local and remote procedures to perform work. For example, the following query makes a *remote procedure call (RPC)* to the remote SALES.ORDER_TYPE member method ORDER_TOTAL:

```
SELECT o.order_total()
  FROM sales.orders@east.compworld o WHERE id = 1;
```

Remote Transactions

A *remote transaction* is a transaction that contains one or more remote statements, all of which reference the same remote database. For example, the following remote transaction updates data in the EAST database only:

```
UPDATE sales.parts@east.compworld
  SET ...
  WHERE ... ;
UPDATE sales.parts@east.compworld
  SET ...
```

```
  WHERE ... ;
UPDATE sales.parts@east.compworld
  SET ...
  WHERE ... ;
COMMIT;
```

Distributed Transactions

A *distributed transaction* is a transaction that includes one or more statements that update data in two or more different databases.
For example, the following distributed transaction updates data in several databases:

```
UPDATE sales.parts
  SET ...
  WHERE ... ;
UPDATE sales.parts@east.compworld
  SET ...
  WHERE ... ;
UPDATE sales.parts@west.compworld
  SET ...
  WHERE ... ;
COMMIT;
```

Oracle's Two-Phase Commit Mechanism

By definition, all statements in the same transaction must either commit or roll back as a unit. To guarantee this fundamental behavior for distributed transactions, Oracle uses a special *two-phase commit mechanism* to coordinate transaction control over a network. A two-phase commit is necessary to address the possibility of network and system failures that might interrupt the commit of distributed transactions.

During a two-phase commit, participating servers meticulously log different phases of the transaction commit process. If an unplanned network or system failure should happen to interrupt the commit process being coordinated over the network, each server participating in the transaction has enough local information in its data dictionary to recover from the failure and ultimately commit or roll back the changes of the transaction. In short, Oracle's two-phase commit mechanism lets servers perform distributed transactions and guarantee the integrity of entire distributed database.

NOTE
The mechanisms of a two-phase commit are completely internal to the Oracle database servers participating in the transaction. All that you have to do is end a distributed transaction with a COMMIT statement and Oracle does the rest of the work for you.

Distributed Database Transparency

The power of a distributed database can be useless if it forces developers to learn a lot of special, complicated SQL syntax just to access remote data. For example, if a team of distributed database developers must reference remote data using fully qualified table and view names (for example, SALES.PARTS@EAST.COMPWORLD), all of the developers must know the current locations of specific data objects in the distributed database system. Furthermore, each developer must be able to understand, create, and use database links to build necessary application SQL statements. No doubt, such complexities can detract from everyone's productivity.

Fortunately, Oracle has several features that you can use to hide the complexities of a distributed database system and make its presence *transparent* to users of the system. When you take the extra time to configure a distributed database with transparency, developers and users of the system can use all databases in the system as though they are accessing a single, local database. For example, the following SQL statement creates a public synonym to establish location transparency for a remote table. *Location transparency* hides the physical location of a schema object in a distributed database system.

```
CREATE PUBLIC SYNONYM parts
   FOR sales.parts@east.compworld;
```

After creating the public synonym, users of the local database can reference the remote PARTS table as though it exists in the local database. Oracle automatically translates the local alias into the remote table name and uses the database link to reach the remote table.

```
SELECT * FROM parts;
```

Synonyms are just one feature that you can use to establish location transparency in a distributed database system. You can also use views, packages, stored procedures, functions, and object type methods to establish location transparency for applications that work in a distributed database system. For example, the local PARTS view points to data in a remote PARTS table.

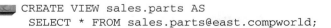
```
CREATE VIEW sales.parts AS
  SELECT * FROM sales.parts@east.compworld;
```

Unique Distributed Database Security Issues

Designing and enforcing a security policy for a single Oracle database can be a challenging task. When you build a distributed database system, you must consider some additional issues in order to design a sound security policy with the entire distributed database system in mind. For example, a database link in your local database establishes connections to the remote database using a specific user account in the remote system. If you forget to create the target user account at the remote database, the database link will not function properly. Furthermore, if the remote database uses Oracle's account management features (account locking, password expiration, etc.), you might have to modify the definition of your database link when the remote account's password changes.

Global Users and Roles

Chapter 6 explains how Oracle can authenticate *global usernames* and *global roles* using an external network service such as Oracle Security Server. Global user and role authentication is especially useful in a distributed database environment for two reasons:

- In most distributed database environments, users require access to several Oracle databases. By centralizing the authentication of users and roles in an external authentication service, you can simplify the administration of the entire distributed database system.

■ In many cases, networks are insecure vehicles used to transport
     sensitive data between computers. Unless you encrypt login packets
     for server-to-server connections in a distributed database system,
     malicious users can sniff an insecure network to read username and
     password combinations and then use the account information to
     illegally access sensitive database information.

Introduction to Data Replication

Distributed database systems are powerful tools that you can use to join
together disparate data sources into a single, global database for application
access. However, distributed databases have fundamental characteristics
that make them unsuitable for certain types of applications. For example,
an application cannot use a distributed database and distributed
transactions unless all of the databases in the system are concurrently
available and remain available most of the time. Considering this
requirement, many types of applications cannot use a distributed database.
For example, you cannot use a distributed database to support a sales force
application where salespeople are typically mobile and disconnected from
the primary system a large percentage of the time.

To support different types of distributed database requirements and
applications, consider using data replication. *Data replication* is the process
of copying and maintaining database objects in multiple databases that
make up a distributed database system. Figure 11-4 illustrates one type of
data replication system.

Data replication offers several benefits that pure distributed database
systems cannot:

■ Data replication can improve the performance of an application
     and a distributed database system's network. That's because the
     application can access replicate data in a local database rather than
     data in a remote database that's available across the network.

■ Data replication can increase the availability of an application
     because replicate data exists at several locations. If one location
     becomes inaccessible due to a system or network failure, alternate
     data access options exist.

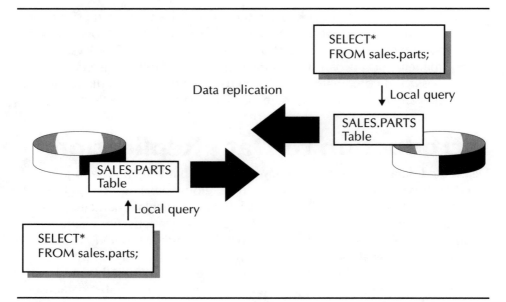

FIGURE 11-4. *A data replication environment*

Uses for Data Replication

Data replication can be useful for many types of applications. The following examples give you an idea of when to consider using data replication to support applications:

- Data replication is useful to distribute copies of useful information. For example, the headquarters of a retail sales chain can replicate its most current product information table to all retail outlets on a nightly basis so that up-to-date product price information is always available and consistent at all stores.

- You can use data replication to transport information from a database to other data stores. For example, you might use Oracle's replication features to periodically copy data from a transaction processing database to data warehouse.

■ Data replication might be the only method that you can use to support transaction processing applications that operate using disconnected components. For example, when users of a transaction processing system are mobile and disconnected for a corporate network most of the time, you can use data replication to synchronize the data of each user's "personal" database with that of the company's "central" database.

■ As Chapter 10 explains, data replication can be useful to build and maintain a failover site that protects the availability of an important database. In contrast with Oracle's standby database feature, failover sites maintained by data replication can also serve as fully functional databases that applications can use to access data, even when the primary site is concurrently operational.

Types of Data Replication

Oracle8 supports two different types of replication to meet different application requirements: basic replication and advanced replication.

■ In a *basic replication environment*, data replicas provide read-only access to the table data that originates from a *primary site*, sometimes called the *master site*. Applications can query data from local data replicas to avoid network access regardless of network availability. However, applications throughout the system must access data at the primary site when updates are necessary.

■ In an *advanced replication environment*, applications can read and update table replicas throughout the system. To support advanced replication, you must configure some special features at each database server that manages data replicas in the system. Oracle8 servers then work to converge the data of all table replicas, while at the same time ensuring global transaction consistency and data integrity.

The remaining sections of this chapter explain the features of Oracle8's basic and advanced replication configurations.

Basic Replication and Read-Only Snapshots

Oracle's basic replication features support applications that require read-only access to the table data that originates from a primary site. To support read-only replication, you create and use read-only table snapshots. A *read-only table snapshot* is a local copy of a table that originates from a remote master table. An application can query the data in a read-only table snapshot, but cannot insert, update, or delete rows in the snapshot. Figure 11-5 shows the architecture of a read-only table snapshot in a basic replication environment.

In one respect, a table snapshot is similar to a view because you define the logical data structure of a table snapshot with a query. For example, the following CREATE SNAPSHOT statement creates a table snapshot of the remote PARTS table:

```
CREATE SNAPSHOT sales.parts AS
   SELECT * FROM sales.parts@central.compworld;
```

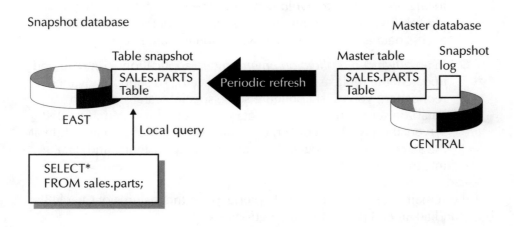

FIGURE 11-5. *A table snapshot is a transaction-consistent view of one or more remote tables.*

NOTE
Oracle's table snapshot mechanism utilizes some of the server's underlying distributed database architecture components to function. For example, a database link is necessary to access remote data.

Unlike a view, a table snapshot stores the table data that it derives through its defining query. When you create a new snapshot, Oracle executes the defining query of the snapshot to populate a local table that holds data for the snapshot.

In general, snapshots defined with simple queries offer advantages over snapshots defined with complex queries. For example, to take advantage of some supplemental table snapshot performance features (namely, snapshot logs and fast refreshes), avoid creating a snapshot with a defining query that contains a distinct or aggregate function, a GROUP BY or CONNECT BY clause, join, complex subqueries, or a set operation. Furthermore, the defining query of a snapshot must always reference all of the primary key columns in the master table so that Oracle can readily identify and compare corresponding rows in a snapshot and its master table.

Complex Snapshots

When the defining query of a snapshot contains a complex query that includes a distinct or aggregate function, a GROUP BY or CONNECT BY clause, join, complicated subquery, or a set operation, you can refer to the snapshot as a *complex snapshot*. For example, the following CREATE SNAPSHOT statement creates a complex snapshot because it joins information from two remote master tables:

```
CREATE SNAPSHOT sales.order_items AS
  SELECT i.id lineid, p.description, i.quantity, p.unitprice, i.total
    FROM sales.items@central.compworld i, sales.parts@central.compworld p
    WHERE i.part_id = p.id;
```

In general, complex snapshots are not recommended because Oracle cannot perform a fast refresh of a complex snapshot. Consequently, the use of complex snapshots forces Oracle to perform complete refreshes for the snapshots, which can saturate the network with data and detract from overall system performance.

Snapshot Data Storage

In reality, a table snapshot is a number of schema objects that you collectively refer to as a "table snapshot." When you create a new read-only table snapshot, Oracle creates a base table to store the snapshot's data, an index for the primary key in the snapshot's base table, and a read-only view of the snapshot's base table—the view takes the name of the snapshot and provides access to the snapshot.

Snapshot Refreshes

When you create a new snapshot, Oracle executes the defining query of the snapshot to populate the snapshot with data from the master table. Subsequently, the data in a snapshot does not necessarily reflect the current data in the snapshot's master table—transactions might update the data in the master table at any time. To keep a snapshot's data relatively current with the data of its master table, you can configure the snapshot so that Oracle periodically refreshes its data. During a *snapshot refresh,* Oracle makes the snapshot reflect a more current state of its master table.

Types of Snapshot Refreshes

Oracle can refresh a snapshot using two different techniques: a complete refresh or a fast refresh. When you configure a snapshot for a *complete refresh*, the server managing the snapshot simply executes the snapshot's defining query. Oracle can perform a complete refresh for any snapshot. To perform the complete refresh of a snapshot, the result set of the snapshot's defining query replaces the current data in the snapshot's base table. When a master table is large, the complete refresh of a snapshot can saturate the network with a lot of data and take a significant amount of time to complete.

Fast refreshes of a snapshot are typically more efficient than complete refreshes. To perform a *fast refresh*, the snapshot server identifies the changes that took place in the master table since the most recent refresh of the snapshot and then applies only those changes to the snapshot. Because a fast refresh requests a subset of master table data from the master database, fast refreshes are typically much more efficient than complete refreshes. However, fast refreshes are available for snapshots only when the master table has a snapshot log. The next section discusses snapshot logs in detail.

Oracle always refreshes a snapshot as part of a refresh group. (See the section "Snapshot Refresh Groups" below for more information about refresh groups.) By default, Oracle attempts to perform a fast refresh of each snapshot in a refresh group. If the snapshot server cannot fast refresh a snapshot, the server performs a complete refresh to refresh the snapshot.

Snapshot Logs

When a master table corresponds to one or more snapshots and you want to perform fast refreshes for the snapshots, you must first create a snapshot log for the master table. A master table's *snapshot log* keeps track of fast refresh data for all corresponding snapshots—it is not necessary or possible to create multiple snapshot logs for a single master table.

When a server performs a fast refresh for a snapshot, the server reads information in the master table's snapshot log to identify the new, changed, and deleted rows since the most recent refresh of the snapshot—these changes are more simply referred to as the "deltas." Then, the snapshot server requests only the deltas from the master database to refresh the snapshot efficiently. After all snapshots read a delta during a snapshot refresh, Oracle can safely purge the delta from the log to minimize the storage requirements for the log.

Snapshot Refresh Groups

Snapshot databases often replicate sets of master tables that are related by referential integrity. To preserve the referential integrity and transaction consistency among a set of related master tables, Oracle lets you refresh a corresponding set of table snapshots as part of a *refresh group*. Oracle refreshes all snapshots in a refresh group using a single operation. After refreshing all of the snapshots in a group, the data of all snapshots in the group consistently reflects the same data in the master table with referential integrity intact.

A snapshot database can contain any number of refresh groups to suit application requirements. After you create a refresh group, you can add and remove snapshots in the group as necessary. The refresh settings for the group apply to all members in the refresh group. Therefore, not only do you want to use groups to refresh snapshots bound by referential integrity, but also to refresh snapshots that have similar refresh requirements.

Automatic Snapshot Refreshes

Oracle8 makes it easy to refresh snapshots because you can configure refresh groups to automatically perform snapshot refreshes at specific intervals. When configuring a refresh group for automatic refreshes, first decide how often to refresh the snapshots in the group. Typically, you should refresh a group of snapshots based on how often and how much data changes in the corresponding master tables—if master table data changes frequently and applications that depend on the snapshots require access to the most current master table data, configure the refresh group for frequent refreshes; if master table data is relatively static, it might be more appropriate to configure only occasional refreshes for a group of snapshots.

When you create or alter a refresh group, you specify its automatic refresh interval as a date expression. The date expression that you specify for a refresh interval must evaluate to a future point in time.

Automatic Snapshot Refreshes and Job Queues

Oracle8 supports the automatic refresh of refresh groups using its *job queue mechanism*. To use job queues, an Oracle database server must start at least one job queue background process. A job queue background process wakes up periodically, checks the job queue, and executes all jobs scheduled for execution. Therefore, to perform snapshot refreshes automatically for refresh groups, you must configure the snapshot server with one or more job queue background server processes.

Manual Snapshot Refreshes

In special situations, you might want to force the refresh of a group of snapshots rather than wait for the next scheduled, automatic refresh of the group. For example, suppose you load a large amount of data into a master table. After the bulk data load completes, dependent snapshots are no longer representative of the master table's data. If applications need to see the new data immediately, you can request Oracle to manually refresh a group of snapshots.

Advanced Replication Environments

In advanced replication environments, data replicas throughout the system provide both read and update access to a table's data. You can configure advanced, "*update anywhere*" replication environments using two different Oracle features: multimaster replication or updatable snapshot sites.

Multimaster Replication

Oracle's *multimaster replication* lets multiple sites manage complete groups of replicated schema objects. In a multimaster configuration, all sites operate as equals—there is no one site that is considered the "primary site." Applications can update any replicated table at any site in a multimaster configuration. Figure 11-6 illustrates a multimaster advanced replication system.

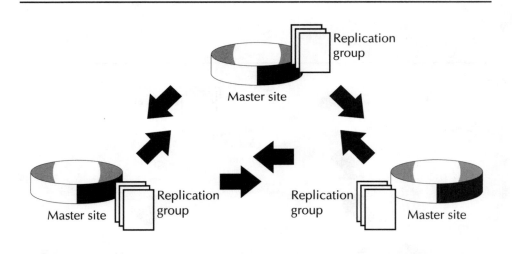

FIGURE 11-6.   *A multimaster configuration*

Snapshot Sites and Updatable Snapshots

Once you create at least one master site in an advanced replication system, you can then create dependent *snapshot sites* with *updatable snapshots*. Oracle's advanced replication facility lets applications insert, update, and delete table rows through updatable snapshots. Updatable snapshot sites are typically configured so that a master site consolidates the information that applications update at snapshot sites stemming from the master site. For example, Figure 11-7 illustrates an advanced replication system with one master site and multiple updatable snapshot sites.

Updatable snapshots are similar to read-only snapshots in several ways, but also have several unique properties. For example, Oracle refreshes an updatable snapshot as part of a refresh group, identical to read-only snapshots. However, Oracle also lets you update data in an updatable snapshot; therefore, the server that manages a snapshot site must regularly propagate the changes made through an updatable snapshot back to the snapshot's remote master table.

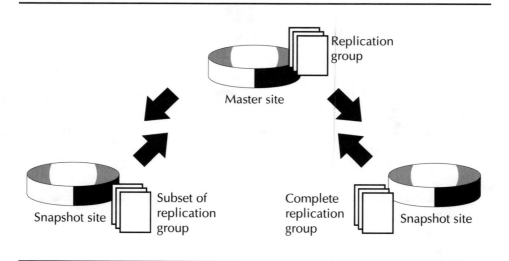

FIGURE 11-7.   *An advanced replication configuration can also support updatable snapshot sites based on a master site.*

NOTE
An updatable snapshot is always a simple, fast-refreshable table snapshot—you cannot define a complex, updatable snapshot.

Comparing Advanced Replication Options

Both multimaster and updatable snapshot advanced replication configurations can support the needs of applications that require an update-anywhere data model in a distributed database system. However, there are a couple of differences to consider when deciding whether to use just multiple master sites or a limited number of master sites and updatable snapshot sites. For example, in multimaster configurations, all master sites must contain identical sets of replicate data (see Figure 11-6). In contrast, a snapshot site can replicate all or subsets of its master site's table data (see Figure 11-7).

Advanced Replication System Architecture

Now that you have an overall understanding of Oracle8's advanced replication options, let's take a look at the underlying architectural components that you must understand.

Replication Objects and Replication Groups

A *replication object* is a schema object that is present in multiple databases in a distributed database system. Oracle8 lets you replicate tables, as well as supporting objects, including views, database triggers, packages, indexes, and synonyms.

Oracle manages related replication objects together in *replication groups*. As with other types of groupings in an Oracle database system (for example, refresh groups), replication groups make it easier to manage the replication of several objects as a unit. In typical advanced replication environments, you create and use a replication group to organize the schema objects necessary to support a specific application. The objects in a replication group can originate all from the same schema, or can originate from several different database schemas.

Master Sites and Snapshot Sites

A *master site* is an instance of a replication group that is a complete copy of all objects in the group (see Figure 11-6). When you configure an advanced replication system with multiple master sites, all master sites communicate directly with one another to transmit replication data and schema changes for the replication group. A replication group at a master site is also called a *master group*.

A *snapshot site* is an instance of a replication group that originates from an associated master site. A snapshot site can include both read-only and updatable snapshots of the table data in the replication group. Additionally, a snapshot site's snapshots can contain all or just a subset of the table data within the replication group (see Figure 11-7), but must be simple snapshots that have an exact correspondence to the tables at the master site. For example, a snapshot site may contain snapshots for only selected tables in a replication group; moreover, an individual snapshot might contain only a selected portion of its master table. A replication group at a snapshot site is also called a *snapshot group*.

NOTE
Every replication group in an advanced replication environment has a master definition site. A replication group's master definition site *is a master site that serves as the control point for managing the replication group and objects in the group.*

Replication Catalogs

Every site in an advanced replication environment manages information about replication objects and groups in a special replication catalog. A site's *replication catalog* is a collection of data dictionary tables and views that maintain information about replication objects and groups at the site. Servers that participate in an advanced replication environment use and coordinate the information in corresponding replication catalogs to handle the replication of objects throughout the system.

Oracle's Replication Management API

To configure and manage an Oracle8 advanced replication environment, you use a set of packaged procedures and functions that are automatically installed in each server's data dictionary. Collectively, these packages of PL/SQL programs are known as Oracle's *replication management application programming interface (API)*.

Oracle's Advanced Replication Software Mechanisms

Oracle uses many internal software mechanisms to manage the replication of information in an advanced replication environment. The next few sections explain how Oracle converges the data of objects in replication groups that use row-level replication with asynchronous data propagation.

Row-Level Replication

With *row-level replication*, applications use basic DML statements (for example, INSERT, UPDATE, and DELETE statements) to modify the data within local tables. When transactions change data in a table, the server managing the table automatically records information about the modifications and then queues corresponding *deferred transactions* to replicate local changes to remote sites that manage the same data.

To support the row-level replication of transactions in an advanced replication environment, it's necessary to generate one or more underlying objects that function to support each replicated object. For example, a replicated table has two internal PL/SQL packages and some internal triggers that its server uses to replicate and queue deferred transactions that involve the table and resolve replication conflicts that involve the table if and when they occur.

Asynchronous (Store-and-Forward) Data Propagation

Typical advanced replication configurations that use row-level replication transmit replication data using asynchronous data replication. *Asynchronous data replication*, also called *store-and-forward data replication*, occurs as follows: when an application updates a local replica of a table, the server builds and queues a corresponding deferred transaction that the server eventually forwards to other sites to replicate the change. Later in this section, you'll see an example of asynchronous data propagation in action.

Pushing the Deferred Transaction Queue

At scheduled intervals, a site *pushes* (forwards) the deferred transactions in its queue to other sites in the advanced replication system. More specifically, at a master site you must schedule a push of deferred transactions to each other master site in the system (that is, you can schedule pushes to different master sites at different times); at a snapshot site, you must schedule a push of deferred transactions to its master site.

Purging the Deferred Transaction Queue

After pushing a deferred transaction to its destination successfully, the site marks the transaction in its queue as "pushed." Then, at schedule intervals, the site *purges* (removes) all successfully pushed deferred transactions from its queue. Periodic purging of the site's deferred transaction queue keeps the queue small.

NOTE

Pushing a deferred transaction to a site successfully is very different from actually executing the transaction successfully at the remote site. After pushing a deferred transaction to a site, the transaction might execute with errors at the destination, perhaps because of a replication conflict or other problem.

Serial and Parallel Propagation

Oracle can propagate a number of deferred transactions to a remote destination serially or using parallel processing. With *serial propagation*, Oracle asynchronously propagates deferred transactions, one at a time, in the same order of commit as on the originating site. In contrast, *parallel propagation* asynchronously propagates multiple deferred transactions to deliver excellent performance and throughput. See Chapter 12 to learn more about Oracle's parallel processing capabilities.

Unique Snapshot Propagation Mechanisms

Updatable snapshots must both "push" and "pull" updates to and from its master table, respectively. After an application updates an updatable snapshot, the snapshot site asynchronously pushes corresponding deferred transactions to update the master table. To update the same snapshot with updates made at the master site, the snapshot site refreshes the snapshot as part of a refresh group, effectively pulling the changes made to the master table.

An Example

As the previous sections explain, each master site and snapshot site in an Oracle8 advanced replication system uses a vast array of internal system objects and mechanisms to enable row-level replication with asynchronous data propagation. To illustrate the interaction of mechanisms explained in the previous sections, please study the following example that demonstrates how it all works together.

1. An application executes an UPDATE statement to update a row in an updatable snapshot.

2. At the snapshot site, an internal trigger fires to capture specific information about the update to the snapshot.

3. Using the snapshot's replication package, the trigger builds a remote procedure call targeting the master table that can reproduce the UPDATE made to the snapshot.

4. The snapshot site stores the RPC produced by the internal trigger in the site's deferred transaction queue.

5. As other updates occur, the snapshot site generates additional RPCs. Oracle also keeps information to delineate transaction boundaries so that it can forward replication information to remote sites in the form of identical transactions.

6. At scheduled intervals, the snapshot site pushes deferred transactions in its queue to its master site.

7. At scheduled intervals, the snapshot site purges all successfully pushed deferred transactions from its queue.

8. At scheduled intervals, the snapshot site refreshes snapshots from the master site.

Replication Conflicts in Advanced Replication Systems

When planning an advanced replication environment, you must consider what happens when transactions originating from different sites change the same data at nearly the same time so as to conflict with each other. Update-anywhere replication systems invite the possibility of such conflicts unless you consciously program applications to avoid such problems. Alternatively, Oracle's advanced replication features allow master sites to automatically resolve conflicts and preserve the integrity of the data that you choose to replicate. The following sections explain the different types of replication conflicts, when they can occur, and how you can configure master sites to detect and resolve replication conflicts automatically.

Types of Replication Conflicts

The three types of conflicts that can occur in an update-anywhere replication environment are uniqueness conflicts, update conflicts, and delete conflicts.

- A *uniqueness conflict* happens when the replication of a row attempts to violate entity integrity (a PRIMARY KEY or UNIQUE constraint). For example, consider what happens when two transactions that originate from two different sites each insert a row into a respective table replica with the same primary key value—replication of the transactions generates a uniqueness conflict.

- An *update conflict* happens when the replication of an update to a row conflicts with another update to the same row. Update conflicts can happen when two different transactions, originating from different sites, update the same row at nearly the same time.

■   A *delete conflict* happens when two transactions originate from
    different sites, with one transaction deleting a row that the other
    transaction updates or deletes. For example, consider a situation
    where one transaction deletes a customer record that another
    transaction updates at nearly the same time. When Oracle attempts
    to converge the customer table replicas, Oracle detects that the
    delete and the update conflict with each other.

Conflict Avoidance

One way to address replication conflicts in an advanced replication
environment is to choose one of several different replicated data ownership
models that simply eliminates the possibility of conflicts altogether. For
example, *primary ownership*, also called *static ownership*, is the replicated
data model that basic read-only replication environments support. Primary
ownership prevents all replication conflicts because the master site in the
system manages all update access to replicated data; applications cannot
update replicate data via read-only snapshots.

Conflict Detection and Resolution

Primary site ownership and other data models that advocate conflict
avoidance are often too restrictive for many database applications. Instead,
many applications must operate using a *shared ownership* replicated data
model. When multiple sites share ownership of replicated data,
applications can update the data of any table replica at any time. Shared
ownership models are also called update-anywhere data models.

   When you choose to operate an application within a shared ownership
data model, you must be sure to configure master sites in the system to
detect and resolve replication conflicts if and when they occur. Fortunately,
Oracle automatically detects all types of replication conflicts in an
advanced replication environment that uses row-level replication with
asynchronous data propagation. To detect replication conflicts, Oracle
compares a minimal amount of row data from the originating site with the
corresponding row information at the receiving site. When there are
differences, Oracle detects the conflict.

   When a receiving site in an advanced replication system detects a
replication conflict in a transaction, the default behavior is to log the
conflict, store the offending transaction as an *error transaction* in the site's

replication catalog, and leave the local version of the data as it is (do not execute the error transaction causing the conflict). When you use this default behavior for conflict detection, it is your responsibility to manually check for error transactions and then resolve conflicts one by one. Alternatively, Oracle has mechanisms that you can configure to automate the resolution of replication conflicts.

Column Groups and Conflict Resolution Methods

Oracle uses column groups to detect and resolve conflicts that happen during data replication. A *column group* is a collection of one or more columns in a replicated table at a master site. If any conflicts occur as the result of changes being made to multiple copies of the same data, master sites detect and resolve the conflicts using column groups.

When configuring master tables, you can create column groups and then assign columns and a list of one or more conflict resolution methods to each group. A *conflict resolution method* is a server-side routine that determines how to safely resolve a replication conflict. When designing column groups you can choose from among many conflict resolution methods offered by Oracle8. For example, to resolve update conflicts, you might choose to have Oracle overwrite the column values at the destination site with the column values from the originating site. Oracle offers many update conflict resolution methods. You can also build custom conflict resolution routines and use them with column groups, if necessary.

Each column group in a replicated table can have several conflict resolution methods. Indicating multiple conflict resolution methods for a group allows Oracle to resolve a conflict in different ways should others fail to resolve the conflict. When trying to resolve a conflict for a group, Oracle executes the group's resolution methods in the order that you list for the group.

By default, every replicated table has a *shadow column group*. A table's shadow column group contains all columns that are not within a specific column group. However, you cannot assign conflict resolution methods to a table's shadow group.

NOTE
Oracle does not support conflict resolution for delete conflicts. Instead, applications must prevent delete conflicts by not using DELETE statements to actually delete rows. Alternatively, applications can mark rows for deletion and configure the system to periodically purge deleted rows using procedural replication. See the next section for more information about procedural replication.

Other Advanced Replication Options

Some applications have special requirements that cannot be met by a traditional advanced replication system that uses row-level replication and asynchronous data propagation. The following sections explain two of Oracle's unique advanced replication options that you can consider using in special circumstances: procedural replication and synchronous data propagation.

Procedural Replication

Batch processing applications can change large amounts of data within a single transaction. In such cases, standard row-level replication mechanisms could bombard a network with a huge quantity of data. To avoid such problems, a batch processing application that operates in an advanced replication environment can use Oracle's procedural replication to replicate simple stored procedure calls that converge data replicas. *Procedural replication* replicates only the call to a stored procedure that an application uses to update a table. Procedural replication does not replicate individual data modifications.

To use procedural replication, at all sites you must replicate the packages that modify data in the system. After replicating a package, you must generate a *wrapper* for the package at each site. When an application calls a packaged procedure at the local site to modify data, the wrapper ensures that the call is automatically made to the same packaged procedure at all other sites in the replicated environment. Procedural replication can happen asynchronously or synchronously.

Conflict Detection and Procedural Replication

When an advanced replication system replicates data using procedural replication, the procedures that replicate data are responsible for ensuring the integrity of the replicated data. That is, you must design such procedures either to avoid or to detect replication conflicts and resolve them appropriately. Consequently, procedural replication is used most typically when databases are available only for the processing of large batch operations. In such situations, replication conflicts are unlikely because numerous transactions are not contending for the same data.

Synchronous (Real-Time) Data Propagation

Asynchronous data propagation is the normal configuration for advanced replication environments using multimaster or snapshot site replication. However, Oracle also supports synchronous data propagation. *Synchronous data propagation* is analogous to distributed transactions because updates to all replicas happen in *real-time*—when an application updates a local replica of a table using synchronous replication, the site managing the replica coordinates updates to all other replicas of the same table as part of the same transaction.

In almost all situations, asynchronous data propagation is the best choice for advanced replication systems. Synchronous replication is useful only when applications require that replicated data remains synchronized at all times.

To support synchronous data propagation, Oracle8 uses the same system of internal database triggers to generate RPCs that replicate data-level changes to other replication sites. However, Oracle does not defer the execution of RPCs when using synchronous data propagation. Instead, data replication RPCs execute as part of the same transaction that modifies the local replica. Consequently, a data-level change must be possible at all sites that manage a replicated table or else a transaction rollback occurs. Replication systems that depend on synchronous data propagation are therefore highly dependent on system and network availability because they can function only when all sites in the system are concurrently available.

Replication Conflicts and Synchronous Data Replication

Replication conflicts are not possible when an advanced system propagates replication information synchronously. With real-time replication, applications use distributed transactions to update all replicas of a table at the same time. As is the case in non-distributed database environments, Oracle's concurrency mechanisms (namely, row locks) prevent all types of destructive interference among transactions.

Summary

This chapter has explained the features of Oracle8 that you can use to join together multiple, independent databases into a global distributed database system. You also learned how to use table snapshots and advanced replication features such as multimaster replication and updatable snapshots to manage replicate data in multiple databases of a distributed database system.

CHAPTER
12

Oracle's Parallel
Processing Options

racle8's parallel processing options extend the capabilities of a standard Oracle Server so that you can fully exploit the parallel processing and high-availability features of different kinds of multiprocessor computer systems. This chapter explains the various multiprocessor computing architectures that you can choose and how to configure an Oracle Server for these systems, including:

- The architecture of multiprocessor computer systems, including shared memory, shared disk, and shared nothing multiprocessor configurations

- How to configure Oracle to process queries and other DML statements with parallel processing so that applications can transparently benefit from the parallel processing capabilities of Oracle running on a multiprocessor computer

- How to configure Oracle's Parallel Server option for shared disk and shared nothing multiprocessor computer systems, as well as how to configure and tune a database for parallel server access

Introduction to Parallel Processing

Many types of demanding applications that operate using a uniprocessor computer system can benefit in some way from the parallel processing capabilities of a multiprocessor computer system. The following sections introduce the basic concepts of parallel processing and multiprocessor computer architectures.

Uniprocessor versus Multiprocessor Computers

When an application submits a demanding job to a uniprocessor computer, the computer's lone processor must tackle the job by itself, not to mention all of the work submitted by other applications. Typically, the goal of parallel processing is to improve the performance of a demanding application. When an application submits a demanding job to a multiprocessor computer, the computer splits the one job into logical subtasks and then processes them in parallel using multiple processors to reduce completion time.

The number of subtasks that result from the one large job is called the *degree of parallelism*. The reduction of processing time necessary to complete a task is directly proportional to its degree of parallelism. Parallel processing systems strive to deliver linear speedup so that they can provide the maximum performance boost from each processor in the system.

Shared Memory Systems

One type of multiprocessor computer architecture is a shared memory system. A *shared memory* system is a computer with multiple processors that all share common memory and disk storage. For this reason, shared memory systems are also commonly referred to as *tightly coupled* systems or *symmetric multiprocessor (SMP)* systems. Figure 12-1 illustrates the architecture of a shared memory system.

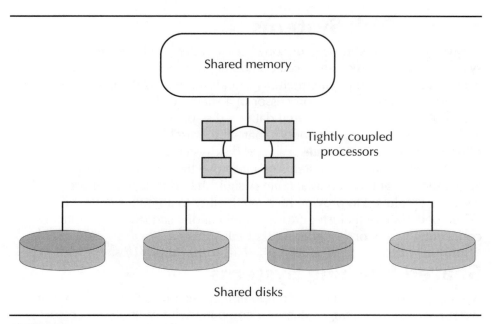

FIGURE 12-1. *A shared memory system*

The operating system of an SMP system safely manages access to shared memory among the computer's multiple processors. To prevent destructive interference, the operating system does not allow more than one processor to access a specific address space in shared memory. Processors communicate using fast inter-processor communication.

Most computer hardware manufacturers offer shared memory systems with two, four, eight, or 16 processors. Even personal computer manufacturers now offer desktop systems with two or four processors—an incredibly inexpensive way to get started with parallel processing. Shared memory systems are very cost-efficient hardware systems that can scale with the needs of most businesses to improve the performance of applications that take advantage of a tightly coupled multiprocessor architecture. However, because of the tightly coupled design of shared memory systems, contention results among multiple processors for the same resources; this architectural characteristic limits the maximum number of processors that can provide significant performance gains for applications. Consequently, SMP systems usually do not scale with more than about 16 processors.

Shared Disk Systems

Another type of multiprocessor computer architecture is the shared disk system. A *shared disk* system is a computer with multiple processors that each have their own private memory but all share a common disk or set of disks for data storage. Each processor in a shared disk system is a node that must coordinate access to shared data on disk using a common distributed lock manager. The group of nodes that shares a set of disks is known as a *cluster*. Figure 12-2 illustrates a shared disk system.

Although shared disk systems can improve the performance of applications that have an adaptable design, shared disk systems are typically employed to provide high availability to an important data store. When one node of a cluster crashes, applications can still access data by connecting to any of the other nodes in the cluster.

Shared Nothing Systems

A third type of multiprocessor computer architecture is the shared nothing system. A *shared nothing* system is a computer with multiple processors that can operate independent of one another because each processor has its

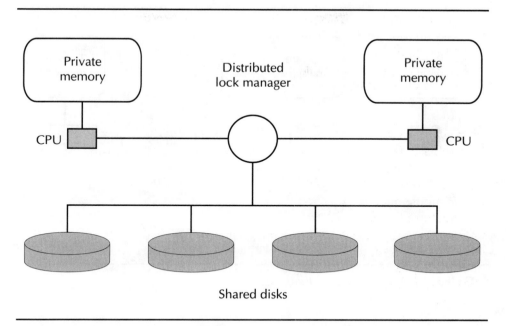

FIGURE 12-2.   *A shared disk system*

own private memory and private disk storage. For this reason, shared nothing systems are also commonly referred to as *loosely coupled* systems. Figure 12-3 illustrates a shared nothing system.

In a shared nothing system, a node is a processor that has private memory and disk storage. There are even hybrid shared nothing systems in which a node is a set of tightly coupled processors that share private memory and disk storage. No matter the configuration, the nodes in a loosely coupled system communicate with each other using an internal high-speed bus.

When you design applications with shared nothing systems in mind, the loosely coupled design of a shared nothing system does not create contention among the multiple processors of the system. Consequently, there is no theoretical limit to the number of nodes that a shared nothing system can have while continuing to offer increased performance for applications that take advantage of the architecture. In fact, many computer hardware manufacturers offer systems that can support hundreds, even

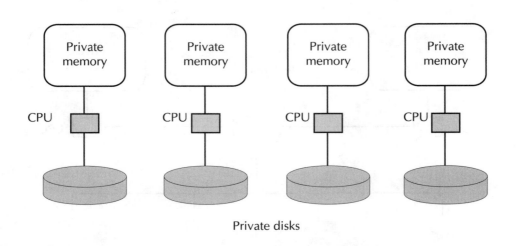

FIGURE 12-3. *A shared nothing system*

thousands, of loosely coupled nodes. When a shared nothing system includes a great number of processors, it is called a *massively parallel processing (MPP)* system. Unfortunately, it is very difficult to develop applications for MPP systems and, as a result, there are not as many software products available that take advantage of this parallel processing architecture.

Now that you understand the basics of multiprocessor computer architectures, let's learn how you can take advantage of them using Oracle's parallel query/DML architecture and Oracle's Parallel Server option.

Processing SQL in Parallel

The first type of parallel processing that we'll focus on is parallel SQL statement processing. Before learning the specifics of Oracle's parallel processing architecture, let's learn the basic concepts of parallel processing in general.

The primary function of a database management system such as Oracle is to service the requests of client applications that read from or write to a shared database. An Oracle database server can process an individual database request on a multiprocessor computer using serial or parallel processing.

Serial Processing

Without parallel processing, the database system processes a database request as a single unit using *serial processing*. For example, when a SQL statement requests a sorted join of two tables, the server might get the rows from one table, then get the rows from the other table, join the rows, sort them, and finally return the rows to the user. In this case, the server uses a single processor to complete each of the operations serially, so the total time to complete the query is the sum of the time it takes to complete each step. Figure 12-4 illustrates a SQL request executed with serial processing.

Notice in Figure 12-4 that without parallel processing, the server executes the many different operations of the SQL request in serial fashion using a single CPU only—while other CPUs sit idle. When a database server uses serial processing to complete SQL requests, complicated database requests or requests for large volumes of data can take a significant amount of time to finish.

Parallel SQL Processing

Divide and conquer is the fundamental concept of parallel SQL processing. To speed things up, a *parallel SQL processing* system takes a single database request, intelligently breaks it up into several smaller subtasks, and then uses all available processors to attack the subtasks in parallel and reduce overall completion time. For example, Figure 12-5 shows how parallel processing can perform a sorted join of two tables: one processor can scan one table while another processor scans the other table, all while other processors are joining and sorting the results. By breaking down a single database request into multiple subtasks and completing them in parallel, the parallel processing server reduces the overall time to complete a query.

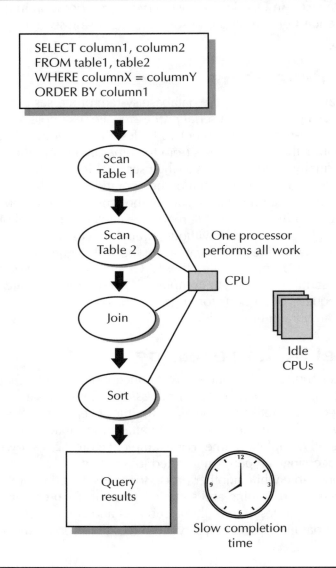

FIGURE 12-4. *A SQL request executed on a multiprocessor computer using serial processing rather than parallel processing*

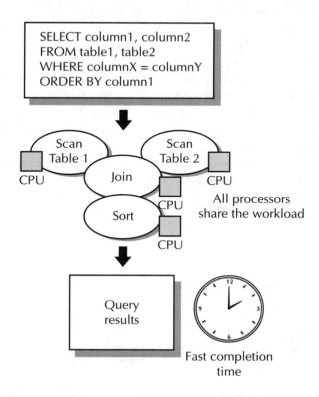

FIGURE 12-5. *A SQL request executed on a multiprocessor computer using parallel processing*

In a good implementation of parallel SQL processing, speed scaleup should be linear with respect to the number of CPUs the system uses to process a query in parallel.

Oracle Server can execute DML operations (for example, SELECT, INSERT, UPDATE, and DELETE statements) and certain DDL operations (for example, CREATE TABLE and CREATE INDEX) using parallel processing. To process a database request with parallel processing, Oracle Server uses a special operating-system process architecture.

Parallel SQL Processing Architecture

When an dispatcher process (see Chapter 8) receives a database request, the dispatcher hands off the request to a query coordinator process (see Figure 12-6). As the name indicates, a *query coordinator* is the focal point of a parallelized database operation. The job of the query coordinator is to intelligently break up a database request into subtasks, which the coordinator then passes to available query servers for processing. The query coordinator also merges results returned from query servers and returns the result of the database request.

A *query server* process is a simple server process that performs the task requested of it by a query coordinator. Oracle8 keeps available a pool of shared query servers that any query coordinator can use to perform work. Once you configure an Oracle instance with a parallel processing

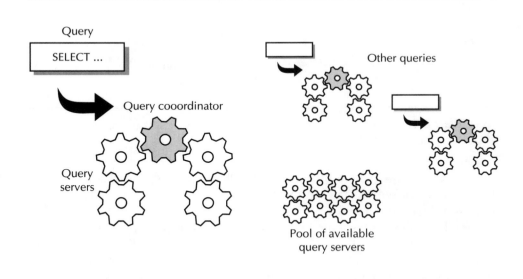

FIGURE 12-6. *Oracle's parallel processing architecture*

configuration, the instance can dynamically tune itself as workloads fluctuate—Oracle varies the number of query servers depending on the current load of the system. When the load increases, Oracle starts more query servers to handle user requests without waiting. With lighter loads, Oracle terminates query servers to reduce the process overhead on the server. At server initialization, you can set the minimum and maximum number of query servers to ensure that there is an adequate number of query servers, but not so many as to overburden the system.

To maximize performance, Oracle's parallel processing architecture automatically takes advantage of available processors on a multiprocessor server computer. Query coordinator and query server processes do not need to be associated with specific processors, but rather should be free to float around and use computer resources as they become available.

Data Partitioning and Parallel SQL Processing

Processing database operations in parallel—such as a scan, join, and sort—is only one part of effective parallel SQL processing; data partitioning is often a requirement for linear speedup in some areas of database processing. As Chapter 7 explains, data partitioning is the distribution of data across multiple disks to relieve bottlenecks associated with the limited I/O bandwidth of a single disk. Parallel queries might not be able to perform their best when they access data that is not partitioned. For example, Figure 12-7 illustrates how a single query that requests a sorted scan of all rows in a large database table can perform slowly due to bandwidth limitations of disk access.

Figure 12-7 illustrates a condition known as *pipelined parallelism.* Pipelined parallelism is an appropriate name for the condition because even though the query can execute with parallel processing, it is limited by a "pipe," in this case the bandwidth of a single disk that stores the entire table. To avoid pipelined parallelism in your parallel SQL processing system, use data partitioning. For example, Figure 12-8 shows how the same parallel query executes much faster after you partition the data of the large table across several disks.

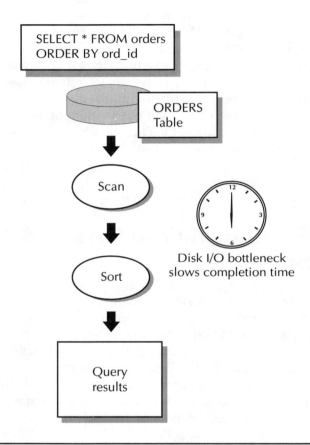

FIGURE 12-7. *Parallel SQL processing without partitioned data creates pipelined parallelism.*

Partitioning Strategies

There are many different types of data partitioning strategies. In Chapter 7 you learned how you can use Oracle8's table and index partitioning options to divide large tables and indexes into smaller, more manageable

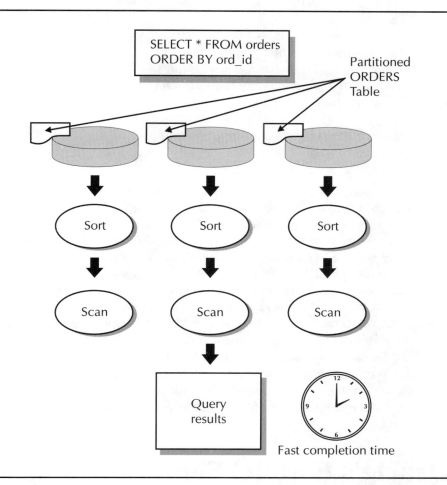

FIGURE 12-8.   *Parallel SQL processing can perform best when you partition large tables and indexes.*

parts. When you configure an Oracle database for parallel SQL processing, strongly consider using Oracle8's range partitioning options for tables and indexes to maximize your system's performance.

NOTE
Oracle8's query optimizer is "partition aware"
of table and index data that you divide using
the server's built-in data partitioning features.
For example, if a parallel query requests data
from only one partition of a large table,
Oracle's query optimizer automatically
eliminates the need to scan all other partitions
of the table.

Unfortunately, not all application queries can benefit best from the range partitioning that Oracle8 offers. Another common partitioning strategy to consider with an Oracle database is round-robin partitioning. With *round-robin* partitioning, the server randomly scatters a table's rows among available table partitions. In general, round-robin partitioning can improve the performance of all parallel SQL executions because the distribution of data is not tailored to the needs of any specific database request. To distribute the physical storage of data in an Oracle database using round-robin partitioning, you will most likely want to rely on external operating system services that can spread data across multiple disk drives. For example, most multiprocessor computer operating systems provide a disk striping utility that you can use to randomly scatter the blocks of operating system files across a number of disk drives. Use such a facility with an Oracle database's data files to achieve round-robin data partitioning.

Oracle's Parallel Server Option—Multiple Instances for High-Availability

The next type of parallel processing that this chapter focuses on is parallel database access. The following sections of this chapter explain the unique functionality of Oracle's Parallel Server option for loosely coupled multiprocessor computer systems.

What Is Parallel Database Access?

Oracle8's Parallel Server option enables an Oracle database system to take full advantage of the high-availability benefits of shared disk and shared nothing multiprocessor computer systems. With Oracle's Parallel Server option, multiple instances of Oracle Server can concurrently provide access to the same Oracle database. Each instance of Oracle executes on a separate node in a clustered or loosely coupled system. Figure 12-9 illustrates a parallel server database configuration.

Each instance in an Oracle Parallel Server is a distinct set of Oracle background processes and memory caches. Every instance in an Oracle Parallel Server mounts and opens the same Oracle database in "parallel"

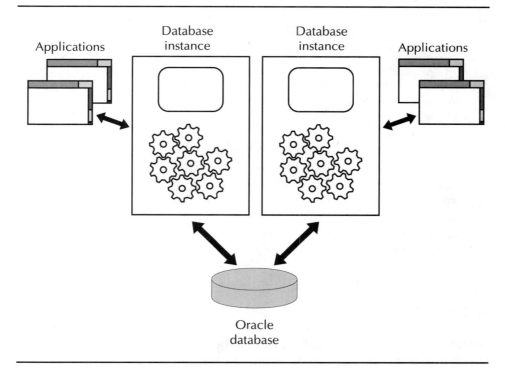

FIGURE 12-9.   *A parallel server allows multiple instances of Oracle to access the same database concurrently.*

mode to provide different pathways for applications to connect with and use the shared database.

Not all types of application environments can benefit from an Oracle Parallel Server configuration. The next few sections explain more about how an Oracle Parallel Server manages data to preserve database integrity, and provide some insight as to what types of applications work well in an Oracle Parallel Server configuration.

Parallel Server Architecture

To preserve the integrity of a database's data that multiple, concurrent Oracle instances are accessing, an Oracle Parallel Server employs special concurrency mechanisms. To determine what type of applications are appropriate for a parallel server system, you must understand the unique data locking architecture of a parallel server.

NOTE
Chapter 9 explains how Oracle Server's internal data concurrency mechanisms work to protect the integrity of a shared database—targeted row locks prevent destructive interference and provide excellent concurrency among multiple transactions that work with the same set of shared data, while Oracle's multiversioning mechanism allows read and write operations to proceed independent of one another. Review this chapter if you are not familiar with these concepts.

Distributed Locks

Applications at work in a parallel server environment request and modify data through an Oracle instance just as applications do in a basic single-instance configuration. For example, when a transaction updates a row in a table, the transaction acquires an exclusive lock on the row; the server reads the data block containing the row into the corresponding instance's data buffer cache, and then updates the row.

Because multiple instances have access to the same database, an Oracle Parallel Server must also use distributed locks. A *distributed lock* is a special type of data lock that prevents two instances from destructively interfering with one another while working with database resources such as rollback segments, cached data dictionary entries, and cached data blocks. An instance in a parallel server configuration acquires a distributed lock when the request of a resource places that resource in the instance's SGA. An instance relinquishes a distributed lock only when another instance requests the same resource. Each instance of an Oracle Parallel Server uses one or more special *Lock (LCK) background processes* and the distributed lock manager of the underlying operating system to coordinate distributed locks and access to shared resources in a database.

Parallel Cache Management (PCM) Locks

To manage coordinated access to database data blocks, an Oracle Parallel Server uses a specific type of distributed lock called a *parallel cache management (PCM) lock*. An instance acquires a PCM lock for a data or index block that it caches in its SGA. Only one instance can have an exclusive PCM lock for a specific block, but many instances can cache and have read-only PCM locks for the same data block. Oracle automatically performs cache coherency so that all instances caching the same block are sure to have the most current version of that block.

Pinging

When one instance must write a block back to a data file because another instance requests the same data block for update, this situation is called *pinging*. Pinging of data blocks among the instances of a parallel server causes disk I/O, which typically decreases overall server performance. Considering this, the interaction of applications that use different instances of an Oracle Parallel Server should not create excessive pinging situations. Optimally, applications that access the same set of database data should access the database through the same instance of a parallel server, and applications that access different sets of data should use different instances of the parallel server. For example, OLTP applications that update mutually exclusive sets of data within the same database will work fine with different instances of an Oracle Parallel Server. Before investing in and using an Oracle Parallel Server, consider your specific application environment to determine whether it will work well.

Transaction Log Threads

Most database operations in an Oracle Parallel Server environment work the same or similar to the way they do in a standard Oracle database instance. However, there are several special configuration steps necessary to get an Oracle Parallel Server up and running. Perhaps the most significant job in preparing a database for use by an Oracle Parallel Server is building the database's transaction log.

NOTE
Review the information in Chapter 10 if you are unfamiliar with Oracle's database protection mechanisms, including the transaction log.

Every instance that accesses a database produces its own *thread* of log entries in the database's transaction log. In a traditional database setting where only one instance mounts and opens a database at a time, there is only one thread of log entries in the database's transaction log. Furthermore, all log groups correspond to the one thread in the transaction log.

In an Oracle Parallel Server, each instance that mounts and opens a database generates its own thread of log entries. To record a thread of log entries, each instance uses its own set of transaction log groups. Together, the threads in a parallel server combine to form the database's overall transaction log.

To prepare a database for use by an Oracle Parallel Server, you must configure a distinct set of log groups for each instance that plans to mount the database. In general, you configure each instance's set of log groups much as you would in a typical, one instance database setting—there must be at least two or more log groups per thread, and you should mirror each log group to protect it from a single point of failure.

Assuming that the database operates with media recovery enabled, you must also configure archiving for the various threads in the database's transaction log. To accomplish this, you must set the server parameters associated with log archiving on an instance-by-instance basis.

Server Startup

When using an Oracle Parallel Server, many typical database administration operations can work differently. When starting up the various instances of an Oracle Parallel Server, there are several issues to consider. Most importantly, each instance must mount the database in "parallel" mode. This differs from a typical database server, where a single instance mounts a database in "exclusive" mode.

The maximum number of instances that a database can ever support is set during database creation. When you create a database and plan to use it in a parallel server configuration, simply make sure that each instance's parameter file identifies itself with a unique instance number.

Parallel Server Database Administration

A database administrator can perform management operations for the database in an Oracle Parallel Server after connecting to any instance in the server. Unless you indicate otherwise, an administrative utility directs all the operations that you execute to the default instance of your server. Oracle's Enterprise Manager and other administrative utilities let you indicate a target instance when establishing a server connection, and switch the setting for your session's default instance.

Several administrative operations in an Oracle Parallel Server can have a "global" or "local" effect. Global operations are those that affect all instances of an Oracle Parallel Server, while a local operation affects only the instance to which you are currently connected.

Automatic Instance Recovery

A system crash is always a possibility in a computer system. When a server in a parallel server configuration crashes, the remaining instances in an Oracle Parallel Server automatically work to perform instance recovery on any failed instances. Keep in mind that recovery from an instance failure is automatic in environments in which at least one instance remains operational after a system crash. When all servers crash in a Parallel Server, Oracle performs crash recovery during the next instance startup operation.

Transparent Application Failover

The primary benefit of an Oracle Parallel Server is that it provides multiple points of access for applications that want to use its database. To maintain application availability, you can configure Net8 clients in a parallel server environment to transparently reconnect to another parallel server instance after the application's current instance becomes unavailable. When a server in the system crashes, disconnected applications automatically reconnect to the database using another server that remains available. Of course, Oracle must roll back all active transactions lost due to the system crash.

Database Recovery from Media Failure

When a database operates with media recovery enabled, Oracle can fully recover the database, even from significant problems such as disk failures. When using an Oracle Parallel Server, you can perform media recovery through a single instance that mounts the database exclusively or through multiple instances that mount the database in parallel. Keep in mind that the necessary archived log groups corresponding to all threads in a Parallel Server's transaction log must be available for recovery from disk failure.

Unique Database Features for Parallel Server Configurations

Contention for various database system resources (memory, disk access, data blocks, and so on) is a common performance inhibitor that exists in any Oracle database environment. The following sections explain some special situations that can exist within an Oracle Parallel Server and corresponding ways to reduce the resulting contention problems.

Sequence Generation

Chapter 2 explains how to use Oracle's sequence generator to quickly generate unique primary keys for the tables in an application schema. When designing applications to work with an Oracle Parallel Server, developers should consider how applications generate sequence numbers across multiple instances. Specifically, you can create a sequence and enable caching to reduce disk access as applications repeatedly reference a sequence. By caching sequence numbers, each instance can pregenerate mutually exclusive sets of unique sequence numbers in memory to reduce disk I/O.

NOTE

In some database designs, a row's primary key value has particular meaning relative to the primary keys of other rows in the same table. For example, a row's primary key value might implicitly indicate when the row was inserted relative to other rows in the same table. In such cases, sequences at work in an Oracle Parallel Server setting should enable ordering. However, note that when ordering is enabled for a sequence, instances cannot pregenerate and cache sequence numbers. Consequently, a disk I/O is necessary to update the database's data dictionary each time an application requests a new sequence number.

Data Block Free Lists

When applications using different instances of an Oracle Parallel Server are inserting rows into the same table, contention can result as a server reads the table's free lists and subsequently attempts to place new rows into the same set of data blocks. To reduce contention for free list lookups, you can create tables with multiple free list groups so that multiple instances do not contend for the same free lists.

Instance-Specific Extent Allocation

When using an Oracle Parallel Server, you can allocate extents to a table's data segment on an instance-specific basis. This way, applications that insert rows into the same table through different instances of an Oracle Parallel Server do not contend for access to the same data blocks.

Private Rollback Segments

All instances at work within an Oracle Parallel Server can use online public rollback segments. Consequently, transactions originating from multiple instances are likely to contend for the same set of public rollback segments. To reduce contention for rollback segments in an Oracle Parallel Server configuration, consider using private rather than public rollback segments.

At instance startup, each instance explicitly acquires exclusive access to all private rollback segments that the instance's parameter file lists. When using private rollback segments with an Oracle Parallel Server, make sure that each instance's initialization parameter file references a mutually exclusive set of private rollback segments.

Reverse Key Indexes

A *reverse key index* is a special type of B-tree index. In a reverse key index, the bytes of each key value are the reverse from what they would normally be in a standard B-tree index. In a parallel server configuration, the unique arrangement of data in a reverse key index can often help to distribute index key values across the leaf blocks of an index that would otherwise be concentrated in a small set of index blocks on a per-instance basis.

Mixing Parallel SQL and Parallel Server Processing

In many cases, an Oracle Parallel Server configuration can benefit from parallel SQL processing capabilities. Oracle can distribute parallel SQL processing operations across all available instances in a parallel server. For example, when you create a table, you can set the table's parallel processing settings so that statements referencing the table use parallel query processes in two or more instances of a parallel server configuration. Additionally, you can cache small lookup tables evenly across several instances of a parallel server to reduce disk I/O and improve application performance.

Summary

This chapter taught you how to use the parallel processing options of Oracle Server to extend the capabilities of standard Oracle Server so that you can fully exploit the parallel processing and high-availability features of multiprocessor computer systems. In this chapter, you learned:

- The basic concepts of parallel processing and all about multiprocessor computer systems, including shared memory, shared disk, and shared nothing multiprocessor configurations

- How Oracle Server's parallel SQL processing architecture can dramatically improve the performance of demanding database operations with parallel query processing

- How to provide high availability and extra horsepower to a parallel processing system using Oracle Server's Parallel Server option

INDEX

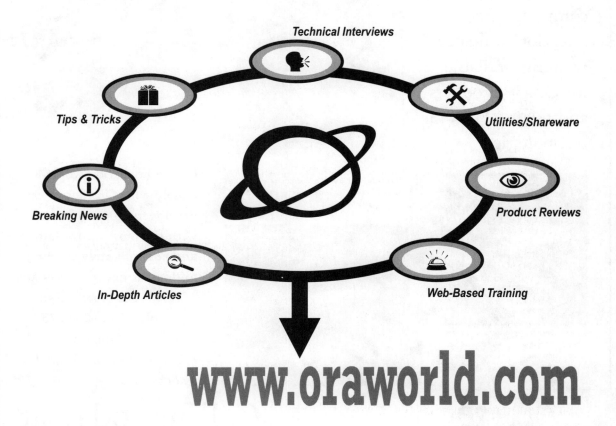

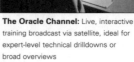

Get Your **FREE** Subscription to Oracle Magazine

Stay informed and increase your productivity with every issue of *Oracle Magazine.* Inside each FREE, bimonthly issue, you'll get:

- Up-to-date information on the Oracle RDBMS and software tools
- Third-party software and hardware products
- Technical articles on Oracle platforms and operating environments
- Software tuning tips
- Oracle client application stories

Three easy ways to subscribe:

1 MAIL: Cut out this page, complete the questionnaire on the back, and mail to: *Oracle Magazine,* 500 Oracle Parkway, Box 659952, Redwood Shores, CA 94065.

2 FAX: Cut out this page, complete the questionnaire on the back, and and fax the questionnaire to **+ 415.633.2424.**

3 WEB: Visit our Web site at **www.oramag.com.** You'll find a subscription form there, plus much more!

If there are other Oracle users at your location who would like to receive their own copy of *Oracle Magazine,* please photocopy the form on the back, and pass it along.

☐ YES! Please send me a FREE subscription to <u>Oracle Magazine</u>.   ☐ NO, I am not interested at this time.

If you wish to receive your free bimonthly subscription to *Oracle Magazine,* you must fill out the entire form, sign it, and date it (incomplete forms cannot be processed or acknowledged). You can also subscribe at our Web Site at **http://www.oramag.com/html/subform.html** or fax your application to *Oracle Magazine* at **+415.633.2424.**

SIGNATURE (REQUIRED) [✓]   DATE [ ]

NAME _____   TITLE _____

COMPANY _____

STREET/P.O. BOX _____

CITY/STATE/ZIP _____

COUNTRY _____   TELEPHONE _____

You must answer all eight of the questions below.

1 What is the primary business activity of your firm at this location? *(circle only one)*
01. Agriculture, Mining, Natural Resources
02. Communications Services, Utilities
03. Computer Consulting, Training
04. Computer, Data Processing Service
05. Computer Hardware, Software, Systems
06. Education—Primary, Secondary, College, University
07. Engineering, Architecture, Construction
08. Financial, Banking, Real Estate, Insurance
09. Government—Federal/Military
10. Government—Federal/Nonmilitary
11. Government—Local, State, Other
12. Health Services, Health Institutions
13. Manufacturing—Aerospace, Defense
14. Manufacturing—Noncomputer Products, Goods
15. Public Utilities (Electric, Gas, Sanitation)
16. Pure and Applied Research & Development
17. Retailing, Wholesaling, Distribution
18. Systems Integrator, VAR, VAD, OEM
19. Transportation
20. Other Business and Services ____

2 Which of the following best describes your job function? *(circle only one)*
CORPORATE MANAGEMENT/STAFF
01. Executive Management (President, Chair, CEO, CFO, Owner, Partner, Principal, Managing Director)
02. Finance/Administrative Management (VP/Director/Manager/Controller of Finance, Purchasing, Administration)
03. Other Finance/Administration Staff
04. Sales/Marketing Management (VP/Director/Manager of Sales/Marketing)
05. Other Sales/Marketing Staff ____
TECHNICAL MANAGEMENT/STAFF
06. Computer/Communications Systems Development/Programming Management
07. Computer/Communications Systems Development/Programming Staff
08. Computer Systems/Operations Management (CIO/VP/Director/Manager MIS, Operations, etc.)
09. Consulting
10. DBA/Systems Administrator
11. Education/Training
12. Engineering/R&D/Science Management
13. Engineering/R&D/Science Staff
14. Technical Support Director/Manager
15. Other Technical Management/Staff ____

3 What is your current primary operating system environment? *(circle all that apply)*
01. AIX
02. HP-UX
03. Macintosh OS
04. MPE-ix
05. MS-DOS
06. MVS
07. NetWare
08. OpenVMS
09. OS/2
10. OS/400
11. SCO
12. Solaris/Sun OS
13. SVR4
14. Ultrix
15. UnixWare
16. Other UNIX
17. VAX VMS
18. VM
19. Windows
20. Windows NT
21. Other ____

4 What is your current primary hardware environment? *(circle all that apply)*
01. Macintosh
02. Mainframe
03. Massively Parallel Processing
04. Minicomputer
05. PC (IBM-Compatible)
06. Supercomputer
07. Symmetric Multiprocessing
08. Workstation
09. Other ____

5 In your job, do you use or plan to purchase any of the following products or services *(check all that apply)*

SOFTWARE	Use	Plan to buy
01. Accounting/Finance	☐	☐
02. Business Graphics	☐	☐
03. CAD/CAE/CAM	☐	☐
04. CASE	☐	☐
05. CIM	☐	☐
06. Communications/Networking	☐	☐
07. Database Management	☐	☐
08. Education	☐	☐
09. File Management	☐	☐
10. GIS	☐	☐
11. Image Processing	☐	☐
12. Laboratory Control	☐	☐
13. Materials Resource Planning (MRP, MRP II)	☐	☐
14. Multimedia Authoring Tools	☐	☐
15. Office Automation	☐	☐
16. Order Entry/Inventory Control	☐	☐
17. Programming/Systems Development	☐	☐
18. Project Management	☐	☐
19. Scientific and Engineering	☐	☐
20. Spreadsheets/Financial Planning	☐	☐
21. Systems Management Products	☐	☐
22. Workflow	☐	☐
HARDWARE		
23. Macintosh	☐	☐
24. Mainframe	☐	☐
25. Massively Parallel Processing	☐	☐
26. Minicomputer	☐	☐
27. PC (IBM-Compatible)	☐	☐
28. Supercomputer	☐	☐
29. Symmetric Multiprocessing	☐	☐
30. Workstation	☐	☐
PERIPHERALS		
31. Bridges/Routers/Hubs/Gateways	☐	☐
32. CD-ROM Drives	☐	☐
33. Disk Drives/Subsystems	☐	☐
34. Tape Drives/Subsystems	☐	☐
35. Video Boards/Other Multimedia Peripherals	☐	☐
NETWORK/COMMUNICATIONS		
36. Communications Controllers	☐	☐
37. Local Area Networks	☐	☐
38. Modems	☐	☐
39. Wide Area Networks	☐	☐
SERVICES		
40. Computer-Based Training	☐	☐
41. Education/Training	☐	☐
42. Maintenance	☐	☐
43. Online DatabaseServices	☐	☐
44. Support	☐	☐
45. **None of the above**	☐	☐

6 What Oracle products are in use at your site? *(circle all that apply)*
SERVERS
01. Oracle7
02. Oracle Media Server
03. Oracle7 Workgroup Server
04. Personal Oracle7
05. Oracle Rdb
TOOLS
06. Designer/2000 (CASE)
07. Developer/2000 (CDE, Forms, Reports, Graphics)
08. Oracle Media Objects
09. Oracle Power Objects
APPLICATIONS
10. Oracle Financials
11. Oracle Human Resources
12. Oracle Manufacturing
13. Other ____
14. **None of the above**

7 What other database products are in use at your site? *(circle all that apply)*
01. CA-Ingres
02. DB2
03. DB2/2
04. DB2/6000
05. dbase
06. Gupta
07. IMS
08. Informix
09. Microsoft Access
10. Microsoft SQL Server
11. Progress
12. Sybase System 10
13. Sybase System 11
14. Sybase SQL Server
15. VSAM
16. Other ____
17. SAP
18. Peoplesoft
19. BAAN
20. **None of the above**

8 During the next 12 months, how much do you anticipate your organization will spend on computer hardware, software, peripherals, and services for your location? *(circle only one)*
01. Less than $10,000
02. $10,000 to $49,999
03. $50,000 to $99,999
04. $100,000 to $499,999
05. $500,000 to $999,999
06. $1,000,000 and over

OMG